A Treatise On Hydrostrtics

A TREATISE ON HYDROSTATICS.

BY

JAGJIT SINGH M. A., F. R. S. S.

CONTENTS.

(i)

Errata

Page	Line	For	...	Read
(ii)	Foot note	d'Etolo	...	d'Ecolo
3	1	ahsolutely	...	absolutely
5	1	th	...	the
6	24	denisty	...	density
7	10	$(1-\frac{1}{n})^3+\mathsf{P}\;\frac{\sigma}{n}$	...	$(1-\frac{1}{n})^3\mathsf{P}+\frac{\sigma}{n}$
8	3	$(\mathsf{P}-\sigma)e^{-/uv}$	...	$(\mathsf{P}-\sigma)e^{-u/v}$
12	12	conponents	...	components
19	10	equal and	...	and equal
29	23	$\Sigma(y^2+yz+z^2)dz$	.	$\Sigma(y^2+yz+z^2)dx$
34	7	Π	...	π
38	7	$dp=\{(X+w^2)dx$	...	$dp=\mathsf{P}\{(X+w^2x)dx\}$
56	4	mnst	...	must
59	14	§ 3 4	...	§ 3.3
62	14	$\bar{x}^2+y^2+z$	.	$\bar{x}^2+\bar{y}^2+\bar{z}^2$
78	11	5 Sin θ − 3 Sin θ cos−2θ		5 Sin θ-3 Sin θcosθ-2θ
78	26	anes	...	axes
82	20	aken	..	taken ...
86	13	$-\mathsf{P}(A\bar{x}+H\bar{y}G\bar{z}+u)t$		$(A\,x+H\bar{y}+Gz+u)$
91	13	unleess	...	unless
93	1	lenght	...	length
105	13	$p=\frac{1}{2}\mu M\mathsf{P}(A^4-r^2)^{\frac{1}{2}}$		$p=\frac{1}{2}\mu M\mathsf{P}(A^2-r^2)$
112	28	$-z\lambda$	...	$-z-\lambda$
125	2	horzoutal	...	horizontal
129	21	Than	...	Then
139	9	veries	..	varies
148	9	corressponds	...	corresponds.
151	20	13.15	...	13.5
155	22	Add the following after "respectively"—The height of B above D is 36 inches.		
163	5 & 7	U		u

Page.	Line	For		Read
166	11	5·10	...	5.11
188	4	molo of the umloss imaoginary shall	...	the molecules of the imaginary shell
188	15	ds	...	$d\mathrm{S}$
201	7	$\mathrm{Sin}\dfrac{8\,i}{2}$	..	$\mathrm{Sin}\dfrac{3\,i}{2}$
212	1	insert "of the heights"		after "difference"
212	12	$\tfrac{4}{3}\Pi a^{3}$	...	$\tfrac{4}{3}\pi a^{3}$
213	13	ballen	...	balloon
213	13	appraximately	...	approximately
215	2	tha	...	the
221	4	F'	..	F_{1}
238	15	$c^{2}\alpha$	—	$c^{2}\phi$
247	15	$\Psi(l)$	...	$f(l)$
249	5	equilibrium	..	Maclaurin
263	2	Boths	..	Both
267	13	$\dfrac{E-E}{A}$	..	$\dfrac{E-E_{1}}{A}$
269	10	$\dfrac{\delta u}{\partial n}$	...	$\dfrac{\partial U}{\partial n}$

Historical Introduction.

The foundations of the science of Hydrostatics were laid down as early as 250 B. C. by Archimedes (287—212 B. C) in his treatise on Floating Bodies. He formulated the theorem that pressure at any point of a fluid mass in equilibrium is the same in every direction. He inquired into the conditions according to which a solid body floating in a fluid assumes and preserves a position of equilibrium, and proceeded so far as to give a complete investigation of the positions of rest and stability of a right segment of a parabloid of revolution wholly above or below the surface of the fluid,—an investigation which has been characterised as a "veritable tour de force" by Sir Thomas Heath,* the historian of Greek mathematics.

In spite of the brilliant and sweeping range of Archimedes' researches, the science of Hydrostatics made no progress at all for a long time to come. For, as Hogben has pointed out, Greek science had reached a stage when having been divorced from the social heritage of the age it had degenerated into a hobby of the unemployed intellectuals of a leisured class. Long long after when the Reformation had stimulated interest in the practical problems of craftsmen and mariners, the study of Hydrostatics was resumed. By the beginning of the 17th century a few hydraulic machines such as the forcing pump and the siphon had been invented. In 1603, Marinus Ghetaldus in his 'Promotus Archimedes' made the first serious attempt to apply the principles already enunciated by Archimedes more than eighteen centuries ago. But the laws of equilibrium of fluids were for the first time demonstrated in the most perspicuous and simple fashion by Blaise Pascal in his posthumous work,— Sur l' Equilibre des Liquers. The Galilean spirit of scientific enquiry animating this work coupled with ample experimental confirmation of the

---

* P, 91 History of Greek Mathematics Vol II by Sir T. Heath

laws enunciated invested Hydrostatics with the dignity of a science

The next considerable advance in Hydrostatics is associated with the name of Torricelli, who invented the barometer and discovered that atmosphere exerts pressure. Here again Pascal carried on Torricelli's work a stage further. It was at his suggestion that his brother-in-law, M. Percier, performed the experiment of carrying a barometer up the Pury de Dome in Auvergne and noting the fall of the column of mercury as the atmospheric pressure decreased.

The problem of equilibrium of floating bodies was taken up by Christian Huygens in 1650 after the epic making work of Archimedes on the same subject. Huygens treated the problem by a new method based on the principle that in equilibrium the centre of gravity of the whole mass of the floating body and of the liquid is as low as possible. A century later two geometrers occupied themselves with this problem about the same time; Bouguer in his Traitè du Navire, and Euler, in his Scientia Navalis. Dupin introduced the surface of floatation and completed the theorems of Bouguer and thus gave the principal general methods now-a-days in use. His memoir with the report of Carnot is reproduced in "Les Applications Geometric et Me'canique, par Charles Dupin." Bouger was the first to study the question of the stability of equilibrium of floating bodies; but he only considered the particular case in which the displacement was such that the volume displaced remained constant. Duhamel[1] showed the insufficiency of Bouguer's reasoning. He attempted to complete the study of the small movement of the system in the neighbourhood of the position of equilibrium; but he made the arbitrary assumption that in this movement the pressures can be determined according to the laws of Hydrostatics. Nevertheless the conditions of stability of equilibrium, which he found, are exact. The hypotheses made

(1) Duhamel : Note sur divers Principles de Mèeanique, observations Sur la Stabilitè de l'equilibre des corps flottants (Journal d'Etole Polytechnique XXIV Cahier 1835).

by Duhamel were criticised by Clebsch[2], who saw that certain terms neglected by Duhamel were of the same order of magnitude as others retained. Besides, Duhamel did not give under one simple form the necessary and sufficient conditions of equilibrium.

The first rigorous exposition of the theory of the stability of floating bodies was given by Guyou[3], following an idea put forward by Bravais in his thesis. This theory which rests on the same principle as that of Huygens and which is rendered rigorous by the theorem of Lejeune-Dirichlet is supported by a simple and elegant geometrical demonstration. A very detailed history of the problem will be found in a memoir by Duhem[4].

A question of the same category but much more complex,—equilibrium of a ship floating in a changing liquid,—has been the object of recent studies by Guyou, Duhem, Greenhill and Appell.

Further progress in the field of Hydrostatics during recent years has been almost exclusively concerned with the determination of shapes assumed by stationary or rotating fluid masses subject to their own gravitation. This problem is of particular importance in Astronomy and Cosmogony. So voluminous is the work done on the solution of this problem that its study has by now become a separate branch of higher mathematics A historical account of this subject will be given in chapter VII

---

(2) Clebsh . Uber das Gleichgewicht schwimmender Körper. (Journal de crelle, 57, 1860).

(3) Guyou : Theorie nouvelle de la Stabilité de l'equilibre des corps flottant et Théorie du Navire.

(4) Duhem, Sur la stabilité de l' equilibre des, Corps flottant (Journal de Mathématiques, 5° série, t. I; 1895.)

CHAPTER I.

The Fundamental Property of a Perfect Fluid.

1 1. It is a well known fact of common experience that matter so far as we know exists in three states *viz.* solid, liquid and gaseous. Matter in the last two states is also referred to as fluid. What distinguishes the solid from the fluid state ?

Matter in the solid state is supposed to be rigid *i. e.* to have definite shape and volume, which are not altered by the action of any external forces. Yet, even the hardest solid, however rigid, succumbs to the action of force if sufficiently strong. In practice, therefore, there exists no perfectly rigid body, solid bodies are rigid only to an extent. Still for the purposes of mathematical analysis we visualise a perfectly rigid body as one which does not yield to the action of any force *i. e* the particles constituting it retain the relative distances between themselves unchanged even when it is acted upon by any force, however great. Let us now consider a small plane area inside a body. The two portions of the body on either side of it exert on each other equal and opposite action. Let this action be R. Resolve it into two components, T in the plane and S normal to it; then T is called tangential or shearing stress and S normal stress. The deformations produced by the action of stress are called strains. The effect of the shearing stress (T) is to cause the portion of the body on either sides of the plane area to slide over that on the other side; this deformation is known as shearing strain e. g. the action of a pair of scissors in cutting through a piece of cloth. It may be mentioned in passing that the normal stress (S) is either one of tension or compression according as the two portions of the body on either side of the plane tend to exert a pull or a thrust respectively on one another. It follows at once that a perfectly rigid body can resist shearing stress to

an indefinite extent. On the other hand fluids *i. e.* 'substances
we have classed as liquids and gases have very little cohesion.
If a plane is passed through water or air it meets with little
resistance. Hence shearing stress between the parts of water or
air is very small. Just as for purposes of mathematical analysis
we evolved a definition of a perfectly rigid body, so also we
define our ideal or perfect fluid as one between the various parts
of which no shearing stress can exist. In other words, "a perfect
fluid is an aggregation of particles which yield at once to the
slightest effort made to separate them from each other."

Consider now a small plane area round a point P in a fluid
mass. The action of the fluid mass on one side of it is a force
R, having components T along the plane and S normal to it.
But by hypothesis, since the mass is a perfect fluid, T$=$O, hence
the direction of R is normal to the plane. The action of the fluid
mass on a small plane area is always normal to the plane area.
Thus the fluid pressure is normal to any surface with which it
is in contact.

Actually however, all fluids do more or less offer resistance
to separation or division e. g. if a jug of coal tar be poured over
a slab, it takes much longer to spread over the surface than water.
This is due to difference in the degree of viscosity of the fluid.
We can amend our definition of fluid in such a way as to include
fluids of all degrees of viscosity. "A fluid is an aggregation of
particles which yield to the slightest effort made to separate them
from each other, if it be continued long enough". In a viscous
fluid at rest there can be no shearing stress as in the case of a
perfect fluid. Hence the fundamental property of a perfect fluid
proved above is also that of a viscous fluid *at rest.* It follows
that all propositions in Hydrostatics are true for all fluids whatever their viscosity.

REMARK :—Fluids which are easily compressible e. g. air,
are known as gases; while incompressible fluids e. g. water or
mercury, are known as liquids. A prefect liquid is a perfect

fluid which is absolutely incompressible *i. e.* which can resist normal stress (S) to an indefinite extent.

1·2. **Pressure.** Consider an area A of a plane surface exposed inside a fluid. We have already seen that the action of the fluid is a force R normal to the plane. If the action of the fluid on A be uniform, then $\frac{R}{A}$ is the thrust per unit area. This thrust per unit area is called the pressure at each point of the surface.

When the thrust on a surface is not uniformly distributed, then the pressure will vary from point to point. Consider an indefinitely small area δA of the plane area A round a point P and let δR be the thrust on it Then $\frac{\delta R}{\delta A}$ is the average force per unit area. In the limiting case when δA tends to zero, $\frac{\delta R}{\delta A}$ ultimately tends to $\frac{dR}{dA} = p$; then p is defined to be the measure of pressure at the point P.

1·3. The pressure at any point of a fluid at rest is the same in every direction.

Let O be any point in the fluid and let us take any three mutually perpendicular lines as axes of co-ordinates. Consider a small tetrahedron formed by the fluid mass enclosed by the 3 coordinates planes and the plane ABC. Let p_1, p_2, p_3 be the pressures on the 3 faces BOC, COA, AOB and q, the pressure on ABC.

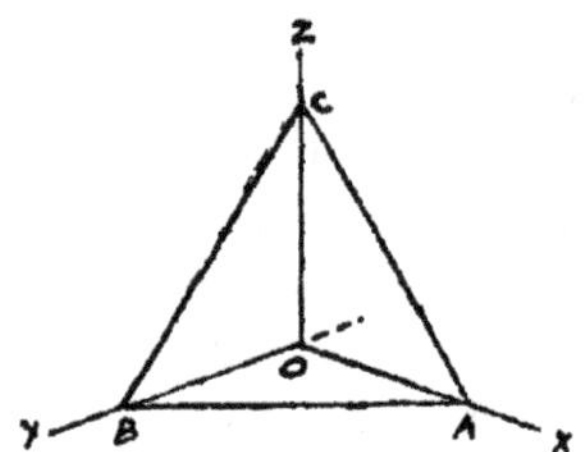

Let $\triangle$ be the area of the triangle ABC, and l, m, n the direction cosines of the perpendicular from O to the plane ABC and let h be the length of this perpendicular.

Then areas of the triangles BOC, COA and AOB are respectively $\triangle l, \triangle m,$ and $\triangle n.$ Also the volume of the tetrahedron OABC is $\frac{1}{3} \triangle h.$

Now since p_1 is the pressure on the face BOC, the force on this face is $p_1 \triangle l$ acting normally to the face BOC *i e.* parallel to OX. Forces on the faces AOB, and AOC have no component parallel to OA. Force on the face ABC has a component, $q \triangle l$ parallel to OA.

Let the fluid be at rest under the action of forces (X, Y, Z) per unit mass.

Hence the tetrahedron under consideration is in equilibrium under the pressures normal to the 4 faces of the tetrahedron and the extraneous forces.

Resolving along OX, we have

$$p_1 \triangle l - q \triangle l + \tfrac{1}{3} \triangle P\, hX = 0,$$

P being the density of the fluid, for the mass of the volume of the fluid in the tetrahedron is $\tfrac{1}{3} \triangle P\, h$,

Hence $\qquad (p_1 - q)\, l + \tfrac{1}{3} P\, X\, h = 0 .. \ldots \ldots (1)$

Now let us diminish the size of the tetrahedron by letting the plane ABC move parallel to itself towards O. Ultimately when the tetrahedron is reduced to almost a mere point, h becomes an infinitesimal and may be neglected in equation (1), hence

$$p_1 - q = 0$$
$$\text{or, } p_1 = q$$

Similarly $\qquad p_2 = q, p_3 = q.$

Hence, $\qquad p_1 = p_2 = p_3 = q.$

But as the three directions OX, OY, OZ are perfectly arbitrary it follows that the pressure p at O along any direction is the same. Of course at any other point, P in the fluid mass the pressure may be very different from what it is at O, this difference always depending on forces which act bodily on the fluid mass.

1·4. Density and Specific gravity.

Density of any homogeneous substance is the mass per unit volume of that substance. Hence if M be the mass of a body whose density is d and volume V, then $d = \dfrac{M}{V}$ or, $V = \dfrac{M}{d}.$

(5)

The specific gravity of a substance is the ratio of the weight of any volume of the substance to the weight of an equal volume of some standard substance. Usually this substance is distilled water at $4°C$ in the case of solids or liquids.

It is evident that specific gravity of a substance is the ratio of the densities of the substance to that of the standard substance.

$$S = \frac{d}{d'}$$

where,　　　$d =$ density of the substance,

　　　　　　$d' = $　　,,　　,,　　standard substance.

$$\therefore d = Sd'.$$

Since in the C. G. S. system of units $d' = 1$, specific gravity of a substance is equal to its density.

If W be the weight of a body whose volume is V and specific gravity is S, then density $= Sd' = \dfrac{W}{V}$.

Hence　　　　　　$W = Sd'V.$

1·5.　*Specific gravity of Mixtures.*

Let $v_1, v_2, v_3, \ldots$ be the volumes of the different substances, and let $s_1, s_2, s_3, \ldots$ be their specific gravities, and let d' be the weight of unit volume of the standard substance. Let v be the volume of the mixture and s its specific gravity.

Assuming that no chemical action takes place and therefore there is no change in the volume,

$$v = v_1 + v_2 + v_3 + \ldots\ldots\ldots \tag{1}$$

Also weights of the various constituents of the mixture are

$$v_1\, s_1\, d', \ v_2\, s_2\, d', \text{ etc.}$$

Hence the total weight of the mixture vsd' must be equal to the sum of the weights of its constituent,

$$\therefore vsd' = v_1\, s_1\, d' + v_2\, s_2\, d' + v_3\, s_3\, d' + \ldots$$

$$\text{or, } s = \frac{v_1\, s_1 + v_2\, s_2 + v_3\, s_3 + \ldots}{v_1 + v_2 + \ldots\ldots}, \ \ldots\ldots \qquad \text{by (1)}$$

(6)

If. however, there occurs a diminution in the total volume when the substances are mixed so that the actual volumo of the mixture is a fractional part k of the sum of the volumes of the different components we have

$$v = k \ (v_1 + v_2 + v_3 + \ldots\ldots)$$

$$\text{Hence } s = \frac{v_1 \ s_1 + v_2 \ s_2 + \underline{\qquad}}{k \ (v_1 + v_2 + \ . \ .\ )} \ .$$

Example 1. If the specific gravity of pure milk be 1.031 and of an adulterated specimon 1.021, find the percentage of added water (*i. e.* the number of gallons of water which must have been added to 100 gallons of pure milk).

Let us suppose x gallons of water are added to 100 gallons of pure milk to have the specific gravity 1.024.

Total volume of the mixture $= 100 + x$

Total weight of the mixture $= (x + 100) \times 1.031 \ d'$

$$\therefore \text{specific gravity} = 1.024$$

$$= \frac{(x + 103.1)d'}{(x + 100)d'}$$

where d' is the wt. of a unit volume of water.

$$\therefore x = 29.17.$$

Example 2. From a vessel full of a liquid of density P is removed $\frac{1}{n}$ th of its contents and it is filled up with a liquid of density σ.

If this operation be repeated m times find the resulting density in the vessel.

Deduce the denisty in a vessel of volume v, originally filled with liquid of density P, after a volume u of liquid of density P has dripped into it by infinitesimal drops.

Let v be the original volume of the liquid; $\dfrac{v}{n}$ has been removed and replaced by a liquid of density σ; hence the mass of the mixture $= (1-\dfrac{1}{n})v\rho + \dfrac{v}{n}\rho\,\sigma$

$\therefore d_1 =$ density after the first operation $= \dfrac{\text{mass of the mixture}}{\text{volume}}$

$$= (1-\dfrac{1}{n})\rho + \dfrac{\sigma}{n}.$$

Similarly, $d_2 =$ density after the second operation.

$$= (1-\dfrac{1}{n})d_1 + \dfrac{\sigma}{n}$$

$$= (1-\dfrac{1}{n})^2\rho + (1-\dfrac{1}{n})\dfrac{\sigma}{n} + \dfrac{\sigma}{n}$$

$$= (1-\dfrac{1}{n})^2\rho + \dfrac{\sigma}{n}\left\{ 1 + (1-\dfrac{1}{n}) \right\}.$$

$$d_3 = (1-\dfrac{1}{n})^3\rho + \dfrac{\sigma}{n}\left\{ 1 + (1-\dfrac{1}{n}) + (1-\dfrac{1}{n})^2 \right\}.$$

So, $d_m =$ density after the completion of the m th operation

$$= (1-\dfrac{1}{n})^m \rho + \dfrac{\sigma}{n}\left\{ 1 + (1-\dfrac{1}{n}) + \ldots (1-\dfrac{1}{n})^{m-1} \right\}$$

$$= (1-\dfrac{1}{n})^m \rho + \dfrac{\sigma}{n}\left\{ \dfrac{1 - (1-\dfrac{1}{n})^m}{1 - (1-\dfrac{1}{n})} \right\}$$

$$= (1-\dfrac{1}{n})^m \rho + \sigma \left\{ 1 - (1-\dfrac{1}{n})^m \right\} \ldots\ldots\ldots (1)$$

Cor. If m and n be made to tend to ∞ so that $\dfrac{v}{n}$, an infinitesimal quantity, is removed m times where $\dfrac{m}{n}v = u$, we have

$$\mathrm{Lt}\,\dfrac{m}{n} = u/v, \quad \text{when } m \text{ and } n \longrightarrow \infty$$

Hence from (1) the density required is the limit of

$$(1-\dfrac{1}{n})^m \rho + \sigma \left\{ 1 - (1-\dfrac{1}{n})^m \right\}$$

(8)

when m, n tend to ∞ in such a way that $\mathrm{Lt}\,\dfrac{m}{n}=\dfrac{u}{v}$

Hence, required density $= \mathsf{P}\,e^{-u/v} + \sigma\,(1-e^{-u/v})$

$$= \sigma +(\mathsf{P}-\sigma)\,e^{-u/v}$$

1·6. Density of a heterogeneous fluid

Consider a point P of a fluid in which density varies from point to point. Consider δm an elementary mass of the fluid round P. Let its volume be δv, then if P be the average density of the mass δm,

$$\mathsf{P}=\delta m/\delta v.$$

In the limit when δm and $\delta v \longrightarrow o$, $\mathsf{P}\left(=\dfrac{dm}{dv}\right)$ becomes the actual density at the point P.

Example 1. The density at any point of a liquid contained in a cone having its axis vertical and vertex downwards is greater than the density at the surface by a quantity varying as the depth of the point. Show that the density of the liquid, when mixed up so as to be uniform, will be that of the liquid originally at the depth of $\frac{1}{4}$th of the axis of the cone.

Let h be the height of the cone.

Consider a circular disc of liquid at distance x from vertex O and of thickness dx. Since the depth of every point on the disc is $(h-x)$ below the base, density at every point of the elementary disc is the same $viz.$ $\mathsf{P}_o+(h-x)\,\lambda$, P_o being the density at the top.

Mass of the disc is, therefore,

$$\{\,\mathsf{P}_o+(h-x)\,\lambda\,\}\,\pi x^2\tan^2\alpha\,dx.$$

$\therefore$ Total mass $= \displaystyle\int_o^h \{\,\mathsf{P}_o+(h-x)\lambda\,\}\,\pi x^2\tan^2\alpha\,dx$

Total volume $= \tfrac{1}{3}\pi h^3\tan^2\alpha$

$\therefore$ Mean density $= \quad P_o + \lambda\, h - \frac{3\lambda}{4}\, h$

$$= \quad P_o + \lambda\, \frac{h}{4}$$

$=$ density of the liquid originally at the depth of one-fourth of axis of the cone.

Example 2.   Show that the specific gravity of a mixture of n fluids is greater when equal volumes are taken than when equal weights are taken, assuming that no change in volume occurs as the result of mixing.

CHAPTER II

Equilibrium of Fluids.

2. 1. The Fundamental Equation of Equilibrium :—

Consider a mass of fluid, compressible or incompressible, homogeneous or heterogeneous, at rest under the action of any system of given forces. Let the component of the given force at any point P (x, y, z) along the three rectangular axes be respectively X, Y, Z per unit mass of the fluid.

Let ρ be the density of the fluid at any point P (x, y, z). We shall suppose that ρ, X, Y, Z are all functions of (x, y, z) We require to find p, the pressure at any point P as a function of (x, y, z).

Let $p = f(x, y, z)$.

Take a point Q $(x + \delta x, y, z)$ adjacent to P and with P Q as axis, construct a cylinder of the fluid with an infinitesimal cross section α.

This cylinder is kept in equilibrium by the following forces:—

(i) the thrust of the fluid acting along P Q on the cross section at P. This thrust is $p\alpha = \alpha f(x, y, z)$;

(ii) the thrust of the fluid acting along Q P on the cross section at Q. This thrust is $p'\alpha = \alpha f(x + \delta x, y, z)$;

iii) the external force acting on the mass of the fluid; the component of this force parallel to OX or PQ is plainly $X\alpha\rho\delta x$, $\alpha\rho\delta x$, being the mass of the fluid in the cylinder;

(iv) The fluid pressures acting on the curved surface of the cylinder. They have no component along PQ, being everywhere perpendicular to PQ.

Hence resolving along PQ, we have for equilibrium

$$\{ f(x+\delta x,\ y,\ z)-f(x,y,z)\ \}\ a= X a \rho \delta x,$$

$$\text{or} \quad \frac{f(x+\delta x,\ y,\ z)-f(x,\ y,\ z)}{\delta x}=\rho\, X$$

Proceeding to the limit when δx is made indefinitely small,

$$\frac{\partial f}{\partial x}=\rho\, X;$$

Similarly,

$$\frac{\partial f}{\partial y}=\rho\, Y,$$

$$\frac{\partial f}{\partial z}=\rho\, Z.$$

In other words,

$$\frac{\partial p}{\partial x}=\rho\, X,\ \frac{\partial p}{\partial y}=\rho\, Y,\ \frac{\partial p}{\partial z}=\rho\, Z,\ \dots\dots\ (1)$$

Again since, $dp=df=\left(\dfrac{\partial f}{\partial x}d\,x+\dfrac{\partial f}{\partial y}d\,y+\dfrac{\partial f}{\partial z}d\,z\right)$

$$=\rho(X\,d\,x+Y\,d\,y+Z\,d\,z);$$

$$\therefore\quad dp=\rho\,(\,X\,dx+Y\,dy+Z\,dz\,).\ \ \dots\dots\ (2)$$

This is the differential equation which determines the pressure.

Remark : Let PQ be the axis of a very small cylinder bounded by planes perpendicular to PQ, PQ being drawn in *any* direction. Let p be the pressure at P and $p+\delta p$ at Q, α the area of cross section and δ s the length of PQ. Let S δm be the component of the forces acting on the infinitesimal fluid mass δm at P, in the direction of PQ.

Then as before, considering the equilibrium of this cylinder of the fluid we have

$$(p+\delta\,p\,)\alpha-p\alpha=S\delta m=S\rho\alpha\delta s,$$

$$\text{or, } dp=\rho S\ ds\dots\dots\dots(3)$$

Now if (x, y, z) be the coordinates of P, then the direction cosines of P Q are $\frac{dx}{ds}, \frac{dy}{ds}, \frac{dz}{ds}$. Hence if X δm, Y δm, Z δm are the components the force acting on an elementary mass δm in the direction of the coordinate axes, then the component of these forces along PQ is

$$(X \frac{dx}{ds}+Y \frac{dy}{ds}+Z \frac{dz}{ds}) \, \delta m,$$

So that

$$S \, \delta m =(X\frac{dx}{ds}+Y \frac{dy}{ds}+ Z\frac{dz}{ds}) \, \delta m$$

Hence from (3)

$$dp=\rho \, (X \, dx+Y \, dy+Z \, dz).$$

If the position of P is given in terms of the cylinderical coordinates r, θ, and z, and P, T, Z be the conponents of S in in the direction of r, θ, z,

$$S = P \frac{dr}{ds} + T \, r \frac{d\theta}{ds} + Z\frac{dz}{ds},$$

for the cosines of the angles made by P Q with O P, PM, (perpendicular to O P in the plane Z O P), and O Z are $\frac{dr}{ds}$, $r\frac{d\theta}{ds}$, $\frac{dz}{ds}$ respectively.

Hence, $\quad dp=\rho \, (Pdr+Tr \, d\theta+Z \, dz) \ldots\ldots$ (4).

Again if the position of P be given by the ordinary polar coordinates r, θ, ϕ and if the components of S in the direction of r, θ, and ϕ be R, N, T then

$$S = R\frac{dr}{ds} + N \, r \, \text{Sin } \theta \, \frac{d\phi}{ds}+Tr\frac{d\theta}{ds}.$$

Hence, $\quad dp=\rho \, (R \, dr+N \, r \, \text{Sin } \theta \, d\phi+T \, r \, d\theta) \ldots\ldots(5)$

2·2. For equilibrium of the fluid we must have

(13)

$$\frac{\partial p}{\partial x} = \rho \, X, \quad \frac{\partial p}{\partial y} = \rho \, Y, \quad \frac{\partial p}{\partial z} = \rho \, Z \quad . (1)$$

But p being a function of the independent variables x, y, z

$$\frac{\partial^2 p}{\partial y \, \partial z} = \frac{\partial^2 p}{\partial z \, \partial y}, \quad \frac{\partial^2 p}{\partial z \, \partial x} = \frac{\partial^2 p}{\partial x \, \partial z}, \quad \frac{\partial^2 p}{\partial x \, \partial y} = \frac{\partial^2 p}{\partial y \, \partial x}$$

Hence from (1) we have

$$\frac{\partial}{\partial y} (\rho Z) = \frac{\partial}{\partial z} (\rho Y)$$

$$\frac{\partial}{\partial z} (\rho X) = \frac{\partial}{\partial x} (\rho Z) \dots \dots \dots \dots \dots (2)$$

$$\frac{\partial}{\partial x} (\rho Y) = \frac{\partial}{\partial y} (\rho X).$$

From these we obtain

$$Z \frac{\partial \rho}{\partial y} - Y \frac{\partial \rho}{\partial z} = \rho \left(\frac{\partial Y}{\partial z} - \frac{\partial Z}{\partial y} \right)$$

$$X \frac{\partial \rho}{\partial z} - Z \frac{\partial \rho}{\partial x} = \rho \left(\frac{\partial Z}{\partial x} - \frac{\partial X}{\partial z} \right) \dots \dots (3)$$

$$Y \frac{\partial \rho}{\partial x} - X \frac{\partial \rho}{\partial y} = \rho \left(\frac{\partial X}{\partial y} - \frac{\partial Y}{\partial x} \right)$$

Remark I. In the case of heterogeneous fluids, whose law of density is known (*i. e* when ρ is a known function of x, y, z,) conditions of equilibrium are given by equations 2, or (3), above.

Remark II. Elastic fluids under the action of a conservative system of force.

Let V be the potential function of the system so that

$$X \, dx + Y \, dy + Z \, dz = -dV.$$

In the case of elastic fluids we have

$$p = k \, \rho$$

hence, the equation $dp = \rho \, X \, dx + Y \, dy + Z \, dZ)$ becomes

$$\frac{dp}{p} = -\frac{dV}{k}$$

Integrating

$$p = c\,e^{-V/k}, \text{ and } P = \frac{c}{k}\,e^{-V/k}.$$

Multiplying equations (3) by X, Y, Z respectively and adding, we obtain

$$X\left(\frac{\partial Y}{\partial z} - \frac{\partial Z}{\partial y}\right) + Y\left(\frac{\partial Z}{\partial x} - \frac{\partial X}{\partial z}\right) + Z\left(\frac{\partial X}{\partial y} - \frac{\partial Y}{\partial x}\right) = 0,$$

which is therefore a necessary condition of equilibrium.

The geometric interpretation of this equation is obvious *viz.* that for equilibrium to be possible the lines of force, $\dfrac{dx}{X} = \dfrac{dy}{Y} = \dfrac{dz}{Z}$, can be intersected orthogonally by a system of surfaces.

Remark I. : If the fluid be homogeneous and incompressible *i. e.* if P is constant the *necessary and sufficient condition* for the equilibrium of the fluid is that $(X\,dx + Y\,dy + Z\,dz)$ be a perfect differential, or in other words, the force system be conservative, or capable of representation by a potential function. That is, there exists a function $V\,(x, y, z)$

such that $X = -\dfrac{\partial V}{\partial x},\ Y = -\dfrac{\partial V}{\partial y},\ Z = -\dfrac{\partial V}{\partial z}.$

For if this is so, then clearly by taking $p = -VP$, the equations (1) of § 2.1 are satisfied since P is constant. Conversely if equations (1) of § 2.1 hold *i. e.* if the fluid is in equilibrium, then there exists a function $p\,(x, y, z)$

such that $X = \dfrac{1}{P}\dfrac{\partial p}{\partial x},\ Y = \dfrac{1}{P}\dfrac{\partial p}{\partial y},\ Z = \dfrac{1}{P}\dfrac{\partial p}{\partial z}$

so that the force system is conservative and its potential function is $-\dfrac{p}{P}$.

2. 3. Superposed Fluids :—Let two fluids be superposed so that p, P and (X, Y, Z) are the pressure, density, and force components per unit mass of one fluid and p', P', (X', Y', Z') are similar quantities for the second fluid.

The two fluids being in equilibrium, we have for the 1st

$$dp = \text{P} (\text{X } dx + \text{Y } dy + \text{Z } dz).$$

and for the second

$$dp' = \text{P}' (\text{X}' dx + \text{Y}' dy + \text{Z}' dz)$$

Along, the surface of separation S, the difference $(p - p')$ is zero, for any element of this surface must be subject to the same pressure on both sides for equilibrium to exist. We have therefore, the result that for any displacement ds along the surface S,

$$\text{P } (\text{X } dx + \text{Y } dy + \text{Z } dz = \text{P}' (\text{X}' dx + \text{Y}' dy + \text{Z}' dz),$$

which is the differential equation of the surface of separation.

Remark I. When the force systems (X, Y, Z) and (X', Y', Z') are conservative or derivable from potential functions V and V', we have

$$\text{P}' d\text{V} - \text{P}' d\text{V}' = 0.$$

Remark II. When the force system is the same in two cases
$$(\text{P} - \text{P}') d\text{V} = 0,$$

Since $\text{P} - \text{P}' \neq 0$, $d\text{V} = 0$ along the surface of separation.

The surface of separation is therefore an equipotential surface.

Remark III. If P, P' be supposed to be constants the equation of the surface of separation is given by

$$\text{PV} - \text{P}'\text{V}' = \text{cons.}$$

2. 4. Pascal's Principle :— In the case of an incompressible homogeneous liquid subject to a conservative system of forces derivable from a potential function V, we have

$$\frac{dp}{\rho} = -d\,\mathrm{V}$$

$$\therefore (p - p_o) \,/\, \rho = (\mathrm{V}_o - \mathrm{V}),$$

giving the pressure at any point when that at any other point P_o is known.

Suppose now that by any process whatever the pressure at P_o is altered to $p_o + \delta\, p_o$; a new condition of equilibrium is established and the value of the pressure at any point P will become $p + \delta p$.

The new equation of equilibrium is

$$\frac{p + \delta p - (p_o + \delta p_o)}{\rho} = \mathrm{V}_o - \mathrm{V}$$

$$\therefore \delta p = \delta p_o.$$

It follows then that in a liquid in equilibrium any pressure applied at any part of the liquid is transmitted equally to all the parts of the liquid.

This is known as Pascal's Principle for a homogeneous incompressible liquid and is applied in Bramah's Press.

In the case of a fluid in which density ρ is a function of pressure, the equation of equilibrium is

$$\int_{p_o}^{p} \frac{dp}{f(p)} = \mathrm{V}_o - \mathrm{V},$$

where $\rho = f(p)$ and p_o is the pressure at the given point P_o.

If we now change the pressure at P_o to $p_o + \delta p_o$ the new value of the pressure at P is $p + \delta p$, which is given by

$$\int_{p_o + \delta p_o}^{p + \delta p} \frac{dp}{f(p)} = \mathrm{V}_o - \mathrm{V}$$

$$= \int_{p_0}^{p} \frac{dp}{f(p)},$$

$$\text{or} \quad \int_{p}^{p+\delta p} \frac{dp}{f(p)} = \int_{p_0}^{p_0+\delta p_0} \frac{dp}{f(p)}.$$

This equation gives δp in terms of δp_0 and expresses the generalised Principle of Pascal.

In the particular case, where δp_0 is infinitesimally small, so is δp.

$$\therefore \int_{p}^{p+\delta p} \frac{dp}{f(p)} = \frac{\delta p}{f(p+\theta\delta p)}, \text{ where } 0<\theta<1,$$

$$\text{and} \int_{p_0}^{p_0+\delta p_0} \frac{dp}{f(p)} = \frac{\delta p_0}{f(p_0+\theta'\delta p_0)}, \text{ where } 0<\theta'<1.$$

$$\text{Hence} \quad \frac{\delta p}{\rho} = \frac{\delta p_0}{\rho_0}$$

The infinitesimally small variations of pressure are, therefore, transmitted at every point in proportion to the density at the point.

2. 5. Surfaces of Equal pressure. In all cases in which equilibrium is possible, we obtain by integration

$$p = f(x, y, z).$$

This shows that locus of all points at which pressure is constant is the surface

$$f(x, y, z) = \text{cons} \dots \dots \quad (1)$$

This is known as a surface of equal pressure. It is evident that by varying the value of the constant we obtain a whole series of surfaces of equal pressure.

If this constant be taken as equal to the pressure external to the fluid we obtain the equation of the free surface or the external surface.

(18)

If the external pressure is zero, the free surface is given by

$$f'x,\ y,\ z) = 0.$$

We shall now prove an important theorem regarding the surfaces of equal pressure *viz.* "The surfaces of equal pressure are the surfaces intersecting orthogonally the lines of force".

For the direction cosines of the normal to a surface of equal pressure at a point P $(x,\ y,\ z)$ are by (1) proportional to

$$\frac{\partial f}{\partial x},\ \frac{\partial f}{\partial y},\ \frac{\partial f}{\partial z}$$

But these quantities are respectively equal to PX, PY, PZ.

Hence the direction cosines of the normal at P to the surface of equal pressure passing through it are proportional to X, Y, Z. The direction of this normal is, therefore, also the direction of the line of force at P. The line of force at P consequently intersects the surface of equal pressure passing through P orthogonally.

Remark I. In the case of a homogeneous liquid at rest under the action of a given system of forces, the surfaces of equal pressure are equipotential surfaces. For, we have already seen that when P is constant the system of force must be conservative, *i. e.* must have a potential function V.

$$\therefore dp = P\ (X\ dx + Y\ dy + Z\ dz)$$

$$= -P\ dV$$

or, $p + PV = \text{cons.}$

Hence if p is constant over any surface so is V, and vice versa.

Remark II. If a fluid is at rest under the action of a conservative force system, surfaces of equal pressure are equipotential, and are also surfaces of equal density.

For if the force-system is conservative, then

$$X\, dx + Y\, dy + Z\, dz = -dV$$

Hence for equilibrium $dp = -P\, dV$.

Also since the fluid is in equilibrium, dp is a perfect differential. Hence P must be a function of V, for if not—$P\, dV$, and therefore dp will not be a perfect differential.

Hence both p aud P must be functions of V. Consequently if V is constant over any surface so must p and P be over it and vice versa. Surfaces of equal pressure are therefore also surfaces of equal potential equal and density.

2. 6. Curves of Equal pressure and density in the case of heterogeneous incompressible fluids.—

The identity of the surfaces of equal pressure and density proved in § 2.5 depends on the conservative character of the force system. If the force system be not conservative, the two surfaces will not be coincident. Suppose we ave a surface of equal pressure given by

$$p = f\,(x,\, y,\, z), \text{ where p is taken as constant. } \ldots (1)$$

Let $P = \phi\,(x,\, y,\, z)$ be a surface of equal density,

$$\text{where } P \text{ is assigned a constant value.. } \ldots \ldots \ldots (2)$$

We require the intersection of these two surfaces which will be the curve of equal pressure and density $i.\,e.$ the locus of all points where both the density and pressure of the fluid are the same.

If we consider the totality of surfaces of equal pressure and the totality of the surfaces of equal density, these two series of surfaces define for us a family. of curves whose differential equation we proceed to discover.

Let $P\,(x,\, y,\, z)$ and $Q\,(x+dx,\, y+dy,\, z+dz)$ be any two neighbouring points on a curve of this family, which for the sake of definiteness we may assume to be given by the interesection of (1) and (2).

Since P and Q are points on the same surface of equal-pressure

$$f(x, y, z) = f(x+dx, y+dy, z+dz)$$

$$= f(x, y, z) + (\frac{\partial f}{\partial x}dx + \frac{\partial f}{\partial y}dy + \frac{\partial f}{\partial z}dz);$$

Neglecting infinitesimals of higher order than the first,

$$\frac{\partial f}{\partial x}dx + \frac{\partial f}{\partial y}dy + \frac{\partial f}{\partial z}dz = 0.$$

or, $\quad \frac{\partial p}{\partial x}dx + \frac{\partial p}{\partial y}dy + \frac{\partial p}{\partial z}dz = 0.$

or $\mathrm{P}\ (\mathrm{X}\ dx + \mathrm{Y}\ dy + \mathrm{Z}\ dz) = 0 \ldots\ldots(3)$

Again, since P and Q are points on the same surface of equal density, we have similarly

$$\frac{\partial \rho}{\partial x}dx + \frac{\partial \rho}{\partial y}dy + \frac{\partial \rho}{\partial z}dz = 0 \ldots\ldots (4,$$

dx, dy, dz therefore satisfy equations (3) and (4).

Hence,

$$\frac{dx}{Z\frac{\partial \rho}{\partial y} - Y\frac{\partial \rho}{\partial z}} = \frac{dy}{X\frac{\partial \rho}{\partial z} - Z\frac{\partial \rho}{\partial x}} = \frac{dz}{Y\frac{\partial \rho}{\partial x} - X\frac{\partial \rho}{\partial y}} \cdot (5)$$

But from equations (3) of § 2·2 we have as conditions of equilibrium of the fluid

$$Z\frac{\partial \rho}{\partial y} - Y\frac{\partial \rho}{\partial z} = \rho\left(\frac{\partial Y}{\partial z} - \frac{\partial Z}{\partial y}\right), \text{ etc.}$$

Hence equations (5) become

$$\frac{dx}{\frac{\partial Z}{\partial y} - \frac{\partial Y}{\partial z}} = \frac{dy}{\frac{\partial X}{\partial z} - \frac{\partial Z}{\partial x}} = \frac{dz}{\frac{\partial Y}{\partial x} - \frac{\partial X}{\partial y}} \ldots\ldots(6)$$

These are the differential equations of the curves of equal pressure and density.

2·7. Fluids at rest under the action of gravity :—

Take vertical measuring down wards as the axis of Z, then

$$X = Y = o, \quad Z = g.$$

Hence equation (2) of § 2·1 becomes

$$dp = \rho \, g \, d z$$

If ρ is constant $i.\ e.$ if the fluid is a homogeneous liquid,

$$p = g \rho \; z + c$$

Thus surfaces of equal pressure are horizontal planes. The free surface must therefore be horizontal. Let us take the origin in the free surface and Π as the external pressure,

then $p = \Pi$, when $z = o$, so that $c = \Pi$.

Hence $\qquad p = g \, \rho \, z + \Pi.$

If there is no external pressure on the free surface

$$, \qquad p = g \, \rho \, z.$$

(ii). In the case of a heterogeneous liquid we have

$$dp, = g \, \rho \, dz,$$

so that ρ must be a function of z alone.

It follows that density and pressure are constant for all points in the same horizontal plane. In other words surfaces of equal pressure and also of equal density are horizontal planes.

(iii . In the case of an elastic fluid,

$$p = k \, \rho$$

$$\therefore \frac{dp}{p} = \frac{g}{k} dz$$

or, $p = c\, e^{\,g\,z/k}$

Thus the surfaces of equal pressure are again horizontal planes.

Ex 1. A mass of fluid rests upon a plane subject to a central attractive force $\frac{\mu}{r^2}$, situated at a distance c from the plane on the side opposite to that on which the fluid is; if a is the radius of the free spherical surface of the fluid show that the pressure at any point is given by

$$\mu\, \rho\, \left(\frac{1}{r} - \frac{1}{a}\right).$$

Let O be the centre of force. O M perpendicular from O on the given plane.

Using equation (5) of § 2·1 we have

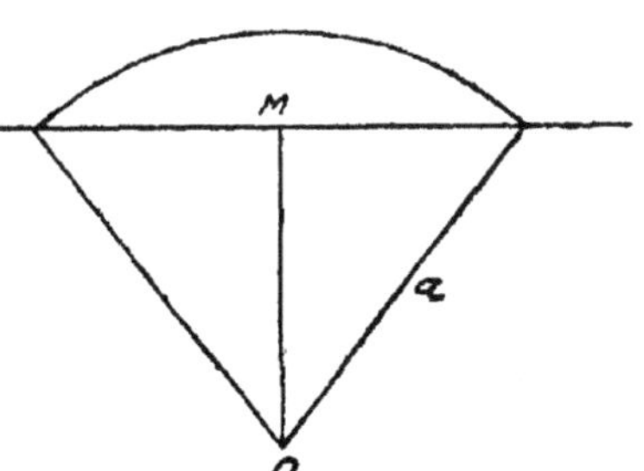

$$dp = -\,\frac{\mu\rho}{r^2}dr$$

$$\therefore p = \frac{\mu\rho}{r} + c$$

Thus if $p =$ const., $r =$ const. so that locus of all points at which pressure of the liquid is the same is a sphere with centre O   External pressure is zero, therefore, the free surface is a sphere of radius a, given by

$$0 = c + \frac{\mu\rho}{a};$$

$$\therefore p = \mu\, \rho\, \left(\frac{1}{r} - \frac{1}{a}\right).$$

This gives pressure at any point of the fluid.

Ex. 2.   A mass M of gas at uniform temperature is diffused through all space and at each point (x, y, z), the components of the force per unit mass are $-Ax$, $-By$, $-Cz$. The pressure and density at the origin are p_0 and ρ_0 respectively.

Prove that

$$A\ B\ C\ \rho_0\ M^2 = 8\ \pi\ ^3 p_0{}^3.$$

We have by equation (1) of § 2·1

$$dp = -\rho\ (A\ x\ d\ x + B\ y\ d\ y + C\ z\ d\ z),$$

and $\qquad p = k\rho$

$$\therefore \frac{dp}{p} = -\frac{A\ x\ d\ x + B\ y\ d\ y + C\ z\ d\ z}{k}$$

or $\qquad p = D\ e^{-\left(\dfrac{A\ x^2 + B\ y^2 + C\ z^2}{2\ k}\right)}$

Since $p = p_0$ and $\rho = \rho_0$ when $x = y = z = 0$,

$$p_0 = D, \frac{p_0}{\rho_0} = k.$$

Accordingly, $\qquad p = p_0\ e^{-\frac{\rho_0}{2p_0} - (Ax^2 + By^2 + Cz^2)}$

Also density at any point (x, y, z) is given by

$$\rho = \rho_0\ e^{-\frac{\rho_0}{2 p_0}\ Ax^2 + (By^2 + Cz^2)}$$

Now, the total mass of the gas diffused throughout whole space is

$$\int_{-\infty}^{\infty} \int_{-\infty}^{\infty} \int_{-\infty}^{\infty} \rho\ dx\ dy\ dz.$$

(24)

$$\therefore M = \int_{-\infty}^{\infty} \int_{-\infty}^{\infty} \int_{-\infty}^{\infty} \rho_0\, e^{-\frac{\rho_0 (A x^2 + B y^2 + C z^2)}{2p_0}} \, dx\, dy\, dz$$

$$= \rho_0 \int_{-\infty}^{\infty} e^{-\frac{A\rho_0}{2p_0} x^2}\, dx \times \int_{-\infty}^{\infty} e^{-\frac{B\rho_0}{2p_0} y^2}\, dy \times \int_{-\infty}^{\infty} e^{-\frac{C\rho_0}{2p_0} z^2}\, dz$$

$$= \rho_0 \sqrt{\frac{2\pi p_0}{A\rho_0}} \times \sqrt{\frac{2\pi p_0}{B\rho_0}} \times \sqrt{\frac{2\pi p_0}{C\rho_0}}$$

$$= \rho_0 \left(\frac{8\pi p_0{}^3}{ABC\rho_0{}^3}\right)^{\frac{1}{2}}$$

$$= \left(\frac{8\pi p_0{}^3}{ABC\rho_0}\right)^{\frac{1}{2}}$$

$$\therefore ABC\rho_0 M^2 = 8\pi p_0{}^3.$$

Ex 3. A compressible liquid is at rest under gravity. Defining the compressibility, k, by the relation $\dfrac{\rho - \rho_0}{\rho_0} = k\,(p - p_0)$ where ρ, p are the density and pressure, respectively, and ρ_0 and p_0 refer to the free surface, and assuming k to be constant, show that at a depth z below the free surface

$$\frac{dp}{dz} = \rho_0 g \left\{ 1 + k\,(p - p_0) \right\}$$

and hence that $\qquad \rho = \rho_0\, e^{kg\rho_0 z}.$

A mine shaft has the same horizontal cross section at all depths It is filled with water to a depth h. Show that if the density. of the water were everywhere equal to that at the surface, the water would rise in the shaft a distance $\dfrac{kg\rho_0 h^2}{2}$. It may be assumed that k is very small. (Tripos Part I, 1925. I. C. S. Higher Applied 1937).

Ex. 4. An infinite mass of homogeneous fluid surrounds a closed surface and is attracted to a point (O) within the surface with a force which varies inversely as the cube of the distance. If the pressure on any element of the surface about a point P be resolved along PO, prove that the whole radial pressure thus estimated, is constant, whatever the shape and size of the surface, it being given that the pressure of the fluid vanishes at an infinite distance from the point O.

Take O as the origin and use 3-dimensional polar coordinates. Equation (5) of § 2·1 gives

$$dp = -\rho\,\mu\frac{dr}{r^3}$$

Hence, $p = \dfrac{\mu\rho}{2r^2} + c$

But $p = 0$, when $r \longrightarrow \infty$,

$$\therefore\ p = \frac{\mu\rho}{2\,r^2}.$$

Consider now any surface and let P, where $OP = r$, be any point on it. Taking an element dS of it we find that the radial pressure along O P is $p\cos\varepsilon$, ε being the angle between the normal at P to the surface and the radius vector O P.

Hence the whole radial pressure

$$= \int\!\int p\cos\varepsilon\,dS$$

$$= \tfrac{1}{2}\int\!\int \frac{\mu\rho}{r^2}\cos\varepsilon\,dS$$

$$= \frac{\mu\rho}{2}\int\!\int \frac{l\,x + m\,y + n\,z}{r^3}dS \ \dots\ (1)$$

where (l, m, n) are the direction cosines of the normal at P to the surface and (x, y, z) the Cartesian Coordinates of P.

Now by Greens' theorem we have

$$\int\!\int (lf + m\phi + n\psi)\,dS = \int\!\int\!\int \left(\frac{\partial f}{\partial x} + \frac{\partial \phi}{\partial y} + \frac{\partial \psi}{\partial z}\right)dx\,dy\,dz.$$

Hence the surface integral (1) becomes

$$\frac{\mu P}{2} \iiint \left\{ \frac{\partial}{\partial x}\left(\frac{x}{r^3}\right) + \frac{\partial}{\partial y}\left(\frac{y}{r^3}\right) + \frac{\partial}{\partial z}\left(\frac{z}{r^3}\right) \right\} dx\, dy\, dz$$

$$= \tfrac{1}{2} \mu P \iiint \sum \left\{ \frac{1}{r^3} - \frac{3x^2}{r^5} \right\} dx\, dy\, dz$$

$$= \tfrac{1}{2} \mu P \iiint \left(\frac{3}{r^3} - 3\,\frac{x^2+y^2+z^2}{r^5} \right) dx\, dy\, dz$$

$$= o.$$

Note : The whole radial pressure has no physical significance whatsoever, being merely a sum of the magnitudes of a number of forces acting in different directions.

Ex. 5. A hollow sphere of radius a, just full of homogeneous liquid of unit density is placed between two external centres of attractive forces $\frac{\mu^2}{r^2}$ and $\frac{\mu'^2}{r'^2}$, distance c apart, in such a position that the attraction due to them at the centre are equal and opposite. Prove that the pressure at any point is

$$\frac{\mu^2}{r} + \frac{\mu'^2}{r'} - \frac{\sqrt{\mu\mu'}\,(\mu+\mu')^2}{\left\{ (\mu+\mu')^2 a^2 + \mu\mu' c^2 \right\}^{\frac{1}{2}}}$$

Let A, B be the centres of force and O, on A B be the centre of the sphere then $\frac{AO}{OB}$ is given by

$$\frac{\mu^2}{AO^2} = \frac{\mu'^2}{OB^2}, \text{ and } AO + OB = c.$$

$$\therefore \frac{\mu}{AO} = \frac{\mu'}{OB} = \frac{\mu+\mu'}{c};$$

$$\text{or } AO = \frac{\mu c}{\mu+\mu'}, OB = \frac{\mu' c}{\mu+\mu'}.$$

Adopting the bipolar coordinates (r, r') of any point of the fluid P referred to A, B as origins we have

(27)

$$dp = - \left\{ \frac{\mu^2}{r^2} \, dr + \frac{\mu'^2}{r'^2} \, dr' \right\} \text{ density being 1.}$$

$$\therefore \; p = C + \frac{\mu^2}{r} + \frac{\mu'^2}{r'}.$$

To determine the constant C, we observe that since the sphere is only just full, there must be a point on the sphere at which the pressure p is zero.

If the bipolar coordinates of this point, Q be (r_1, r_1') then

$$C + \frac{\mu^2}{r_1} + \frac{\mu'^2}{r_1'} = 0 \ldots\ldots\ldots(1)$$

Also if OQ makes an angle θ with OB, then

$$r_1'^2 = OB^2 + a^2 - 2a.OB \cos\theta$$
$$r_1^2 = OA^2 + a^2 + 2a \, OA \cos\theta \; \cdots\cdots\cdots(2)$$

Evidently Q is the point on the sphere at which p is minimum, so that $dp = 0$.

Hence $\dfrac{\mu^2}{r_1^2} dr_1 + \dfrac{\mu'^2}{r_1'^2} dr_1' = 0 \ldots\ldots\ldots(3)$

From (2) $dr_1' = \dfrac{a.OB \sin\theta \, d\theta}{r_1'}$

$$dr_1 = \frac{aOA \sin\theta \, d\theta}{r_1}$$

Hence from (3) we have

$$\frac{\mu^2}{r_1^2} = \frac{\mu'^2}{r_1'^2}$$

or, $\dfrac{r_1'}{r_1} = \dfrac{\mu'}{\mu} \ldots\ldots\ldots(4)$

Again from (2)

$$\frac{OB^2 + a^2 - 2a \, OB \cos\theta}{OA^2 + a^2 + 2a \, OA \cos\theta} = \frac{r_1'^2}{r_1^2} = \frac{\mu'^2}{\mu^2}$$

or substituting the values of OA and OB we get

$$a\,(\mu^2 - \mu'^2) = 2\,c\mu\mu'\,\cos\theta. \quad \ldots\ldots (5)$$

From (1), $C = -\left(\dfrac{\mu^2}{r_1} + \dfrac{\mu'^2}{r'_1}\right)$

$$= -\,\frac{\mu'\,(\mu+\mu')}{r_1'}\ \text{by (4)}$$

$$= -\mu'(\mu+\mu')\left\{\frac{1}{\mathrm{OB}^2 + a^2 - 2a\,\mathrm{OB}\,\cos\theta}\right\}^{\frac12},$$

Substituting for OB and for $\cos\theta$ from (5)

$$= -\mu'(\mu+\mu')\left\{\frac{\mu\,(\mu+\mu')^2}{c^2\mu\mu'^2 + a^2\mu'\,(\mu+\mu')^2}\right\}^{\frac12}$$

$$= -\frac{\sqrt{\mu\mu'}\,(\mu+\mu')^2}{\{c^2\mu\mu' + a^2\,(\mu+\mu')^2\}^{\frac12}}$$

Hence, $p = \dfrac{\mu^2}{r} + \dfrac{\mu'^2}{r'} - \dfrac{\sqrt{\mu\mu'}\,(\mu+\mu')^2}{\{c^2\mu\mu' + a^2\,(\mu+\mu')^2\}^{\frac12}}$

Ex. 6. If the components parallel to the axes of the forces acting on an element of fluid at (x, y, z) be proportional to

$$y^2 + 2\lambda yz + z^2,\ z^2 + 2\mu zx + x^2,\ x^2 + 2vxy + y^2,$$

show that equilibrium is only possible, if

$$2\lambda = 2\mu = 2v = 1.$$

Find the most general possible expression for the density of the fluid.

If the density $a\dfrac{1}{(dist)^2}$ from the plane $x+y+z=0$, the curves of equal pressure and density will be circles.

Equations (3) of § 2·2 give for equilibrium

$$\Sigma\,\mathrm{X}\left(\frac{\partial \mathrm{Y}}{\partial z} - \frac{\partial \mathrm{Z}}{\partial y}\right) = 0.$$

or, $2\ \Sigma\ (y^2 + 2\lambda yz + z^2)\ \{(z-y) + (\mu-v)\,x\} = 0$

(29)

or, $\Sigma\ (y^2+z^2)\ (z-y)+2\Sigma\ \lambda yz\ (z-y)$

$$+\Sigma\ (y^2+z^2)\ (\mu-v)\ x+2\ xyz\ \Sigma\ \lambda\ (\mu-v)=o$$

or, $\Sigma\ yz\ (y-z)+\Sigma\ (z^3-y^3)+2\Sigma\ \lambda yz\ (z-y)$

$$+\Sigma\ x\ (y^2+z^2)\ (\mu-v)=o$$

or, $\Sigma\ yz\ (y-z)\ (1-2\lambda)+\Sigma\ x(y^2+z^2)\ (\mu-v)=o$

or, $\Sigma\ y^2z\ (1-\lambda-\mu)-z^2y\ (1-\lambda-\iota)=o$

$$\text{Hence}\quad 1-\lambda-\mu=o,\ 1-\lambda-v=o,$$

$$\text{and}\quad 1-\mu-v=o,\ 1-\mu-\lambda=o,$$

$$\text{and}\quad 1-v-\lambda=o,\ 1-v-\mu=o,$$

$$\therefore\quad \lambda=\mu=v=\tfrac{1}{2}$$

Thus the necessary condition for equilibrium is

$$2\lambda=2\mu=2v=1.$$

We have, therefore, from Equation 2 of § 2.1

$$dp=P\ (X\ dx+Y\ dy+Zdz)$$

$$=Pk\ \Sigma\ (y^2+yz+z^2)dx,$$

where $X=k\ (y^2+yz+z^2)$ etc.

In order that equilibrium be possible we must have P such a function of $x,\ y,\ z$, that

$P\Sigma\ (y^2+yz+z^2)\ dx$ is a perfect differential,

say of $\phi\ (x,\ y,\ z)$.

To find the form of ϕ, we proceed to find the primitive of the total differential equation

$$\Sigma\ (y^2+yz+z^2)\ dz=o\dots\dots\dots\dots 1)$$

That this primitive does exist is known for the condition of integrability, (which is the same as the condition of equilibrium expressed by Equations 3 of § 2·2), is satisfied.

Treating z as constant in the 1st instance,

$$(y^2+yz+z^2)\,dx+(z^2+zx+x^2)\,dy=0 \text{ leads to}$$

$$\frac{x+y+z}{z^2-2\,xy-xz-zy}=u=\text{cons.}$$

$$\therefore \frac{\partial u}{\partial x}=\frac{2\,(y^2+yz+z^2)}{(z^2-2\,xy-xz-zy)^2}\,,\quad \frac{\partial u}{\partial y}=\frac{2\,(z^2+zx+x^2)}{(z^2-2\,xy-xz-zy)^2}\,,$$

and, $\dfrac{\partial u}{\partial z}=\dfrac{x^2+y^2-2\,z\,x-2\,z\,y-z^2}{(z^2-2\,x\,y-x\,z-z\,y)^2}\,.$

Hence if we multiply (1) by $\dfrac{2}{\{z^2-2\,x\,y-x\,z-z\,y\}^2}$,

(1) becomes

$$\frac{\partial u}{\partial x}\,dx+\frac{\partial u}{\partial y}\,dy+\frac{2\,(x^2+xy+y^2)\,dz}{(z^2-2\,xy-xz-zy)^2}=0$$

or, $\dfrac{\partial u}{\partial x}\,dx+\dfrac{\partial u}{\partial y}\,dy+\dfrac{(x^2+y^2-2\,z\,x-2z\,y-z^2)}{(z^2-2\,x\,y-x\,z-z\,y)^2}\,d\,z+$

$$\frac{(x+y+z)^2}{(x^2-2\,x\,y-x\,z-z\,y)^2}\,dz=0$$

or, $\left(\dfrac{\partial u}{\partial x}\,d\,x+\dfrac{\partial u}{\partial y}\,d\,y+\dfrac{\partial u}{\partial z}\,d\,z\right)+u^2\,d\,z=0$

or, $\dfrac{du}{u^2}+dz=0$

or, $z-\dfrac{1}{u}=\text{cons.}$

or, $\dfrac{x\,y+y\,z+z\,x}{x+y+z}=\text{cons}$

Thus setting $\phi\,(x,\,y,\,z)=\dfrac{x\,y+y\,z+z\,x}{x+y+z}$

we have $\dfrac{\partial\phi}{\partial x} = \dfrac{y^2 + y\,z + z^2}{(x+y+z)^3}$, etc.

Hence $P\ \Sigma\,(y^2 + y\,z + z^2)\,dx$ becomes

$$P\,(x+y+z)^2\ \Sigma\ \frac{(y^2 + y\,z + z^2)}{(x+y+z)^3}\,dx,$$

or, $\quad P\,(x+y+z)^2\,d\phi$

$\therefore\quad dp = P\,k\,(x+y+z)^2\,d\phi$, where

$$\phi = \frac{x\,y + y\,z + z\,x}{(x+y+z)^2}$$

It follows, therefore, that $P\,(x+y+z)^2$ must be some function

of ϕ or of $\left[\dfrac{x\,y + y\,z + z\,x}{(x+y+z)}\right]$

$$\text{i. e. } P\,(x+y+z)^2 = f\left(\frac{x\,y + y\,z + z\,x}{x+y+z}\right)$$

Hence $P = \dfrac{1}{(x+y+z)^2}\,f\left(\dfrac{x\,y + y\,z + z\,x}{x+y+z}\right),$

giving the most general possible expression for the density of
the fluid in equilibrium under the action of the given forces.
Curves of equal density and pressure are given by the differential equations,

$$\frac{dx}{\dfrac{\partial Z}{\partial y} - \dfrac{\partial Y}{\partial z}} = \frac{dy}{\dfrac{\partial X}{\partial z} - \dfrac{\partial Z}{\partial x}} = \frac{dz}{\dfrac{\partial Y}{\partial x} - \dfrac{\partial X}{\partial y}},$$

which become in the present case

$$\frac{dx}{y-z} = \frac{dy}{z-x} = \frac{dz}{x-y}$$

$$= \frac{dx + dy + dz}{0}\quad \ldots\ldots\ \text{(i)}$$

$$= \frac{x\,dx + y\,dy + z\,dz}{0}\ \ldots\ldots\ \text{(ii)}.$$

Eq. i) leads to $x+y+z=\text{cons}$; and

Eq. (ii) leads to $x^2+y^2+z^2=\text{cons}$.

Thus the curves of equal pressure and density are circles.

Ex. 7. If a fluid is at rest under the action of a system of forces whose components along three rectangular axes are proportional to

$$(a\,y-b\,z),\ (c\,z-a\,x),\ (b\,x-c\,y)$$

show that in order that equilibrium be possible density must be equal to

$$F\left(\frac{a\,x-c\,z}{a\,y-b\,z}\right)\Big/(a\,y-b\,z)^2$$

F being any arbitrary function.

Show that the lines of equal density and equal pressure are straight lines.

Ex. 8. Find the value of pressure at any point in the preceeding example.

$$\left[p=\frac{1}{a}\int F\left(\frac{a\,x-c\,z}{a\,y-b\,z}\right)d\left(\frac{a\,x-c\,z}{a\,y-b\,z}\right)\right]$$

Ex. 9. A fluid is in equilibrium under a given system of forces; if $P_1=\phi\,(x,\,y,\,z)$, $P_2=\psi\,(x,\,y,\,z)$ be two possible values of the density at any point, show that the equations of the surfaces of equal pressure in either case are given by

$$\phi\,(x,\,y,\,z)+\lambda\,\psi\,(x,\,y,\,z)=0,$$

λ being an arbitrary const.

Ex. 10. A mass of gas at constant temperature is at rest under the action of forces of potential ψ at any point of space, with any boundary conditions. At the point where ψ is zero the pressure is π and the density P_o. The gas is now removed from the action of the forces and confined in a space so that it is at a uniform density P_o. Prove that the loss of intrinsic potential energy by the gas, due to expansion, is

$$P_o \iiint \psi e^{-\frac{P_o \psi}{\pi}} dv,$$

where the integrations are taken throughout the gas in its original state.

Ex. 11. A uniform spherical mass of liquid of density P and radius a is surrounded by another incompressible liquid of density σ and external radius b. The whole is in equilibrium under its own gravitation, but with no external pressure or forces. Show that the pressure at the centre is

$$\tfrac{2}{3} \pi P^2 a^2 + \tfrac{2}{3} \pi \sigma \left\{ \frac{2 a^2}{b} (P - \sigma) + \sigma (a + b) \right\} (b - a).$$

For our purpose we may assume that a liquid of density σ occupies the entire space enclosed in the outer sphere of radius b and a liquid of density $P - \sigma$ occupies the space enclosed in the inner sphere of radius a.

Hence gravitational attraction at any point of the fluid inside the inner sphere is

$$\frac{4\pi}{3} \sigma r + \frac{4\pi}{3} (P - \sigma) r = \frac{4\pi}{3} P r,$$

r being the distance of the point from the centre

Also the gravitational attraction at any point inside the outer sphere and outside the inner sphere is

$$\frac{4\pi}{3} \sigma r + \frac{4\pi}{3} (P - \sigma) \frac{a^3}{r^2}$$

Hence pressure at any point inside the inner sphere is given by

$$dp = -\rho\frac{4\pi}{3}\,\rho\,r\,dr\ldots\ldots\ldots \text{(i)}$$

and at any point outside the inner sphere but inside the outer sphere

$$dp = -\sigma\frac{4\pi}{3}\left\{ \sigma r + (\rho - \sigma)\frac{a^3}{r^2} \right\} \qquad \ldots \quad \text{(ii)}$$

$\therefore p = c - \frac{2}{3}\,\pi\,\rho^2 r,^2 c$ being the presure at the centre. This gives the presure at any point inside the inner sphere.

Hence presure on the boundary of the inner sphere is

$$c - 2\frac{\pi}{3}\rho^2 a^2 \qquad \ldots \qquad \ldots \qquad \ldots \quad \text{(iii)}$$

Again pressure at any point outside the inner sphere but inside the outer sphere is given by

$$p = c' - \frac{4\pi}{3}\sigma\left\{ \frac{\sigma r^2}{2} - (\rho - \sigma)\frac{a^3}{r} \right\}$$

But $p = o$, when $r = b$

$$\therefore c' = \frac{4\pi}{3}\,\sigma\left\{ \frac{\sigma b^2}{2} - (\rho - \sigma)\frac{a^3}{b} \right\}$$

$$\therefore p = \frac{2\pi}{3}\,\sigma^2\,(b^2 - r^2) + \frac{4\pi}{3}\,\sigma\,(\rho - \sigma)a^3\left(\frac{1}{r} - \frac{1}{b}\right)$$

Hence pressure at the boundary of the the two liquids *i. e.* at $r = a$, is given by

$$\frac{2\pi}{3}\sigma^2(b^2 - a^2) + \frac{4\pi\sigma}{3}(\rho - \sigma)a^3\left(\frac{1}{a} - \frac{1}{b}\right)$$

$$= c - \frac{2\pi}{3}\,\rho^2\,a^2, \qquad \ldots \qquad \ldots \quad \text{by (iii)}$$

$$\therefore c = \frac{2\pi}{3} \rho^2 a^2 + \frac{2\pi}{3} \sigma \left\{ \sigma(b+a) + \frac{2a^2}{b}(\rho - \sigma) \right\} (b-a)$$

Ex. 12.   Two homogeneous liquids of density ρ and ρ_1, and volumes V and V_1, are superposed in a cylinderical vase having the form of a cylinder of revolution with vertical generators. The upper liquid is simply heavy, but the lower liquid ρ_1 is heavy and in addition its elements are attracted by the centre O of the bottom of the vase, the force of attraction being proportional to distance and mass.   The attraction of the point O on a unit mass at unit distance is λ.   Determine the figure of equilibrium and the law of pressure.

Ex. 13.   A uniform incompressible fluid is of mass M in gravitational units, and forms a sphere of radius a when undisturbed under the influence of its own gravitation. It is placed in a weak field of force of gravitational potential $\Sigma \ \mu_n \dfrac{r^n}{a^{n+1}} S_n (\theta, \phi)$ $(n > 1)$, where r is measured from the centre of the mean spherical surface of the liquid and the squares of quantities of the type μ_n can be neglected. Prove that the Equation of the free surface is

$$\frac{r}{a} = 1 + \Sigma \ \frac{\mu_n}{M} \frac{2n+1}{2n-2} S_n (\theta, \phi),$$

S_n being a Spherical Harmonic of nth order.

Let ρ be the density of the liquid, then

$$M = \frac{4\pi}{3} a^3 \rho \quad \ldots \qquad \ldots \qquad \ldots \quad (1)$$

Let the Equation of the free surface be

$$\frac{r}{a} = 1 + \Sigma \ a_n S_n (\theta, \phi), \quad \ldots \qquad \ldots \quad (2)$$

We first proceed to find the potential of a gravitating mass of matter enclosed within equation (2). Since a_n may be assumed to be small, we may consider that the potential is the same as that of a solid sphere of radius a *plus* the potential of a distribution of matter of surface density $a \, P \, \Sigma \, \alpha_n \, S_n \, (\theta, \phi)$ spread over the sphere. It is known from the theory of Potential that potential of a solid sphere of homogeneous density P at an internal point is $2 \pi P \, a^2 (1 - \dfrac{r^2}{3a^2})$. Likewise the potential of a distribution of matter of surface density

$$a \, P \, \Sigma \, \alpha_n \, S_n \, (\theta, \phi)$$

over a sphere of radius a is $4 \pi \, P a^2 \, \Sigma \dfrac{\alpha_n \, S_n}{2n+1} \left(\dfrac{r}{a} \right)^n$ at an internal point.

The total potential of the external field and that of the gravitation of the liquid is, therefore,

$$2 \pi P a^2 (1 - \frac{r^2}{3a^2}) + 4 \pi a^2 P \, \Sigma \frac{\alpha n S n'}{2n+1} \left(\frac{r}{a} \right)^n + \Sigma \frac{\mu_n S_n}{a} \left(\frac{r}{a} \right)^n$$

Now we know that in the case of liquids subject to a conservative system of forces derivable from a potential function V, we have

$$\frac{p}{\rho} + V = \text{const} = C.$$

If $p = o$ over the free surface, the Equation of the free surface is, therefore, $V = C$

or, $2 \pi P a^2 (1 - \dfrac{r^2}{3a^2}) + 4 \pi P a^2 \, \Sigma \dfrac{\alpha n \, Sn}{2n+1} \left(\dfrac{r}{a} \right)^n + \Sigma \dfrac{\mu_n \, S_n}{a} \left(\dfrac{r}{a} \right)^n = C$

In order that this be identical with the equation $\dfrac{r}{a} = 1 + \Sigma \, \alpha_n \, S_n$ that it is necessary and sufficient,

$$4 \pi P a^2 \alpha_n \left(\frac{1}{2n+1} - \frac{1}{3} \right) + \frac{\mu_n}{a} = o \text{ for } n > 1$$

$$\therefore a_n = \frac{2n+1}{2n-2} \ \frac{\mu_n}{\frac{4\pi a^3 \rho}{3}} = \frac{2n+1}{2n-2} \ \frac{\mu_n}{M}, \text{ by } (\text{i})$$

Hence the Equation of the free surface is

$$\frac{r}{a} = 1 + \Sigma \ \frac{2n+1}{2n-2} \ \frac{\mu_n}{M} S_n (\theta, \phi)$$

Ex. 14.   A solid gravitating sphere of radius a and density ρ is surrounded by a gravitating liquid of volume $\frac{4\pi}{3} (b^3 - a^3)$ and density σ The whole is placed in a field of force whose potential is $\frac{1}{3} \omega^2 r^2 [1 - P_2 (\cos \theta)]$. Shew that the form of the free surface of the liquid is a spheroid of small ellipticity ε given by

$$r = b \ \{ 1 - \tfrac{2}{3} \varepsilon P_2 (\cos \theta) \},$$

where $\varepsilon = \dfrac{15\omega^2 b^3}{8\pi \{ 5(\rho - \sigma)a^3 + 2\sigma b^3 \}}$

P_2 being Legendre's coefficient of the second order.

2.8   Rotating Fluids.—If a particle of mass m moves in a circle of radius r with constant angular velocity ω, the effective force acting on the particle i. e. the product of mass and its acceleration, is $m \omega^2 r$, acting along the radius and directed towards the centre. Consider now a quantity of fluid revolving uniformly and without any relative displacement of its particles i. e. as if rigid, about a fixed axis. The "effective force" on any particle m of the fluid is $m \omega^2 r$ directed towards the axis, where r is the distance of the particle from the axis and ω is the angular velocity of the fluid. This force must be supplied by the external forces and fluid pressure acting on the particle. Hence the resultant of the external forces and fluid pressure on the particle is a force $m\omega^2 r$ acting *towards* the axis. It follows then that the fluid pressure, external forces, and forces $m\omega^2 r$ acting *from* the axis are in equilibrium. We may accordingly consider the fluid at rest and

(38)

apply the equations of §2. 1 provided that we consider each particle as acted on by a force $(\omega^2 r)$ per unit mass from the axis in addition to other forces.

Take the axis of rotation as z axis. If the system of external forces acting on the fluid is derivable from a potential function V, the equation of equilibrium, therefore, becomes

$$dp = P\ \{\ (X + \omega^2)dx + (Y + \omega^2 y)dy + Zdz\ \}$$

$$= P\ \{\ (-\frac{\partial V}{\partial x} + \omega^2 x\ )dx + (-\frac{\partial V}{\partial y} + \omega^2 y)\ dy - \frac{\partial V}{\partial z}dz\ \}$$

$$= -PdV + \tfrac{1}{2}\omega^2 Pd(x^2 + y^2)$$

$$= -Pd\ \{\ V - \tfrac{1}{2}\omega^2(x^2 + y^2)\ \}$$

Or $\frac{p}{P} + [V - \tfrac{1}{2}\omega^2(x^2 + y^2)] = $ cons,

assuming P to be constant.

This shows that fluid pressure is the same as in the case of a fluid at rest subject to an external force derivable from a potential function.

$$V - \tfrac{1}{2}w^2(x^2 + y^2)$$

The effect of rotation is, therefore, merely to add an additional term, $-\tfrac{1}{2}\omega^2(\ x^2 + y^2\ )$ to the potential of the external system.

Ex. 1. A homogeneous mass of liquid contained in a vessel revolves with uniform angular velocity w about a vertical axis Find the pressure at any point and the surfaces of equal pressure.

Take the axis of rotation directed vertically upwards as z, axis and the highest point of the axis as origin. Potential V of the external force system is clearly gz.

Hence $\frac{p}{P} + gz - \tfrac{1}{2}w^2(x^2 + y^2) = $ cons

$$\text{or,} \quad p = P\{ \tfrac{1}{2}w^2(x^2+y^2) - gz \} + c$$

Surfaces of equal pressure are parabloids of revolution.

$\checkmark$ **Ex. 2.** Liquid is rotating as if solid with angular velocity w, about a vertical axis. Shew that the free surface is formed by the revolution of a parabola of latus rectum $\dfrac{2g}{w^2}$ about its axis.

(Tripos part. I 1924)

Ex. 3. A mass m of an elastic fluid enclosed in a cylinder of radius a and height h is rotating round its axis, which is vertical, with uniform angular velocity w. Prove that density at any point distant r from the axis and at a height z is

$$e^{c/k}\; e^{\frac{w^2 r^2 - 2gz}{2k}}$$

Where c is given by the equation

$$m = \frac{2\pi k^2}{gw^2}\, e^{c/k}\, (e^{\frac{w^2 a^2}{2k^2}} - 1)\,(1 - e^{-\frac{gh}{k}})$$

Ex. 4. Prove that the common surface of two homogeneous liquids of densities P and P_1, superposed upon one another in a vessel and rotating with uniform angular velicity w about a vertical axis is a paraboloid of revolution. Find the latus rectum of the generating parabola.

(Hint use §2. 3. Ans. $\dfrac{2g}{w^2}$)

Ex. 5. A mass m of elastic fluid is rotating about an axis with uniform angular velocity w, and is acted on by an attraction towards a point in that axis equal to μ times the distance, μ being $> w^2$, prove that the equation of a surface of equal density is.

(40)

$$\mu\left(x^2+y^2+z^2\right)-w^2\left(x^2+y^2\right)=k\,\log\left\{\frac{\mu(\mu-w^2)^2}{8\pi^3}\cdot\frac{m^2}{\rho^2 k^3}\right\}$$

Taking the axis of rotation as z axis and the centre of attraction () on it as the origin, we have from the equation of pressure

$$dp=-\rho dV,$$

and $p=k\rho,$

where V is the potential of the external forces acting.

$$k\,d\rho=-\rho dV$$

or, $k\,\log\rho=c-V$

$$\rho=Ae^{-V/k}$$

Now the potential of the attractive force is $\tfrac{1}{2}\mu(x^2+y^2+z^2)$ and that due to the "centrifugal force" of rotation $-\tfrac{1}{2}w^2(x^2+y^2)$

$$\therefore V=\tfrac{1}{2}(\mu-w^2)x^2+\tfrac{1}{2}(\mu-w^2)y^2+\tfrac{1}{2}\mu z^2$$

$$-\frac{1}{2k}\left\{(\mu-w^2)x^2+(\mu-w^2)y^2+\mu z^2\right\}$$

$$\therefore \rho=A\,e$$

Since the whole mass is $m,$

$$m=\iiint\rho\;dx\,dy\,dz$$

$$=\int_{-\infty}^{\infty}\int_{-\infty}^{\infty}\int_{-\infty}^{\infty}A\,e^{-\frac{1}{2}k\left\{(\mu-w^2)(x^2+y^2)+\mu z^2\right\}}dx\,dy\,dz$$

$$=8A\int_{0}^{\infty}e^{-\frac{(\mu-w^2)}{2k}x^2}dx\cdot\int_{0}^{\infty}e^{-\frac{(\mu-w^2)}{2k}y^2}dy\int_{0}^{\infty}e^{-\frac{\mu}{2k}z^2}dz$$

$$= 8A \left[\frac{\sqrt{2k\pi}}{2\sqrt{\mu-w^2}} \right]^2 \left[\sqrt[2]{\frac{\sqrt{2k\pi}}{\mu}} \right]$$

$$= \frac{A\pi^{\frac{3}{2}}\, 2\sqrt{2}\, k^{\frac{3}{2}}}{(\mu-w^2)\,\sqrt{\mu}}$$

The Equation of a surface of equal density ρ is, therefore,

$$(\mu-w^2)\,(x^2+y^2)+\mu z^2 = k \log \frac{A^2}{\rho^2}$$

$$= k \log \left\{ \frac{m^2(\mu-w^2)^2\mu}{8\pi^3 k^3 \rho^2} \right\}.$$

Ex. 6. A conical vessel of height h and vertical angle 2α contains water whose volume is $\frac{1}{2}$ of the cone ; if the vessel and the water revolve with uniform velocity w, and no water over-flows prove that w must not be $> \sqrt{\dfrac{2g}{3h}}\ \cot \alpha.$

Ex. 7. Liquid is contained in a thin circular tube in a vertical plane which can rotate about the vertical diameter. If the liquid subtend an angle 2α at the centre, show that it will separate into two parts when the angular velocity exceeds $\sqrt{\dfrac{g}{a}}\, \sec \dfrac{\alpha}{2},$ a being the radius of the circle.

(Hint: the liquid will first separate when the pressure at the lowest point is zero.)

Ex. 8. The whole circumference of a circle and a diameter are formed by fine uniform tubes communicating freely with one another. The diameter is vertical and initially tubes are filled with water to the level of the centre of the circle. Prove that all water will be just driven into the circumference if the system be made to rotate with an angular velocity

$$\sqrt{\frac{2g}{a(1-\sin \phi/2)}},$$ about the diameter, where a is the radius and ϕ is the unit circular measure i. e. a radian.

Let O, be the centre of the circle and M its lowest point. Let P and Q be the points on the circle up to which water rises when the water in the diameteral tube is just driven into the circumference. Then clearly arc AP=arc BQ=$\frac{a}{2}$. Therefore

$<$AOP=$<$BOQ=$\frac{\phi}{2}$, ϕ being a radian.

Taking O as origin and the downward vertical as z—axis we have

$$\frac{p}{\rho}=gz+\tfrac{1}{2}w^2(x^2+y^2)+c,$$

c being a constant.

Since the pressure p_o at P must be equal to that at M, we have

$$\frac{p_o}{\rho}=ga+\tfrac{1}{2}w^2(o)+c$$

$$=g(\ -\ a\sin\frac{\phi}{2})+\tfrac{1}{2}w^2a^2\cos^2\frac{\phi}{2}+c$$

$$\therefore w^2\cos^2\frac{\phi}{2}=\frac{2g}{a}(1+\sin\frac{\phi}{2})$$

$$\text{or, } w^2\cos^2\frac{\phi}{2}=\frac{2g}{a}\ \frac{(1-\sin^2\phi/2)}{(1-\sin\frac{\phi}{2})}$$

$$\text{or, } w=\sqrt{\frac{2g}{a}\ \frac{1}{1-\sin\frac{\phi}{2}}}$$

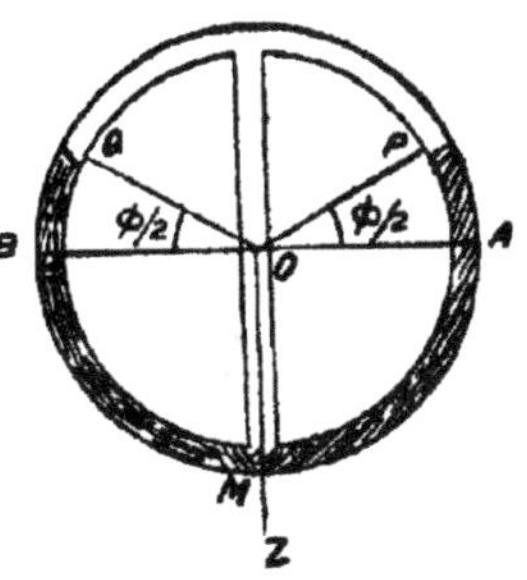

Ex. 9. A circular cylinder with an open top is filled with a liquid of density P. The cylinder is set rotating along with

the liquid with angular velocity w about its axis which is vertical. Show that a volume $(\pi w^2 a^4 P)/4g$ will run out, a being the radius of the cylinder provided that $w^2 \leq \dfrac{2gh}{a^2}$

Examine the case when $w^2 > \dfrac{2gh}{a^2}$

Ex. 10.   A cylinder of radius a is filled with water to a depth h. A fine vertical tube is at a distance d ($\angle a$) from the axis of the cylinder and communicates with the bottom of the cylinder. If the whole is made to rotate uniformly about the axis of the cylinder show that the angular velocity w necessary to make the water rise in the tube to a height x above the bottom of the cylinder is given by

$$w^2 \left(d^2 - \frac{a^2}{2}\right) = 2g\,(x-h)$$

Let x be the height of water in the vertical tube MN at a distance d from the axis OA of the cylinder. Let BAC be the free surface of the water in the cylinder when the system is revolving with angular velocity w. Take O as origin and the upward vertical as axis of z, the equation of pressure is

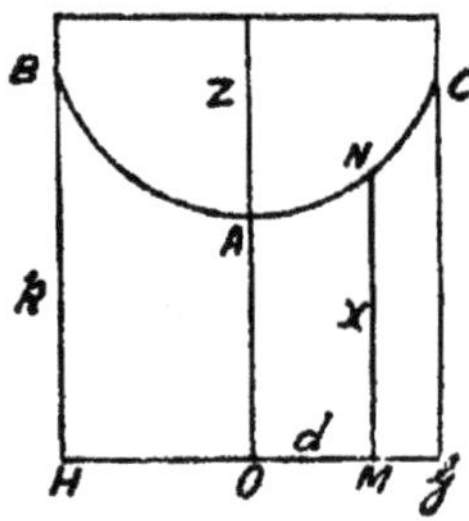

$$\frac{dp}{\rho} = -\,g dz + w^2 r dr$$

$$\therefore \frac{p}{\rho} = C - gz + \tfrac{1}{2} w^2 r^2$$

At N the top point of the vertical tube up to which water rises, $z=x$, and OM$=d$, $p=\pi$ the pressure at the free surface.

$$\frac{\pi}{\rho} = C - gx + \tfrac{1}{2} w^2 d^2 \qquad \ldots \qquad \ldots \quad (1)$$

If the height of B or C above O is k, then

$$\frac{\Pi}{\rho} = C - gk + \tfrac{1}{2} w^2 a^2 \quad \ldots \quad \ldots \quad (2)$$

$$\therefore \frac{p - \Pi}{\rho} = g (k - z) + \tfrac{1}{2} w^2 (r^2 - a^2)$$

The equation of the paraboloid of free surface *viz* BAC is therefore clearly

$$g (k - z) + \tfrac{1}{2} w^2 (r^2 - a^2) = o$$

$$\text{or, } r^2 = \frac{2g}{w^2} \left(z - k + \frac{w^2 a^2}{2g} \right)$$

Now the Volume of the liquid

$$= \text{Volume of the cylinder GHBC} - \text{paraboloid ABC}$$

$$= \pi a^2 k - \pi \int r^2 dz$$

$$= \pi a^2 k - \pi \int_{k - \frac{w^2 a^2}{2g}}^{k} \frac{2g}{w^2} \left(z - k + \frac{w^2 a^2}{2g} \right) dz$$

$$= \pi a^2 k - \frac{\pi w^2 a^4}{4g}$$

But the volume of water was originally $\pi a^2 h$

$$\therefore \pi a^2 h = \pi a^2 k - \frac{\pi w^2 a^4}{4g}$$

$$\text{or } k = h + \frac{w^2 a^2}{4g} \quad \ldots \quad \ldots \quad \ldots \quad (3)$$

Now subtracting (1) from (2) we have

$$g (x - k) + \tfrac{1}{2} w^2 (a^2 - d^2) = o$$

Hence by (3‧ we have

$$w^2 \left(d^2 - \frac{a^2}{2}\right) = 2g\,(x - h).$$

Ex. 11. A straight tube AB of thin uniform bore is closed at the lower end A and filled with water. The length of the tube is l and it rotates with constant angular velocity w about the vertical through A, to which the tube is inclined at an angle α. Show that no liquid excapes if

$$w^2 \leq \frac{g}{l}\,\frac{\cos \alpha}{\sin^2 \alpha};$$

and that all the liquid escapes if

$$w^2 = \frac{2g}{l}\,\frac{\cos \alpha}{\sin^3 \alpha}.$$

Ex. 12. A uniform semi circular closed tube of radius r is tightly filled with equal volumes of two fluids of densities ρ and σ respectively which do not mix, and is rotated with angular velocity w about a vertical radius making an angle α with the line of symmetry. Prove that the pressure at the two ends will be equal if

$$\frac{w^2 r}{2g}\,(\sigma - \rho) = \frac{\sigma}{\cos \alpha + \sin \alpha} - \frac{\rho}{\cos \alpha - \sin \alpha}$$

the fluid of density σ being the lower of the two, and the convexity of the tube being downwards.

Ex. 13. A fine straight tube of length l, closed at both ends, and inclined to the vertical at an angle α is just filled with a liquid of density ρ. If the tube is rotated with unifrom angular velocity w round a vertical axis through the lower end, prove that the pressure at the highest point is

$$\tfrac{1}{2}\,\rho w^2 \sin^2 \alpha \,(l - g \cos \alpha / w^2 \sin^2 \alpha)^2.$$

provided that $w^2 > g \cos\alpha / l \sin^2 \alpha$. What is the pressure if $w^2 <$ this value.

$$\text{Ans. } \tfrac{1}{2} P w^2 \sin^2 \alpha \left(l^2 - \frac{2gl \cos \alpha}{w^2 \sin^2 \alpha} \right)$$

Ex 14. A hollow sphere of radius a, half filled with liquid, is made to rotate with angular velocity w about its vertical diameter. If the lowest point of the sphere is just exposed, prove that

$$2g = a\, w^2 \left(2 - \sqrt[3]{4} \right)$$

Ex. 15. Prove that, if a mass of homogeneous liquid rotates about an axis and is acted upon by a force to a point in the axis, varying inversely as the square of the distance, the curvatures of the meridian curve of the free surface at the equator and pole are respectively $\dfrac{1}{a\,(1-m)}$ and $\dfrac{1}{b}\left(1 - \dfrac{mb^3}{a^3}\right)$ where a and b are the equatorial and polar radii, and m is the ratio of the centrifugal force at the equator to the attraction there.

CHAPTER III

Fluid Pressure on Surfaces

3.1. In the previous chapter we saw how to calculate the pressure at any point of a mass of fluid at rest. We shall now consider the problem of finding the resultant of the pressures exerted by fluids at rest upon surfaces with which they are in contact. Take first the simple case of a horizontal plane surface A B at a depth d below the surface of a homogeneous fluid at rest under gravity. At any point P of this surface we saw that the fluid pressure is $g \, \rho \, d$, ρ being the density of the fluid. The direction of this force is

normal to the surface i. e. vertical. Hence if we consider an infinitesimal area δA of the surface round P, the force on this infinitesimal area would be $g \, \rho \, d \, \delta A$, acting at right angles to the plane.

Splitting up the surface into an infinite number of such infinitesimal areas we find that the problem of finding the resultant fluid pressure is just the same as that of finding the resultant of parallel forces like $g \, \rho \, d \, \delta A$ acting all over the plane. Now the resultant of these parallel forces is known to be

$$\Sigma \, g \, d \, \rho \, \delta A$$

$$= g \, \rho \, d \, \Sigma \, \delta A,$$

since d is the same for every point of the horizontal plane surface we are considering,

$$= g \, \rho \, d \, A,$$

where A is the whole area of the plane

3.2. Let us now take up the more general problem of a plane surface of any kind in a fluid at rest under the action of any given forces.

Take any two rectangular lines in the plane as axes of x and y. Consider any point P (x, y) of the plane. The pressure (i. e. force exerted by the fluid per unit area) at P will dpend on the forces which act upon the fluid 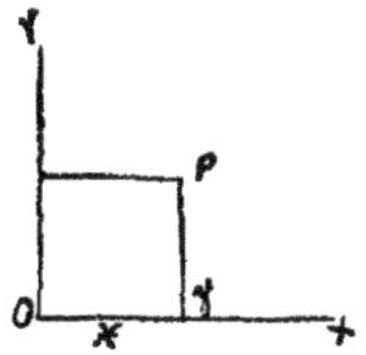 and maintain it in equilibrium. Let it be p, which will in general be a function of (x, y) and the forces acting on the fluid. Moreover, its direction will be normal to the plane. Considering as before an elementary area $dx\,dy$ round P we see that the force acting on this area will be p $dx\,dy$ at r·ght angles to the plane. If we imagine the plane to be split up into an indefinite number of such plane areas, to each such area there will correspond a force of definite magnitude and normal to the plane. We have, therefore, to compound an indefinite number of such parallel forces; the resultant is, therefore,

$$\Sigma\ \mathrm{p}\ dx\,dy$$

$$=\int\int\ \mathrm{p}\ dx\,dy.$$

If we had used polar coordinates, we would have considered an area $rd\theta dr$ round P and the expression for the resultant pressure would have been

$$\int\int\ \mathrm{p}\ rd\theta dr.$$

Remark:—If a homogeneous fluid is at rest under the action of gravity alone, p$=g\,\rho\,z$ where z is the depth of the point P below the horizontal surface. Hence the resultant pressure

$$=\Sigma\ g\,\rho\,z\ \delta \mathrm{A},\ \delta \mathrm{A}\ \text{being an infinitesimal area round P.}$$

$$=g\,\rho\ \Sigma\ z\,\delta \mathrm{A}$$

(49)

$= g\, \mathsf{P}\, \bar{z}\mathrm{A}$, where A = whole area of the plane, and

$\bar{z} =$ depth below the horizontal of the centroid of the plane.

Ex. 1. Calculate the pressure on a triangular lamina immersed in a fluid of density P.

Let the depth of the 3 vertices of the lamina below the horizontal surface be d_1, d_2, d_3.

Then the resultant fluid pressure $= g\, \mathsf{P} \triangle \dfrac{(d_1 + d_2 + d_3)}{3}$

where $\triangle =$ area of the triangle, for, $\bar{z} = \dfrac{d_1 + d_2 + d_3}{3}$.

Ex. 2. Prove that the pressure of a parabolic lamina bounded by latus rectum and inclined at an angle θ to the horizontal is $\frac{8}{3}\, g\mathsf{P}\,(d + \frac{3}{5}\, a \sin \theta)\, a^2$, where d is the depth of of the vertex and $4\,a$ the latus of the lamina.

Ex. 3. An isosceles triangular lamina is immersed in a fluid vertically with its vertex coincident with the surface of the fluid, and base horizontal. Find how to divide the lamina so that the pressure on the upper and lower portions be in the ratio of $1 : n$.

3·3. Centre of pressure. While dealing with plane surfaces immersed in fluids we were able to deduce a simple formula for finding the magnitude of the resultant fluid pressure. We have now to investigate the line of action of the resultant. So far as the direction of this resultant pressure is concerned it must be normal to the plane. Hence if we know the point of the plane where the resultant of the fluid pressure meets it, the line of action of the resultant is known. This point is known as the *centre of pressure*. We may briefly define it as the point at which the direction of the single force, which is equivalent in all respects to the fluid pressures on the surface meets the plane surface.

Take any two rectangular straight lines as axes of x and y in the plane surface. Let p be the fluid pressure at any point P (x, y) of the plane. Then the fluid pressure on an infinitesimal area $dx\,dy$ round P will be $p\,dx\,dy$. We have thus parallel forces like $p\,dx\,dy$ acting at P (x, y).

The resultant fluid pressure will therefore act at the point $(\bar{x}, \bar{y})$ where

$$\bar{x} = \frac{\Sigma\,px\,dx\,dy}{\Sigma\,p\,dx\,dy}, \quad \bar{y} = \frac{\Sigma\,py\,dx\,dx}{\Sigma\,p\,dx\,dy}$$

$$= \frac{\int\int px\,dx\,dy}{\int\int p\,dx\,dy}, \quad = \frac{\int\int py\,dx\,dy}{\int\int p\,dx\,dy},$$

the field of integration being the whole area of the plane.

Hence the coordinates of the centre of pressure are

$$\left(\frac{\int\int px\,dx\,dy}{\int\int p\,dx\,dy}, \ \frac{\int\int py\,dx\,dy}{\int\int p\,dx\,dy} \right).$$

Using polar coordinates, we can similarly prove that the cartesian coordinates of the centre of pressure are

$$\left(\frac{\int\int p\,r^2\cos\theta\,dr\,d\theta}{\int\int pr\,dr\,d\theta}, \ \frac{\int\int p\,r^2\sin\theta\,dr\,d\theta}{\int\int p\,r\,dr\,d\theta} \right)$$

Remark 1: If a homogeneous fluid is at rest under the action of gravity alone then $p = g\,\rho\,z$, where z is the depth of the point below the surface. Hence

$$\bar{x} = \frac{\int\int z\,x\,dx\,dy}{\int\int z\,dx\,dy}, \quad \bar{y} = \frac{\int\int z\,x\,dx\,dy}{\int\int z\,dx\,dy}.$$

Remark 2: Let us take the line of intersection of the plane with the horizontal surface as O x. Then z, the depth of P below the surface $= y \sin \theta$ where θ is the inclination of the plane to the horizontal,

$$\text{Hence} \quad \bar{x} = \frac{\int\int x\, y \sin\theta\, dx\, dy}{\int\int y \sin\theta\, dx\, dy} = \frac{\int\int x\, y\, dx\, dy}{\int\int y\, dx\, dy}$$

$$\bar{y} = \frac{\int\int y^2 \sin\theta\, dx\, dy}{\int\int y \sin\theta\, dx\, dy} = \frac{\int\int y^2\, dx\, dy}{\int\int y\, dx\, dy}$$

This shows that the position of the centre of pressure relative to the plane is independent of its inclination to the horizon. It follows accordingly that if a plane area be immersed in a fluid, and then turned about its line of intersection with the surface as a fixed axis, the centre of pressure relative to the plane will remain unchanged.

3·4. In the case of a plane lamina $\int\int y^2\, dx\, dy$ is plainly the moment of inertia of the lamina about O x.

$$\therefore \quad \bar{y} = \frac{\int\int y^2\, dx\, dy}{\int\int y\, dx\, dy} = \frac{A\, k^2}{A\, \bar{z}},$$

where A $=$ area of the lamina, $k =$ radius of gyration about O x, which is the line of intersection of the lamina with the horizontal free surface, and z is the ordinate of the centroid of the lamina.

Hence $\qquad \bar{y}\, \bar{z} = k^2.$

In particular, if the lamina is vertical, we have:

(depth of the centre of pressure of the lamina) $\times$ (depth of the centre of gravity of the lamina) $= k^2 = K^2 + \bar{z}^2$, where K is the radius of gyration about an axis through the centroid parallel to the horizontal. K is obviously a fixed constant of the lamina.

Hence $\bar{z}\, (\bar{y} - \bar{z}) = K^2$

Or, (depth of the centre of gravity below the free surface) (depth of centre of pressure below the centre of gravity) $=$ const.

This is an important result.

Ex. 1. A plane triangular area is immersed with its plane vertical, one side horizontal, and the opposite corner downwards. Its vertical altitude is h, and the horizontal side is at a depth h below the free surface. Show that its centre of pressure is at a depth $\dfrac{11}{8} h$ below the free surface. (Tripos 1926)

Reducing the triangle to its equimomental particles we see that the moment of inertia of the lamina about the horizontal is the same as that of three particles of mass $\dfrac{\triangle}{3}$ placed at the mid-points of the triangle, or at depths, h, $\dfrac{3h}{2}$ & $\dfrac{3h}{2}$ respectively, $\triangle$ being the area of the triangle.

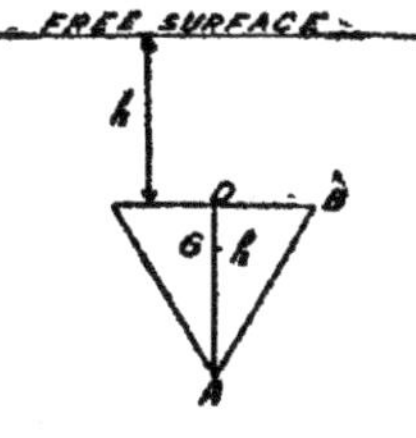

Hence $k^2 = \dfrac{\triangle}{3} \left\{ h^2 + \dfrac{9h^2}{4} + \dfrac{9h^2}{4} \right\} \dfrac{1}{\triangle} = \dfrac{11}{6} h^2;$

k being the radius of gyration of the area about the line of intersection of the area and the free surface.

Now, $\bar{Z} =$ depth of the C. G. of the area $= h + \dfrac{h}{3} = \dfrac{4h}{3}$, for G D $= \dfrac{h}{3}$

Since (depth of centre of pressure below the free surface) $\times$ $(\bar{z}) = k^2,$

$\therefore$ Depth of centre of pressure $= \dfrac{11}{6} h^2 \times \dfrac{3}{4h} = \dfrac{11}{8} h$

Ex. 2. A flat circular plate of radius a, lies in a plane inclined at $30°$ to the horizontal, and is subjected to water pressure on one face.

The centre of pressure is at a distance $\frac{1}{16} a$ from its geometrical centre.

Shew that the geometrical centre is at a depth $2\,a$ below the free surface of water. (Tripos part I 1927)

Ex. 3   Prove that in the case of a plane lamina immersed vertically in a homogeneous liquid at rest under gravity, centre of pressure is always lower than its centre of gravity.

Show that as the lamina is lowered down the liquid, the vertical distance between the centre of pressure and centre of gravity becomes smaller and smaller.

Calculate its rate of variation

[Ans. $\frac{k^2}{\bar{z}^2}$ where k is the radius of gyration of the lamina and $\bar{z}$, the depth of its C. G.]

Ex. 4.   A system of particles of masses m_1, m_2, · ...placed

at $(\,x_1,\,y_1\,)$, $(x_2,\,y_2)$.. .... is equimomental with a lamina immersed in a heavy homogeneous liquid (with its plane not necessarily vertical). The axis of x is the line of intersection of the lamina with the free surface.

Prove that the coordinates of the centre of pressure are the coordinates of the centroid of a system of particles of masses $m_1\,y_1$, $m_2\,y_2$,............ ...placed at $[x_1\,y_1]$, $[x_2,\,y_2]$ etc.

Ex. 5.   Show that the depth of the centre of pressure of a triangular lamina, whose vertices are at depths a, b, c below the free surface, is the same as the C. G. of 3 masses proportional

(54)

to $[2a+b+c]$, $[2b+c+a]$, $[2c+a+b]$ placed at A, B, C respectively.

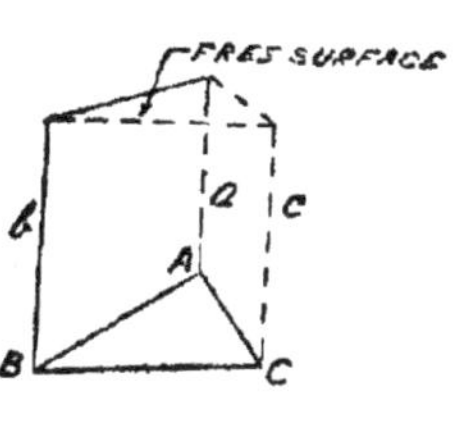

The triangle is reducible to 3 particles of mass $\frac{m}{3}$ each placed at mid-points of the sides, this system being equi-momental with the triangular lamina, where $m =$ mass of the lamina.

Hence $m_1 = m_2 = m_3 = \frac{m}{3}$ and $y_1 = \frac{a+b}{2}, y_2 = \frac{b+c}{2}, y_3 = \frac{c+a}{2}$

We have therefore to find the depth of the C. G. of a system of 3 particles $\frac{m}{3} (\frac{a+b}{2}), \frac{m}{3} (\frac{b+c}{2}) \frac{m}{3} (\frac{c+a}{2})$ placed respectively at depths $\frac{a+b}{2}$, $\frac{b+c}{2}$, $\frac{c+a}{2}$ below the free surface.

Hence the required depth of centre pressure

$$= \frac{\frac{m}{3} (\frac{a+b}{2}) (\frac{a+b}{2}) + \frac{m}{3} (\frac{b+c}{2}) (\frac{b+c}{2}) + \frac{m}{3} (\frac{c+a}{2}) (\frac{c+a}{3})}{\frac{m}{3} \frac{(a+b)}{2} + \frac{m}{3} (\frac{b+c}{2}) + \frac{m}{3} (\frac{c+a}{2})}$$

$$= \frac{1}{3} \cdot \frac{a^2 + b^2 + c^2 + bc + ca + ab }{(a+b+c)}$$

$$= \frac{\Sigma \, a (2a + b + c)}{\Sigma (2a + b + c)}$$

Ex. 6   Show that in the above example the depth of the centre of pressure of the lamina below its C. G. is $\dfrac{\Sigma (b - c)^2}{12 \, \Sigma \, a.}$

Ex. 7.   ABCD is a quadrilateral having its side AD in the surface of a liquid and the sides AB, DC vertical and equal to a and b respectively. Show that the depth of the centre of pressure is

$$\frac{(a^2 + b^2) \, (a+b)}{2 (a^2 + ab + b^2)}$$

(Hint:—Reduce the quadrilateral to two triangles by a diagonal and deduce the system of particles equimomental to the lamina, then apply Ex. 4.)

Ex. 8. A trapezium is immersed vertically in a liquid with one of its parallel sides of length l in the surface and the other of l' at a depth d from the surface. Find the depth of the centre of pressure.

$$\text{Ans.} \quad \frac{(l + 3\,l')\,d}{2\,(l + 2\,l')}$$

Ex. 9 A parallelogram has its corners at depths d_1, d_2, d_3, d_4, below the surface of a liquid and its centre is at a depth d show that the depth of the centre of pressure is

$$\frac{d_1{}^2 + d_2{}^2 + d_3{}^2 + d_4{}^2 + 8\,d^2}{12d}$$

Ex. 10. A square lamina just immersed vertically in water with one side in the surface is then lowered through a depth h. If a be the length of the square, prove that the distance of the centre of pressure from the centre of the square is

$$\frac{a^2}{6a + 12\,h}$$

Ex. 11. A regular hexagon, whose side is a is immersed in a liquid with one side in the surface, prove that the depth of its centre of pressure below the surface is $1.107a$ approximately (I. C. S. 1930)

Ex. 12. A square lamina ABCD is completely immersed in water with its plane vertical so that the side A B is in the surface. Draw a line B E to a point E in C D such that the pressures on the two portions may be equal. Prove that, if this be the case, the distance between the centres of pressure: the side of the square $= \sqrt{505} : 48$.

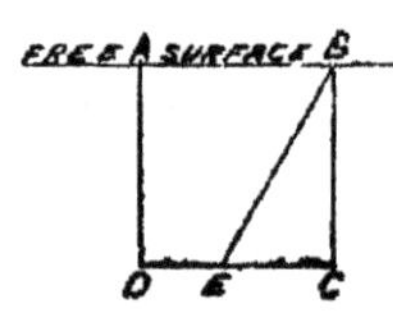

Let E C $= b$.

Pressure on the triangle B C E $=g$ P $(a\ b)(\frac{a}{3})$

Also pressure on the whole square is g P $a^2(\frac{a}{2})$

If the pressure on B E C is equal to that on A B E D then this must be half of the total pressure on the square.   Hence

$$\tfrac{1}{3}\, g\ \text{P}\ a^2\ b = \tfrac{1}{2}\, g\ \text{P}\ a^2\left(\tfrac{a}{2}\right)$$

$$\therefore\ b = \tfrac{n}{4}a$$

$$or,\ \text{D}\ \text{E} = a/4.$$

Now take A B and A D as axes of x and y.

Triangle B E C is equimomental with 3 particles each of mass proportional to $\dfrac{1}{3}\left(\dfrac{a}{2}\right)\left(\tfrac{3}{4}a\right) = \dfrac{a^2}{8}$, and placed at $\left(a,\dfrac{a}{2}\right)$, $\left(\dfrac{5}{8}a,\ a\right)$ and $\left(\dfrac{5}{8}a,\ \dfrac{a}{2}\right)$.

Hence the coordinates of the centre of pressure of the triangle are the same as those of the centre of gravity of the particles of mass $\dfrac{a^2}{8}\left(\dfrac{a}{2}\right),\dfrac{a^2}{8}\left(a\right),\ \dfrac{a^2}{8}\left(\dfrac{a}{2}\right)$ placed at $\left(a,\dfrac{a}{2}\right),\ \left(\dfrac{5a}{8},\ a\right),\ \left(\dfrac{5a}{8}\ \dfrac{a}{2}\right)$

respectively.

$$\therefore\ \bar{x} = \frac{\dfrac{a^2}{8}\left(\dfrac{a}{2}\right)(a) + \dfrac{a^2}{8}(a)\left(\dfrac{5a}{8}\right) + \dfrac{a^2}{8}\left(\dfrac{a}{2}\right)\left(\dfrac{5a}{8}\right)}{\dfrac{a^2}{8}\left(\dfrac{a}{2}\right) + \dfrac{a^2}{8}(a) + \dfrac{a^2}{8}\left(\dfrac{a}{2}\right)}$$

$$= \frac{23}{32}a.$$

$$y = \frac{\dfrac{a^2}{8}\left(\dfrac{a}{2}\right)^2 + \dfrac{a^2}{8}(a)^2 + \dfrac{a^2}{8}\left(\dfrac{a}{2}\right)^2}{\dfrac{a^2}{8}\left(\dfrac{a}{2}\right) + \left(\dfrac{a^2}{8}\right)(a) + \dfrac{a^2}{8}\left(\dfrac{a}{2}\right)}$$

$$= \tfrac{5}{4}a.$$

Hence the coordinates of the centre of pressure are $(\frac{33}{32}a, \frac{3}{4}a)$.

Similarly splitting the trepezium A B D E into equimomental particles, the coordinates of the centre of pressure will be found to be $(\frac{9}{32}a, \frac{7}{12}a)$

$$\therefore \text{The required distance} = \sqrt{\left\{\left(\frac{33}{32}-\frac{9}{32}\right)^2 a^2 + \left(\frac{3}{4}-\frac{7}{12}\right)^2 a^2\right\}}$$
$$= \frac{\sqrt{505}}{48}a.$$

Ex. 13. If an area is bounded by two concentric semicircles with their common bounding diameter in the free surface, prove that the depth of the centre of pressure is

$$\tfrac{3}{16}\,\pi\,(a+b)\,(a^2+b^2)/(a^2+ab+b^2)$$

where a and b are the radii.

By § 3·3 and using the bounding diameter in the free surface as the initial line we have

$$\bar{x} = \frac{\int\int pr^2 \cos\theta\, dr\, d\theta}{\int\int pr\, d\theta\, dr}, \qquad \bar{y} = \frac{\int\int pr^2 \sin\theta\, dr\, d\theta}{\int\int pr\, d\theta\, dr}$$

$$= \frac{\int\int r^3 \sin\theta \cos\theta\, dr\, d\theta}{\int\int r^2 \sin\theta\, d\theta\, dr}, \qquad = \frac{\int\int r^3 \sin^2\theta\, dr\, d\theta}{\int\int r^2 \sin\theta\, dr\, d\theta,}$$

Since $p = g\rho\, r \sin\theta$)

$$= \frac{\int_0^\pi \sin\theta\cos\theta\, d\theta \int_a^b r^3 dr}{\int_0^\pi \sin\theta\, d\theta \int_a^b r^2\, dr}, \qquad = \frac{\int_0^\pi \sin^2\theta\, d\theta \int_a^b r^3\, dr}{\int_0^\pi \sin\theta\, d\theta \int_a^b r^2\, dr}$$

$$= 0 \qquad\qquad = \tfrac{3}{16}\frac{\pi(a+b)(a^2+b^2)}{(a^2+ab+b^2)}$$

Ex. 14. Shew that the depth of the centre of pressure of the area included between the arc and the asymptote of the curve

$$(r-a)\cos\theta = b \text{ is } \frac{a}{4}\,\frac{3\pi a + 16b}{3\pi b + 4a},$$

the asymptote being in the surface and the plane of the curve vertical.

(I.C.S. 1931)

The form of the curve is roughly as shown in the fig. where $T\,T'$ is the asymptote.

Consider an elementry area $rd\theta d_r$ round P. The depth of this point below the surface (or the asymp_tote) is $(r\cos\theta - b)$; hence thedepth of the centre of pressure below the surface

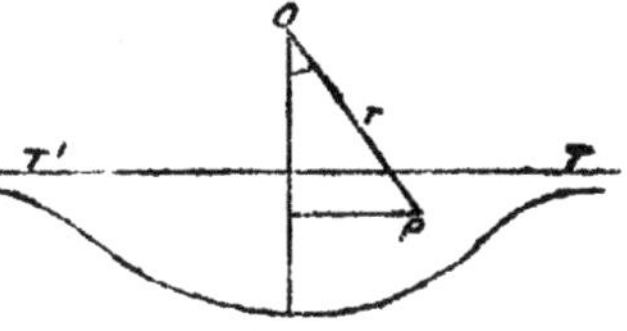

$$= \frac{\iint (r\cos\theta - b)\,pr\,d\theta\,dr}{\iint pr\,\theta\,dr\,d\theta}, \text{ where } p \text{ is the pressure at P}$$

$$= \frac{\iint (r\cos\theta - b)^2\,g\rho\,r\,d\theta\,dr}{\iint (r\cos\theta - b)\,g\rho\,r\,d\theta\,dr}, \text{ since } p = g\rho\,(r\cos\theta - b).$$

$$= \frac{\displaystyle\int_{-\frac{\pi}{2}}^{\frac{\pi}{2}} d\theta \int_{b\sec\theta}^{a+b\sec\theta} (r^2\cos^2\theta - 2\,b\,r\cos\theta + b^2)\,r\,d\,r}{\displaystyle\int_{-\frac{\pi}{2}}^{\pi/2} d\theta \int_{b\sec\theta}^{a+b\sec\theta} (r\cos\theta - b)\,r\,d\,r}$$

$$= \frac{\displaystyle\int_{-\frac{\pi}{2}}^{\pi/2} \left(\frac{a^4}{4}\cos^2\theta + \frac{a^3}{3}b\cos\theta\right) d\theta}{\displaystyle\int_{-\frac{\pi}{2}}^{\pi/2} \left(\frac{a^3}{3}\cos\theta + \frac{a^2\,b}{2}\right) d\theta}$$

$$= \frac{a}{4}\,\frac{3\,\pi\,a + 16\,b}{4\,a + 3\,\pi\,b}.$$

Ex. 15. A plane area, bounded by the parabola $y^2 = 4ax$ the ordinate $x = h$ and the axis $y = 0$, is immersed in a homogeneous liquid with the axis vertical and the vertex in the surface, and is then lowered without rotation. Prove that the centre of pressure moves along the straight line.

$$48\sqrt{h}\, y = 5\sqrt{a}\,(7x + 3h),$$

approaching the centroid of the area as its limiting position.

I.C.S. 1932)

Let ONP be the lamina, where $ON = h$. Let the depth of the vertex O below the free surface in any subsequent position be λ. If $\bar{x},\ \bar{y}$ be the cordinates of the centre of pressure with respect to given axes fixed in the lamina we have by § 3·4

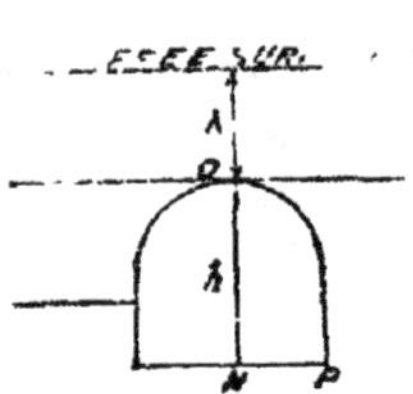

$$\bar{x} = \frac{\int\!\int p\, x\, dx\, dy}{\int\!\int p\, dx\, dy}, \quad \bar{y} = \frac{\int\!\int py\, dx\, dy}{\int\!\int p\, dx\, dy},$$

where p is the pressure at any point Q (x, y) of the lamina.

Now the pressure $p = g\rho$ (depth of Q below the surface)

$$= g\rho\, (x + \lambda)$$

$$\therefore\ \bar{x} = \frac{\int\!\int x(x+\lambda)\, dx\, dy}{\int\!\int (x+\lambda)\, dx\, dy}, \quad \bar{y} = \frac{\int\!\int y(x+\lambda)\, dx\, dy}{\int\!\int (x+\lambda)\, dx\, dy}$$

the field of intergation being the whole of the plane lamina.

Hence

$$\bar{x} = \frac{\displaystyle\int_0^h dx \int_0^{\sqrt{4ax}} x\,(x+\lambda)\, dy}{\displaystyle\int_0^h dx \int_0^{\sqrt{4ax}} (x+\lambda)\, dy} = \frac{3}{7}\ \frac{5h^2 + 7\lambda h}{3h + 5\lambda} \quad \text{...(i)}$$

$$\bar{y} = \frac{\displaystyle\int_{0}^{h} dx \int_{0} y\,(x+\lambda)\,dy}{\displaystyle\int_{0}^{h} dx \int (x+\lambda)\,dy\Big/ \sqrt{4a\,x}} = \frac{5\sqrt{ah}}{4}\;\frac{2h+3\lambda}{3h+5\lambda} \quad\text{...(ii)}$$

To find the locus of $(\bar{x},\ \bar{y})$ we have to eliminate λ from equations (i) and (ii).

From (i) we have
$$\frac{7}{3}\frac{\bar{x}}{h} = \frac{5h+7\lambda}{3h+5\lambda}$$

or, $\dfrac{7}{3}\dfrac{\bar{x}}{h} + 1 = \dfrac{4\,(2h+3\lambda)}{3h+5\lambda}$

Dividing this equation by (ii) we have
$$\frac{7\bar{x}+3h}{3h\,\bar{y}} = \frac{16}{5\sqrt{ah}}$$

or, $48\sqrt{h}\ \bar{y} = \sqrt{a}\,(7\bar{x} + 3h)$.

Ex. 16.   A regular polygon wholly immersed in a homogeneous liquid is movable about its centre of gravity; prove that the locus of the centre of pressure is a sphere.

Take the fixed centre of gravity O of the lamina as origin

Take any three mutually perpendicular lines as axes of x, y and z, taking the vertical through O as z axis.   Let the principal axes of inertia of the lamina be Ox', Oy' and Oz' be normal to the lamina. Then since O, the origin, is the centre of gravity of the lamina,

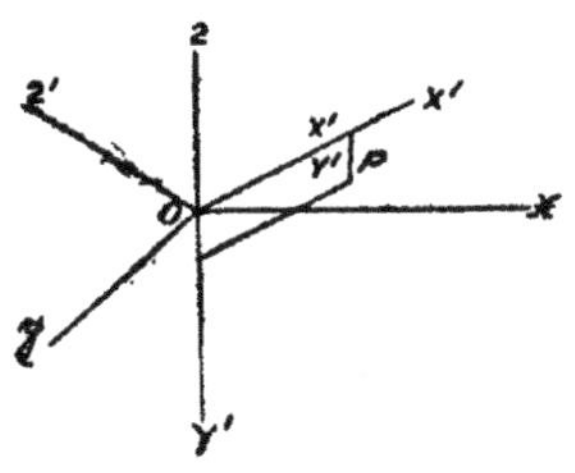

$$\int\!\int x'\, dx'\, dy' = \int\!\int y'\, dx'\, dy' = 0 \qquad\qquad (1)$$

Again since Ox', Oy' are the principal axes of the lamina

$$\int\int x' \, y' \, dx' \, dy' = 0 \qquad (2)$$

Again since the lamina is a regular polygon, by symmetry the moments of inertia of the lamina about Ox' and Oy' are equal.

Hence $\int\int x'^2 \, dx' \, dy' = \int\int y'^2 \, dx' \, dy' = Ak^2$, $\qquad$ (3)

where $\int\int dx' \, dy' = A = $ area of the lamina.

Let P be any point in the lamina. Its coordinates relative to axes $Ox' \, y' \, z'$ (fixed in the lamina) will be (x', y', o) while relative to the axes $O \, x \, y \, z$ (fixed in space) will be (x, y, z). If (l_1, m_1, n_1), (l_2, m_2, n_2), (l_3, m_3, n_3) be the direction cosines of the lines Ox', Oy', Oz' with respect to axes $O \, x \, y \, z$, then by considering the projections of $O \, P$ on Ox etc. in two different ways we have

$$x = l_1 \, x' + l_2 \, y'$$
$$y = m_1 \, x' + m_2 \, y'$$
$$z = n_1 \, x' + n_2 \, y'$$

Let the coordinates of the centre of pressure of the lamina in this particular position be $(\bar{x}, \bar{y}, \bar{z})$ with respect to axes fixed in space and $(\bar{x}', \bar{y}', o)$ with respect to axes fixed in the lamina, since the centre of pressure must plainly be in the lamina.

$$\text{Then, } \bar{x} = \bar{x}' \, l_1 + \bar{y}' \, l_2$$
$$\bar{y} = \bar{x}' \, m_1 + \bar{y}' \, m_2 \qquad (4)$$
$$\bar{z} = \bar{x}' \, n_1 + \bar{y}' \, n_2$$

$$\text{also, } \bar{x}' = \frac{\int\int p \, x' \, dx' \, dy'}{\int\int p \, dx' \, dy'} \, , \; \bar{y}' = \frac{\int\int p \, y' \, dx' \, dy'}{\int\int p \, dx' \, dy'}$$
$$\bar{z}' = 0 \qquad (5)$$

Now pressure at (x', y', o) is $g \, P$ (depth of P below the surface)

Let the depth of the fixed origin O below the free surface be d, then the depth of P below the free surface is $d - z$, z being the corresponding z—coordinate of P with respect to fixed axes

But $z = n_1 x' + n_2 y'$

$\therefore p = g P (d - n_1 x' - n_2 y')$

Hence from (5) we have

$$\bar{x}' = \frac{\int\int (d - n_1 x' - n_2 y') x' \, dx' \, dy'}{\int\int (d - n_1 x' - n_2 y') \, dx' \, dy'}$$

$$= - n_1 \frac{\int\int x'^2 \, dx' \, dy'}{d \int\int dx' \, dy'} \qquad \text{, by (1) and (2)}$$

$$= - \frac{n_1}{d} k^2 \qquad\qquad \text{by} \qquad\qquad (3)$$

So also

$$\bar{y}' = - \frac{n_2}{d} k^2,$$

Now, by squaring and adding each one of the equations (4) we have

$$\bar{x}^2 + \bar{y}^2 + \bar{z}^2 = \bar{x}'^2 + \bar{y}'^2$$

$$= \frac{k^4}{d^2} (n_1^2 + n_2^2)$$

Also $\bar{z} = n_1 \bar{x}' + n_2 \bar{y}'$

$$= - \frac{k^2}{d} (n_1^2 + n_2^2)$$

$$\therefore \bar{x}^2 + \bar{y}^2 + \bar{z}^2 = - \frac{k^2}{d} \bar{z},$$

which is the locus of centre of pressure, with respect to fixed axes. This locus is evidently a sphere.

Ex. 17. Prove that the locus of the centres of pressure of a series of a coaxal circles immersed completely in a homogeneous liquid and having their line of centres horizontal is a parabola.

Ex. 18.   An elliptic area bounded by two conjugate dia-
meters C B, C D and the intercepted arc is immersed vertically
in a homogeneous liquid, C D coinciding with the surface.
Find the centre of pressure.   (Punjab Univ. M A 1928).

Ex. 19.   An area bounded by the curve $r = a (1 + cos\ \theta)$ is
immersed in a flluid, the prime radius vector being coincident
with the surface.   Find the centre of pressur .

3·5.   If a straight line be taken in the plane of the area
parallel to the surface of the liquid and as far below the
centroid of the area as the surface of the liquid is above, the
pole of this straight line with respect to the momental ellipse
at the centroid, whose semi-axes are equal to the principal radii
of gyration at that point, will be the centre of pressure.

Take the principal axes of the lamina through its centroid
as axes of x and y.

Then, if A be the area of the lamina, and b, a the principal
radii of gyration,

$$A\ b^2 = \int\int y^2\ dx\ dy,\ A\ a^2 = \int\int x^2\ dx\ dy,$$

$$\int\int x\ y\ dx\ dy = 0.$$

$$\text{Also,}\ \int\int x\ dx\ dy = \int\int y\ dx\ dy = 0,$$

for the C. G. of the lamina is at the origin.

Hence the equation of the momental ellipse is

$$\frac{x^2}{a^2} + \frac{y^2}{b^2} = 1.$$

Let $x\ cos\ \theta + y\ sin\ \theta = d$ be the equation of the line in the free
surface, and $(\bar{x},\ \bar{y})$ the coordinates of the centre of pressure; then

$$\bar{x} = \frac{\int\int p\ x\ dx\ dy}{\int\int p\ dx\ dy},\ \bar{y} = \frac{\int\int p\ y\ dx\ dy}{\int\int p\ dx\ dy},$$

where p is the fluid pressure at $P(x, y)$.

Hence if the fluid is homogeneous and at rest under the
action of gavity,

$$p = g\mathsf{P} \quad \text{(perpendicular from P on } x \cos\theta + y \sin\theta = d).$$

$$\therefore\ p = g\mathsf{P}\ (d x - \cos\theta - y \sin\theta)$$

Hence $\quad \bar{x} = \dfrac{\int\int (d - x \cos\theta - y \sin\theta)\ x\ dx\ dy}{\int\int (d - r \cos\theta - y \sin\theta)\ dx\ dy}$

$$= -\frac{a^2}{d}\ \cos\theta;$$

and similarly, $\quad \bar{y} = -\dfrac{b^2}{d}\ \sin\theta$

It follows at once that $(\bar{x},\ \bar{y})$ is the pole of the line

$$x \cos\theta + y \sin\theta = -d$$

with regard to the momental ellipse.

Ex. 1. Find the locus of the centre of pressure of an elliptic lamina immersed vertically in a homogeneous fluid at rest under gravity and moving in the vertical plane in such a way as to be always just immersed.

Let $x \cos\theta + y \sin\theta = d$ be the equation of the horizontal line in the free surface touching the elliptic lamina with respect to the principal axes of the lamina. Let the equation of the ellipse be

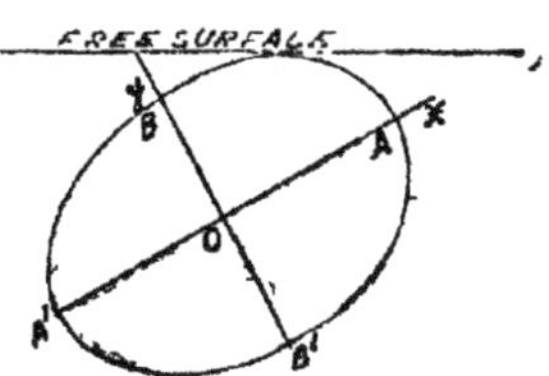

$$\frac{x^2}{a^2} + \frac{y^2}{b^2} = 1$$

Since (the radius of gyration about $ox)^2 = \dfrac{b^2}{4}$,

and, (the radius of gyration about $oy)^2 = \dfrac{a^2}{4}$,

the equation of the momental ellipse will be

$$\frac{x^2}{\frac{a^2}{4}} + \frac{y^2}{\frac{b^2}{4}} = 1 \ldots\ldots \text{(i)}$$

The centre of pressure $(\bar{x},\ \bar{y})$ is the pole of

$$x \cos \theta + y \sin \theta = -d \ldots \ldots (ii)$$

with respect (i)

Hence comparing $\dfrac{x \, \bar{x}}{\dfrac{a^2}{4}} + \dfrac{y \, \bar{y}}{\dfrac{b^2}{4}} = 1$ with (ii), we have

$$\bar{x} = -\frac{a^2}{4d} \cos \theta, \quad \bar{y} = -\frac{b^2}{4d} \sin \theta \ldots \ldots (iii)$$

Now, since $x \cos \theta + y \sin \theta = d$ is tangent to the ellipse

$$\frac{x^2}{a^2} + \frac{y^2}{b^2} = 1,$$

$$a^2 \cos^2 \theta + b^2 \sin^2 \theta = d^2.$$

Substituting in this from (iii) we have

$$\frac{\bar{x}^2}{a^2} + \frac{\bar{y}^2}{b^2} = \frac{1}{16},$$

as the locus of the centre of pressure.

Ex. 2. A quadrant of a circle is just immersed vertically, with one edge in the surface in a liquid, the density of which varies as the depth. Find the centre of pressure.

Take $O x$ as the edge in the surface, $P = \mu \, y$ and $p = \tfrac{1}{2} \mu g y^2$

Hence $\bar{x} = \dfrac{\int\!\int p \, x \, dx \, dy}{\int\!\int p \, dx \, dy} = \dfrac{\int\!\int x \, y^2 \, dx \, dy}{\int\!\int y^2 \, dx \, dy}$

$$= \frac{\displaystyle\int_0^a dx \int_0^{\sqrt{a^2 - x^2}} x \, y^2 \, dy}{\displaystyle\int_0^a dx \int_0^{\sqrt{a^2 - x^2}} y^2 \, dy}$$

$$= \frac{\displaystyle\int_0^a x \, (a^2 - x^2)^{\frac{3}{2}} \, dx}{\displaystyle\int_0^a (a^2 - x^2)^{\frac{3}{2}} \, dx}$$

$$= \frac{16a}{15\pi}$$

Similarly $\bar{y} = \frac{32a}{15\pi}$.

Ex 3. A plane area immersed in a fluid of uniform density moves parallel to itself and with its centre of gravity always in the same vertical straight line. Show (1) that the locus of the centres of pressure is a hyperbola, one asymptote of which is the given vertical, and (2) that if a, $a+h$, $a+h'$, $a+h''$ be the depths of the C. G. in any positions, y, $y+k$, $y+k'$, $y+k'$ those of the centre of pressure in the same positions, then

$$\begin{vmatrix} k & h & h(k-h) \\ k' & h' & h'(k'-h') \\ k'' & h'' & h''(k''-h'') \end{vmatrix} = o$$

Let G be the centre of gravity of the plane area A and, C the centre of the pressure. Suppose the area is moved parallel to itself so that G moves in a vertical straight line. Let a be the depth of G in the first position and $a+h$ be its depth when in the position G' Let C'' be the position of the *new* centre of pressure, C' being the *new* position of the *old* centre of pressure.

In the old position the resultant of pressures p at every point acted at C and was equal to g^{P} A a.

Now in the present position pressure at every point is increased by $g^{P}h$ because every point is now at a depth h below its previous position. Hence the pressure at every point is $p + g^{P}h$; but the resultant of pressures p at the various points of the area is g^{P} A a and acts at C', the present position of the point C. Also the resultant of the constant pressure $g^{P}h$ acting at every point of the area will be clearly $g^{P}h$ A acting at the centroid of the area. Hence the new centre of pressure C'' is the point where the resultant of parallel forces g^{P} A a acting at C' and $g^{P}h$ A acting at G' acts.

Hence taking moments about C'',

$$G' C'' (g P A h) = C' C'' (g P A a)$$

$$\frac{G' C''}{C' C''} = \frac{a}{h}$$

or, $\quad \dfrac{G' C''}{G' C'} = \dfrac{a}{a+h}$

Let us now take the vertical along which G moves as y axis and the projection of G C on the horizontal free surface as x—axis. Let (x_0, y_0) be the coordinates of C in the initial position of the lamina, then in any subsequent position of the lamina when it has been lowered through depth h, the cooidinates of C', the subsequent position of C will clearly be $(x_0, y_0 + h)$. Now if (x, y) be the coordinates of C'', the new centre of pressure, then since $G' C'' : C' C'' = a : h$,

$$x = \frac{a\, x_0}{a+h}\ , y = \frac{a\,(y_0 + h) + h\,(a+h)}{a+h}$$

Locus of (x, y) the centre of pressure is clearly obtained by eliminating the variable parameter 'h'. It is

$$(y_0 - a)\, x^2 - x_0\, x\, y + a\, x_0^2 = 0,$$

which is a hyperbola, whose one asymptote is $x = o$, the vertical along which G moves.

If $y_0,\ y_0 + k,\ y_0 + k',\ y_0 + k''$ be the depths of the centres of pressure corresponding to the depths $a,\ a+h,\ a+h',\ a+h''$, of the C. G., then we have

$$y_0 + k = \frac{a\,(y_0 + h) + h\,(a+h)}{a+h}$$

$$y_0 + k' = \frac{a\,(y_0 + h') + h'\,(a+h')}{a+h'}$$

$$y_0 + k'' = \frac{a\,(y_0 + h'') + h''\,(a+h'')}{a+h''}$$

or, $\quad h\ (y_0 - 2a) + k\ a + h\ (k\ - h\ ) = c$

$\qquad\quad h'\ (y_0 - 2a) + k'\ a + h'\ (k' - h'\ ) = o$

$$h''\ y_0 - 2a) + k''a + h''(k'' - h'') = 0$$

Eliminating $(y_0 - 2a$, a, we have

$$\begin{vmatrix} h & k & (k-h & h \\ h' & k' & (k'-h') & h' \\ h'' & k'' & (k''-h'') & h'' \end{vmatrix} = 0$$

3 6. Resultant pressure on curved surfaces.

We shall first consider the case of curved surfaces immersed in a fluid of uniform density and at rest under the action of gravity.

To find the resultant of the fluid pressures acting on a curved surface let us first find out the vertical component of this resultant We shall later find the components of the resultant in two mutually perpendicular horizontal directions. It will then be possible to deduce the resultant from these three components.

(i) Let the curved surface P Q R S be bounded by the contour P Q R. Let us drop perpendiculars from every point of the contour on the free surface so that the plane curve $p\ q\ r$ is the projection of the skew curve P Q R   These perpendiculars

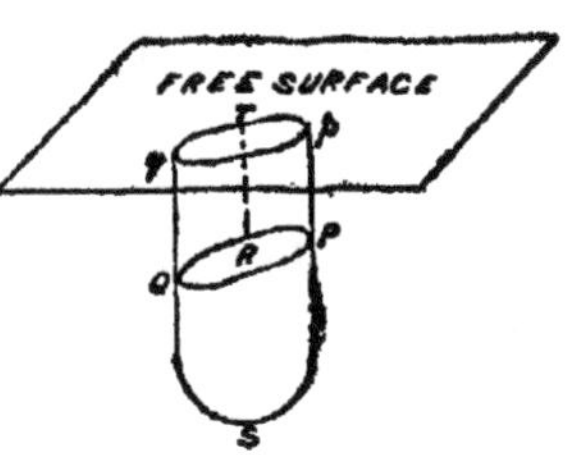

clearly generate a closed surface bounded by the cylinder on the base $p\ q\ r$ and the surface P Q R S   The mass of fluid enclosed in the surface $p\ q\ r$— P Q R S is in equilibrium under the action of fluid pressures acting on the surface $p\ q\ r$—P Q R S, and its own weight acting vertically downwards through the centroid of the enclosed fluid. Hence resolving vertically the resultant of the vertical compon nts of the fluid pressures on the surface $p\ q\ r$—P Q R S is equal to the weight of the fluid enclosed in the surface $p\ q\ r$—P Q R S and acts vertically upwards through the centroid of the fluid enclosed in this surface. But the fluid pressures on the cylinderical part of the surface $p\ q\ r$—P Q R have no vertical components at all. Hence the resultant of the vertical components of fluid pressures acting on the surface P Q R S is equal to the weight of the fluid enclosed in the surface $p \, q \, r$—P Q R S, and acts through the C. G. of this mass.

(ii) Secondly, consider now a surface P Q which is pressed upwards instead of downwards. Let A B be the horizontal surface. Let us project the contour bounding the surface 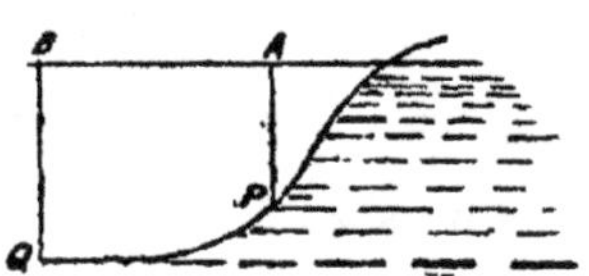 P Q on the surface A B. Consider the surface formed by the surface P Q and the projections of its contour P Q on the free surface A B. If this surface were supposed filled with fluid of the same density, the resultant vertical pressure on the surface P Q will be, by the above argument, equal to the weight of the fluid enclosed in the surface A Q, and act along the vertical through the centroid of this mass.

But the pressure at any point of the surface P Q is just the same in the two cases, for the depth of the point below the free surface remains the same in either case and the pressure in the case of a homogeneous fluid at rest under gravity depends only on depth. Hence .the resultant vertical pressure on the surface P Q in the actual case is also known.

Ex. 1. A hollow spherical vessel is formed by two hemi-spherical cups joined together. The vessel is placed with the plane of the join horizontal and contains liquid up to height h above this plane. Shew that the pressure of the liquid produces a force tending to lift the upper hemisphere from the lower proportional to h^3, but independent of the radius of the vessel.

(Tripos Part I, 1926)

Here we have to find the fluid pressure on the upper hemisphere. In this case the liquid is pressing the surface upwards. Hence the vertical pressure by what has been just said is equal to the weight of the fluid enclosed in the space between a cylinder of height h based on 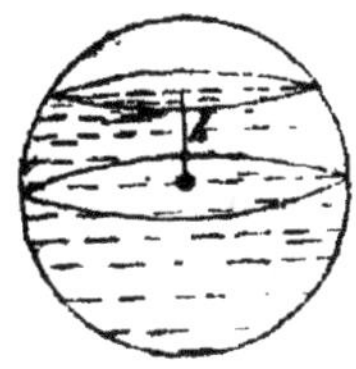 the circle in the plane of the join and the upper hemisphere i. e.

$$= \left\{ \pi\, a^2\, h - \int_0^h \pi\, (a^2 - x^2)\, dx \right\} g\rho$$

$$= \pi g\rho\, \frac{h^3}{3}.$$

(iii) Thirdly, suppose now that the surface is pressed partially upwards and partially downwards, i. e.

part P S of the surface P Q is pressed upwards and the part S Q downwards. 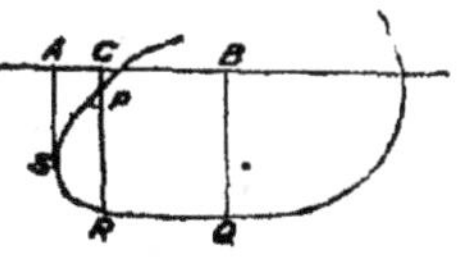 Vertical pressure on the surface S Q is by (i) clearly equal to the weight of the liquid contained in the surface A S Q B acting vertically through its centroid. Now surface S P is wholly pressed upwards so that by (ii) the vertical pressure is equal to the weight of the fluid enclosed in the space A S P C acting vertically through its centroid.

Hence the resultant vertical pressure on the surface P S R Q is equal to the weight of the fluid enclosed in the spaces P S R and B Q R C acting vertically through its centroid.

3. 7. We have next to find the horizontal component of the resultant fluid pressure on a curved surface in any given direction.

Let the curved surface in question be P R Q.

Let us project the surface P R Q on
a vertical plane perpendicular to the
given horizontal direction. Let $p\ q$ be
the curve into which the surface thus
projects.

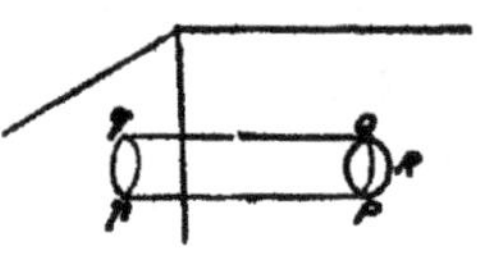

Consider the mass of fluid enclosed in the space $p\ q$—P R Q.
It is in equilibrium under the action of (i) fluid pressure acting
on the given surface P R Q (ii) the fluid pressure on the plane
curve $p\ q$ (iii) the fluid pressure on the cylinderical surface
generated by perpendiculars from points like P of the bounding
contour P Q of the surface P R Q on the vertical plane, and (iv)
the weight of the fluid which acts vertically, (and has therefore
no horizontal component).

Resolving horizontally along the. given direction we see
that fluid pressures on the cylinderical surface being everywhere
at right angles to this direction have no component in this
direction. It follows that the horizontal component in this
direction of the resultant fluid pressure on P R Q must balance
the fluid pressure on the plane area $p\ q$. Hence the required
component is equal to the fluid pressure on the plane area $p\ q$
and passes through its centre of pressure.

To determine the resultant fluid pressure on any surface
we have therefore to find (i) the vertical pressure, and (ii)
resultant horizontal pressure in any two direction.

These three forces may in some cases be compounded
into a single force, in which case the point in which the
line of force meets the surface is called the centre of pressure
of the surface.

Ex. 1. A vessel in the form of an elliptic paraboloid,

whose axis. is vertical and equation $\dfrac{x^2}{a^2}+\dfrac{y^2}{b^2}=\dfrac{z}{h}$, is divided into four equal compartments by its principal planes. Into one of these water is poured to the depth h; prove that, if the resultant fluid pressure on the curved portion be reduced to two forces, one vertical and the other horizontal, the line of action of the latter will pass through the point $(\frac{5a}{16}, \frac{5b}{16}, \frac{3h}{7})$.

Let OACB be one of the four equal parts into which the elliptic paraboloid is divided by the planes $x0z$ and $y0z$, the plane ACB being the horizontal surface of the water. We require the horizontal component of the fluid pressure acting on the curved surface AOB.

The horizontal component of the pressure parallel to Ox is equal and opposite to the fluid pressure acting on the projection of the surface on the plane $y\,0\,z$ i. e. on the parabola BOC, whose equation is $y^2/b^2 = z/h$, $x = o$, BC being the water line.

The coordinates of the centre of pressure are $(\bar{x}, \bar{y}, \bar{z})$ where

$$\bar{x} = o, \quad \bar{y} = \frac{\frac{1}{2}\int py\, y\,dz}{\int p\, y\, d z}$$

$$= \frac{\frac{1}{2}\, g^{\mathrm{P}} \int_{o}^{h} (h-z)\, \frac{b^2}{h}\, z\, d z}{g^{\mathrm{P}} \int_{o}^{h} (h-z\, \frac{b}{\sqrt{h}}\, \sqrt{z}\, d z}$$

$$= \frac{5b}{16};$$

$$\text{and, } \bar{z} = \frac{\int_{o}^{h} pz\, y dz}{\int_{o}^{h} py dz} = \frac{\int_{o}^{h} g^{\mathrm{P}} (h-z)\, z\frac{b}{\sqrt{h}}\, dz}{\int_{o}^{h} g^{\mathrm{P}} (h-z)\, \frac{b}{\sqrt{h}}\, \sqrt{z} d z} = \frac{3h}{7}$$

Hence the horizontal component of the fluid pressure parallel to ox acts at $\left(o, \dfrac{5b}{16}, \dfrac{3h}{7}\right)$

Similarly the horizontal component of the fluid pressure parallel to oy acts at $\left(\dfrac{5a}{16}, o, \dfrac{3h}{7}\right)$.

The line through $\left(o, \dfrac{5b}{16}, \dfrac{3h}{7}\right)$ parallel to ox clearly meets the line through $\left(\dfrac{5a}{16}, o, \dfrac{3h}{7}\right)$ parallel to oy in the point $\left(\dfrac{5a}{16}, \dfrac{5b}{16}, \dfrac{3h}{7}\right)$, which is, therefore, the point through which the resultant of these two horizontal components must pass.

Ex. 2.   A hemisphere is filled with a homogeneous liquid; find the resultant fluid pressure on one of the four portions into which it is divided by two vertical planes through its centre at right angles to each other.

(Resultant force $= \dfrac{1}{6} g\rho\, a^{3}\, \sqrt{\pi^{2}+4}$, acting along $x = y = \dfrac{2}{\pi}z$.)

Ex. 3.   A hemispherical bowl is filled with water, and two vertical planes are drawn through its central radius, cutting off a semi lune of the surface; if 2α be the angle between the planes, prove that the angle which the line of resultant pressure on the surface makes with the vertical is $\tan^{-1}\left(\dfrac{\operatorname{Sin}\alpha}{\alpha}\right)$.

Let ABC be the semi-lune of the hemispherical surface cut off by two vertical planes AOC and BOC inclined to each other at an angle 2α.

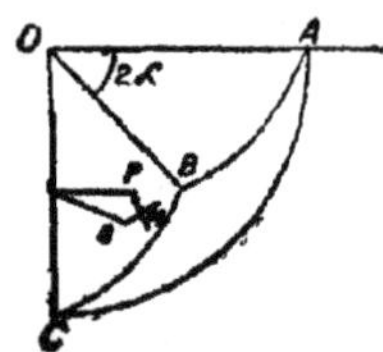

The vertical component of the pressure on the surface is equal to the weight of the fluid enclosed in the semi-lunar surface

ABCO. Now the area of the circular quadrant is $\dfrac{\pi a^2}{4}$ with its centroid G at $(\dfrac{4a}{3\pi},\ \dfrac{4a}{3\pi})$, OB, OC being taken as axes of coordinate.

Volume of the surface thus genarated

= (area of the quadrant) (distance travelled by G as the

quadrant moves from its position BOC to AOC),

$$= \frac{\pi a^2}{4}\ (\frac{4a}{3\pi}\ 2a)\ =\ \frac{2a^3}{3}\alpha$$

Hence the vertical component of the fluid pressure is
$$\tfrac{2}{3}\,g\mathrm{P}\,a^3\alpha.$$

Horizontal component of the fluid pressure perpendicular to the plane BOC is $\dfrac{g\mathrm{P}\,\pi a^2}{4}\ (\dfrac{4a}{3\pi})\ =\ \tfrac{1}{3}\,g\mathrm{P}a^3$, acting at Q.

So also the horizontal component of the fluid pressure perpendicular to the plane AOC is $\tfrac{1}{3}\,g\mathrm{P}a^3$ acting at P.

By symmetry, normals at P and Q to the planes BOC and AOC respectively meet at M so that $\angle\,\mathrm{PMQ} = \pi - 2\alpha$.

Now, the resultant of equal forces $\tfrac{1}{3}\,g\mathrm{P}a^3$ acting along MP and MQ is clearly $\tfrac{2}{3}\,g\mathrm{P}a^3\ \cos\,(\dfrac{\pi - 2\alpha}{2})\ =\ \tfrac{2}{3}\,g\mathrm{P}a^3\,\sin\alpha$. Since the vertical component is $\tfrac{2}{3}\,g\mathrm{P}a^3\alpha$, the angle between the resultant and the vertical is $\tan^{-1}(\dfrac{\tfrac{2}{3}\,g\mathrm{P}a^3\,\mathrm{Sin}\alpha}{\tfrac{2}{3}\,g\mathrm{P}a^3\alpha})\ =\ \tan^{-1}(\dfrac{\mathrm{Sin}\,\alpha}{\alpha})$.

Ex. 4. A vessel full of water is in the form of an eighth part of an ellipsoid (axes a, b, c), bounded by the three principal planes. The axis c is vertical, and the atmospheric pressure is neglected. Prove that the resultant fluid pressure on the curved surface is a force of intensity $\tfrac{1}{3}g\mathrm{P}\ \{\ b^2c^4 + a^2c^4 + \tfrac{1}{4}\pi^2a^2b^2c^2\ \}^{\frac{1}{2}}.$

Ex. 5. A surface in the form of a quarter of a circular cylinder of radius a and axial length b is immersed in a fluid of density ρ with its axis and edge in the free surface. Neglecting atmospheric pressure, show that the resultant pressure of the fluid on the concave surface is $\cdot093g\rho a^2 b$ and is inclined at $32.5°$ to the vertical.

(Tripos, Part I, 1925).

3 8. Fluid pressure on a solid.

We shall now show that the resultant fluid pressure on the surface of a solid either wholly or partially immersed in a fluid at rest under gravity is equal to the weight of the fluid displaced and acts vertically through the centroid of the displaced fluid.

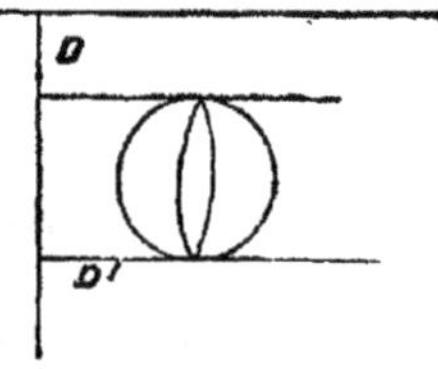

Draw parallel lines D, D′ touching the surface and forming a cylinder which encloses it; the curve of contact divides the surface of the solid into two parts, on which the resultant horizontal pressures parallel to the axis of the cylinder are equal and opposite (§ 3.7). It follows that the fluid pressure on the solid has no horizontal component and is therefore entirely vertical.

Now draw parallel vertical lines E, E′ touching the surface and let C D be the curve of the cylinder generated by E, E′ and the surface of the solid. The curve C D divides 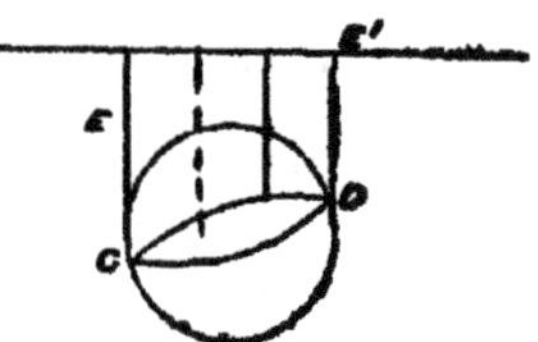 the surface of the solid into two parts, on one of which the resultant vertical pressure act upwards, and on the other downwards, the difference of the two is plainly the weight of the fluid displaced by the solid.

The resultant pressure is therefore equal to the weight of the fluid displaced.

Remark : If the bounding surface of a solid completely immersed in a fluid consists partly of a curved surface and partly of known plane areas, we can easily find the resultant fluid pressure on the curved surface

Suppose for the sake of definiteness the solid consists of two plane areas and a curved surface.

The resultant fluid pressure on the entire curved surface of the solid *viz* S, and the two plane areas is vertical and equal to the weight of the fluid displaced, acting through its centroid. Now the pressures on the plane surfaces can be easily found both in magnitude and direction. . Hence the resultant fluid pressure on S is clearly known.

Ex. 1. An unclosed curved surface which has a plane curve for its boundary, is immersed in a homogeneous liquid. Prove that the thrust of the liquid on one side of the surface is equivalent to two forces, one vertical and the other perpendicular to the plane of the boundary. State precisely the magnitude of each force and the position of its line of action.

Ex. 2. A cubical box of edge a is made of thin metal and has an accurately fitting lid smoothly hinged to one side. The lid has a piece of uniform metal of specific gravity s forged to its inner face, the volume of the metal and the distance of its centre of gravity from the lid being v and h respectively. The box is filled with water and the lid being held closed, is placed with the side to which the hinges are attached on a horizontal table. Prove that, if $6 (s-1) v h > a^4$, the lid will not open when released.

(Tripos Part I 1923.)

Let BCDE be the lid and BC, the line of hinges. Fluid pressure on the lid acts normally to the lid at P which is the centre of pressure. The fluid pressure is clearly $g\rho a^2 \left(-\dfrac{a}{2}\right)$

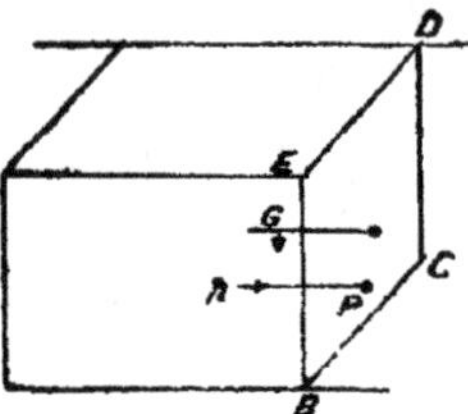

$= \tfrac{1}{2} g\rho a^3$, acting at the centre of pressure P whose depth below ED is $\tfrac{2}{3} a$, or whose height above BC is $\dfrac{a}{3}$, ρ being the density of water. This pressure tends to rotate the lid about BC outwards $i.\,e.$ opens the lid. The weight of the metal of volume v forged to the lid has opposite tendency.

The weight of the metal acting downwards through G is $v\,(s\rho g)$. Also the fluid pressure acting on the solid is equal to the mass of the fluid displaced by it, acting also at G but vertically upwards. This fluid pressure is $g\rho v$

Hence, the net vertical force acting at G is $g\rho v\,(s-1)$. This force tends to counterbalance the effect of the fluid pressure in opening the lid.

Hence, taking moments about BC, the lid will not open so long as

$$g\rho v\,(s-1)\,h > \tfrac{1}{2} g\rho a^3 \left(\dfrac{a}{3}\right)$$

$$\text{or, } 6\,(s-1)\,h\,v > a^4.$$

Ex. 3. A right cone is totally immersed in water, the depth of the centre of its base being given. Prove that, P, P′, P″ being the resultant pressures on its convex surface, when the sines of the angles between its axis to the horizon are S, S′, S″ respectively

$$P^2\,(S'-S'') + P'^2\,(S''-S) + P''^2\,(S-S') = o.$$

Ex. 4. A solid is formed by turning a circular area round a tangent line through an angle θ, and is held under water just immersed with its lower plane face horizontal If ϕ be the inclination between the horizontal and the resultant fluid pressure on the curved part of the surface of the solid,

$$\tan \phi = \tan \frac{\theta}{2} + \operatorname{cosec} \theta.$$

Ex. 5. A solid is formed by turning a parabolic area, bounded by the latus rectum, about the latus rectum, through an angle θ and this solid is held under water, just immersed, with its lower plane face horizontal. Prove that, if ϕ be the inclination to the horizon of the resultant pressure on the curved surface of the solid,

$$3 \sin^2 \theta \tan \phi = 5 \sin \theta - 3 \sin \theta \cos - 2\theta.$$

Ex. 6. A hollow ellipsoid is filled with water and placed with its a axis making an angle α with the horizontal and its c-axis horizontal. Prove that the fluid pressure on the curved surface on either side of the vertical plane through the a-axis is equivalent to a wrench of pitch

$$\frac{3c \sin \alpha \cos \alpha}{2} \cdot \frac{a^2 - b^2}{4c^2 + 9 (a^2 \sin^2\alpha + b^2 \cos^2 \alpha)}.$$

Let OA, OB be the a and b axes of the ellipsoid, OA making an angle α with the horizontal. Since OC, the c-axis is horizontal and normal to the plane of AOB, hence AOB must be a vertical plane. Let OV be the vertical in in th s plane.

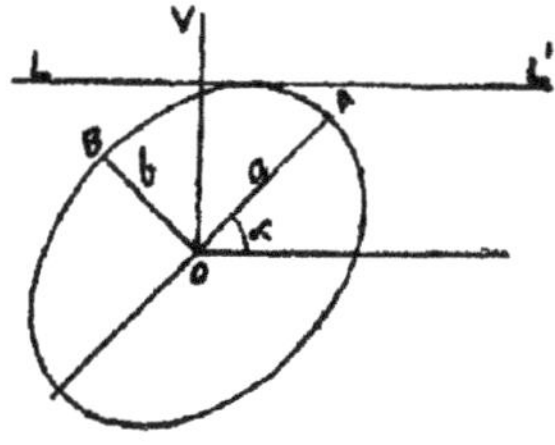

Let us take OA, OB, OC as anes of x, y and z respectively. We have to find out the resultant pressure on the curved surface on either side of the plane AOB.

The horizontal component of this pressure in the direction of OC is the pressure on the curve of projection of this surface on the vertical plane normal to OC $i.\ e.$ on the plane AOB. This projection is precisely the ellipse with axes A A′ and B B′ whose equation with regard to OA, OB as axes is

$$\frac{x^2}{a^2} + \frac{y^2}{b^2} = 1. \qquad \dots \qquad (1)$$

Let LL′ be the horizontal line touching the ellipse, then since it is inclined at an angle α to OA, its equation will be

$$x \sin \alpha + y \cos \alpha = d, \text{ where}$$
$$a^2\sin^2\alpha + b^2\cos^2\alpha = d^2 \qquad \dots \qquad (2)$$

Now the pressure on this plane area bounded ¦by the ellipse (1) is g^ρ (area of the curve) (depth of its C. G. below the horizontal)

$$= g^\rho\pi\ ab\ d, \text{ where } d \text{ is given by (2)}.$$

This pressure of course acts normally to the plane AOB and therefore its line of action has direction cosines (o, o, 1).

Further it must act at P (ζ, η), these being the coordinates of the centre of pressure.

By §3.5, P (ζ, η) is the pole with respect to the momental ellipse of the area, of a line parallel to the horizontal line LL′ and as far below the centroid of the area as LL′ is above it $i.\ e.$ of the line $x \sin \alpha + y \cos \alpha = -d$. Also the equation of the momental ellipse is

$$\frac{x^2}{a^2/4} + \frac{y^2}{b^2/4} = 1.$$

Hence
$$\zeta = - \frac{a^2}{4}\ \frac{\sin \alpha}{d},$$

$$\eta = - \frac{b^2}{4}\ \frac{\cos \alpha}{d}.$$

Thus the horizontal component of the pressure on the curved surface is $\pi\ ab\ dg^\rho$ acting along the line whose direction cosines are (o, o, 1) and which passes through

(80)

$$\left(- \frac{a^2}{4} \frac{\sin \alpha}{d} , \; - \frac{b^2}{4} \frac{\cos \alpha}{d} , \; o \right) \qquad \ldots \; (3)$$

The vertical component of the resultant pressure on the surface is equal to the weight of the liquid enclosed by the surface and acting at its centroid.

Now the volume of the liquid enclosed by the surface is clearly half the total volume of the ellipsoid, *viz.* $\frac{2}{3} \pi abc$.

Hence the vertical component is $\frac{2}{3} \pi abc \, g\rho$ acting vertically *i. e.* parallel to OV whose direction cosines are $(\sin \alpha, \cos \alpha, o)$ and acting at the centroid of the semi-ellipsoid into which the plane divides the ellipsoid *i. e.* at $\left(o, o, \frac{3c}{8} \right)$ (4)

Hence if X, Y, Z, and L, M, N be the resultant pressures parallel to the axes and the resultant couples about the axes, respectively, then from (3) and (4)

$$X = \tfrac{2}{3} \pi abc \, g\rho \sin \alpha,$$

$$Y = \tfrac{2}{3} \pi abc \, g\rho \cos \alpha,$$

$$Z = \pi ab \, d \, g\rho,$$

$$L = - \frac{\pi}{4} g\rho \, ab \, (b^2 + c^2) \cos \alpha$$

$$M = \frac{\pi}{4} g\rho \, ab \, (a^2 + c^2) \sin \alpha,$$

$$N = o.$$

Hence the pitch of the wrench (X, Y, Z, L, M, N), to which the fluid pressure is equivalent

$$= \frac{XL + YM + ZN}{X^2 + Y^2 + Z^2}$$

$$= \frac{\tfrac{2}{3} \pi^2 a^2 b^2 cg^2\rho^2 \dfrac{\sin \alpha \cos \alpha}{4} (a^2 - b^2)}{\tfrac{4}{9} \pi^2 a^2 b^2 c^2 g^2 \rho^2 + \pi^2 a^2 b^2 g^2 \rho^2 d^2}$$

(81)

$$= \frac{3c \sin \alpha \cos \alpha}{2} \quad \frac{a^2 - b^2}{4c^2 + 9 (a^2 \sin{}^2\alpha + b^2 \cos{}^2\alpha)}.$$

3.9. Let us now find the resultant pressure on any surface of a fluid at rest under the action of any given forces.

We have already seen how to find out pressure at any point of a fluid at rest under the action of any given forces.

Consider now a surface S exposed to the action of such a fluid; and let P (x, y, z) be any point on it.

Let (l, m, n) be the direction cosines of the normal to the surface at P. Let p be the pressure at P; p is then a known function of x, y, z and the given forces that act on the fluid.

Considering an element δS of the surface about the point P, the force on this element is $p\delta S$ acting along the normal at P to the surface. This force therefore has components $lp \, \delta S$, $mp \, \delta S$, $np \delta S$ parallel to the axes. We have thus an infinite number of such forces acting at every point of the surface. We know from statics that these forces can be reduced to three forces X. Y, Z acting along the axes of coordinates and three couples L, M, N whose 'axes' are also the coordinate axes, where

$$X = \Sigma \; lp\delta S = \int\int lpdS,$$

$$Y = \Sigma \; mp\delta S = \int\int mpdS,$$

$$Z = \Sigma \; np\delta S = \int\int npdS,$$

$$L = \Sigma \; p \, (ny - mz) \, \delta S = \int\int p \, (ny - mz) \, dS$$

$$M = \Sigma \; p \, (lz - nx) \, \delta S = \int\int p \, (lz - nx) \, dS,$$

$$N = \Sigma \; p \, (mx - ly) \, \delta S = \int\int p \, (mx - ly) \, dS,$$

the integrations being made to include the whole of the surface under consideration.

Again, since $l \, dS$ is the projection of the element dS on the $z \, o \, y$ plane therefore $l \, dS = dy \, dz$; hence the three components of the force X, Y, Z, are also equivalent to

(82)

$$X = \int\int p\,dy\,dz, \quad Y = \int\int p\,dz\,dx, \quad Z = \int\int p\,dx\,dy;$$

and the couples L, M, N, are equal to

$$L = \int\int p\,(ydy - zdz)\,dx, \quad M = \int\int p\,(zdz - x\,dx)\,dy$$
$$N = \int\int p\,(xdx - ydy)\,dz.$$

In the particular case of a fluid at rest under gravity let us take the free surface of the fluid which is known to be a horizontal plane as $x\,o\,y$ plane. Let P″ be the projection of any point P (x, y, z) on the $x\,o\,y$ plane.

We know by the above that the component of the fluid pressure along the vertical is

$$Z = \int\int p\,dx\,dy, \quad \ldots\ldots\ldots (1)$$

the field of integration being the curve into which the surface projects on the $x\,o\,y$ plane. Now the weight of a column of liquid with a small area $dx\,dy$ at P″ as base and height P″ P is

$$dx\,dy \int_{o}^{z} g\rho\,dz$$

But $dp = g\rho\,dz$,

∴ the weight of the fluid in the column P″ P is

$$dx\,dy \int_{o}^{p} dp = p\,dx\,dy,$$

where p is the pressure at P, (the presure at the free surface is taken to be zero).

Hence by (1) Z is equal to the weight of the fluid enclosed in the surface and its projection on the free surface.

3. 10. We proceed to deduce now the results of § 3. 6 analytically. Suppose that the fluid, homogeneous or heterogeneous, is at rest under the action of gravity only, then taking z— axis as vertical dp $= g\rho\,d\,z$, so that p is a function of z only. Let

$$p = \phi(z).$$

$$X = \int\int p \, dy \, dz = \int\int \phi \, (z) \, dy \, dz$$

This expression clearly shows that the horizontal component of the pressure on the surface along $o\,x$ is the same as the pressure on the curve, which is the projection of the surface S on the yoz plane. For if P' be the projection of any point P of S on yoz then P and P' have the same z—coordinate so that the pressure at P' is also $\phi\,(z)$, the same as at P.

Similarly Y is equal to the pressure on the projection of S on $x\,o\,z$.

3. 11. If the surface S is closed, we have by applying Green's Theorem,

$$X = \int\int\int \frac{\partial p}{\partial x} \, dx \, dy \, dz, \text{ etc. and}$$

$$L = \int\int\int \left(y\frac{\partial p}{\partial z} - z\frac{\partial p}{\partial y} \right) dx \, dy \, dz, \text{ etc.,}$$

the integrations being made over the entire space enclosed by the surface, and p being the value of the pressure function at the point (x, y, z) of the enclosed space which is supposed to contain fluid with the same law of pressure as the surrounding fluid.

Ex. 1. A small solid body is held at rest in a fluid in which the pressure p at any point is a given function of the rectangular coordinates (x, y, z); prove that the components of the couple which tends to make it rotate round the centre of gravity of its volume are

$$(C-B)\frac{\partial^2 p}{\partial y \partial z} - D\left(\frac{\partial^2 p}{\partial y^2} - \frac{\partial^2 p}{\partial z^2}\right) - E\frac{\partial^2 p}{\partial y \partial x} + F\frac{\partial^2 p}{\partial z \partial x}$$

and two similar expressions, where A, B, C, D, E, F, are the moments and products of inertia of the solid with respect to axes through the centre of gravity.

We know that, with centroid as origin

(84)

$$A = \iiint (y^2 + z^2)\, dx\, dy\, dz, \quad B = \iiint (z^2 + x^2)\, dx\, dy\, dz$$

$$C = \iiint (x^2 + y^2)\, dx\, dy\, dz;$$

$$D = \iiint y\, z\, dx\, dy\, dz, \quad E = \iiint z\, x\, dx\, dy\, dz,$$

$$F = \iiint x\, y\, dx\, dy\, dz.$$

Now
$$L = \iiint \left(y\frac{\partial p}{\partial z} - z\frac{\partial p}{\partial y} \right) dx\, dy\, dz, \quad\ldots\ldots\ldots\ldots\ldots (1)$$

integration to be made over the space enclosed by the solid. But the solid by hypothesis is small and origin is the centroid of the solid. Let $(x, y, z,)$ be the coordinates of a neighbouring point so that x, y, z are small. Hence

$$\frac{\partial p}{\partial z} = \left(\frac{\partial p}{\partial z}\right)_0 + \left(\frac{\partial^2 p}{\partial z\partial x}\right)_0 x + \left(\frac{\partial^2 p}{\partial z\partial y}\right)_0 y + \left(\frac{\partial^2 p}{\partial z^2}\right)_0 z$$

$$\frac{\partial p}{\partial y} = \left(\frac{\partial p}{\partial y}\right)_0 + \left(\frac{\partial^2 p}{\partial y\partial x}\right)_0 x + \left(\frac{\partial^2 p}{\partial y^2}\right)_0 y + \left(\frac{\partial^2 p}{\partial y\partial z}\right)_0 z$$

Substituting in (1) we have,

$$L = \iiint \left\{ \left(\frac{\partial p}{\partial z}\right)_0 y + \left(\frac{\partial^2 p}{\partial z\partial x}\right)_0 xy + \left(\frac{\partial^2 p}{\partial z\partial y}\right)_0 y^2 + \right.$$

$$\left(\frac{\partial^2 p}{\partial z^2}\right) z\, y \Big\} - \Big\{ \left(\frac{\partial p}{\partial z}\right)_0 z + \left(\frac{\partial^2 p}{\partial x\partial y}\right)_0 x\, z + \left(\frac{\partial^2 p}{\partial y^2}\right)_0 y\, z +$$

$$\left(\frac{\partial^2 p}{\partial y\partial z}\right)_0 ^2 \Big\} dx\, dy\, dz$$

$$= \left(\frac{\partial^2 p}{\partial z\partial x}\right)_0 F + \left[\left(\frac{\partial^2 p}{\partial z^2}\right)_0 - \left(\frac{\partial^2 p}{\partial y^2}\right)_0\right] D - \left(\frac{\partial^2 p}{\partial x\partial y}\right)_0 E$$

$$+ \left(\frac{\partial^2 p}{\partial y\partial z}\right)_0 (C - B).$$

For, $\iiint y\, dx\, dy\, dz = \bar{y}\, v = o$, etc.

Ex. 2   Prove that the resultant thrust on the curved surface of a right circular cylinder completely submerged with its axis at an angle α to the vertical is $w\, \mathrm{Sin}\, \alpha$ and acts at right angles to the axis through its middle point, w denoting the weight of the liquid displaced by the cylinder

(Punjab Univ. 'M.A.' 1935).

Ex. 3. A plane lamina is immersed in a liquid with its plane vertical. It is rotated in its plane about a fixed point lying in the surface of the liquid. Prove that the locus of the centre of pressure of the lamina is part of a straight line so long as the lamina is totally immersed (atmospheric pressure is neglected).

A plane lamina in the form of a regular polygon having n sides of length a is totally immersed. Prove that centre of pressure lies within or on a similar polygon of side

$$\frac{a}{12}\left[\, 2\cos\frac{\pi}{n} + Sec\,\frac{\pi}{n}\,\right]$$

(Tripos Pt. II 1927)

Ex. 4. A uniform sphere of weight w, sp. gravity σ and radius a is wholly immersed in water with its centre at a depth h. Show that if the sphere is divided by a vertical plane through its centre and the hemispheres are smoothly hinged together at their highest point the magnitude of the least horizontal force through the centre that would have to be applied in order to separate them is $\dfrac{3}{16}\,w\left(1+\dfrac{4h}{a\sigma}\right).$

(Tripos Pt. II, 1925).

Ex.5. A mass of homogeneous liquid is at rest under the action of a force whose potential is a quadratic function of rectangular coordinates, so that the surfaces of equipressure are ellipsoids. Show that, if a body of any shape is held immersed in the liquid, the resultant thrust on the body may be represented as a force acting through G, the centroid of its volume, and directed along the normal to the surface of equi-pressure through G, together with a couple which depends on the orientation of the body but not on the position of G in the liquid.

(Tripos. Pt. II, 1924).

Let V be the potential so that

$$V = \Sigma\,(Ax^2 + 2Fyz + 2ux)$$

We also know that $\dfrac{p}{\rho} + V = \text{cons.}$

By § 3.11 we know that the components of the force system due to the pressure of the liquid are given by (X,Y,Z, L,M,N) where

$$X = \int\!\!\int\!\!\int \frac{\partial p}{\partial x}\,dx\,dy\,dz,$$

$$L = \int\!\!\int\!\!\int \left(y\frac{\partial p}{\partial z} - z\frac{\partial p}{\partial y}\right)\,dx\,dy\,dz \ \text{etc},$$

the field of integration being the region enclosed by the solid body.

$$\therefore X = \int\!\!\int\!\!\int \frac{\partial p}{\partial x}\,dx\,dy\,dz$$

$$= -\rho \int\!\!\int\!\!\int \frac{\partial V}{\partial x}\,dx\,dy\,dz$$

$$= -2\rho \int\!\!\int\!\!\int (Ax + Hy + Gz + u)\,dx\,dy\,dz$$

$$= -2\rho(A\bar{x} + H\bar{y}\ G\bar{z} + u)\,t$$

where t is the volume of the solid and $(\bar{x},\ \bar{y},\ z)$ the co-ordinates of its C. G.

Transferring the point of action of the force components (X, Y, Z) to the centroid of the mass viz $(\bar{x},\ \bar{y},\bar{z})$ the components of the force acting at G are proportional to

$$(A\bar{x}, + H\bar{y} + G\bar{z} + u) : (H x + B\bar{y} + F\bar{z} + v) : (G\ \bar{x} + F\bar{y} + Cz + w)$$

$$\text{or,}\left[\frac{\partial V}{\partial x}\right]_{x,y,z\,=\,\bar{x},\,\bar{y},\,z} : \left[\frac{\partial V}{\partial y}\right]_{x,y,z\,=\,\bar{x},\,\bar{y},\,z} : \left[\frac{\partial V}{\partial z}\right]_{x,y,z\,=\,\bar{x},\,\bar{y},\,z}$$

or, proportional to the direction cosines of the normal at G to the surface of equipressure passing through G. Thus the resultant force is in the direction of the normal to this surface. The transference of the point of application of the forces (X, Y, Z) to G involves the introduction of a couple, whose components are

$$\bar{z}\, Y - \bar{y}\, Z, \quad \bar{x}\, Z - \bar{z}\, X, \quad \bar{y}\, X - \bar{x}\, Y.$$

Thus the system reduces to a force through G and a couple of components

$$L + \bar{z}\, Y - \bar{y}\, Z, \; \text{etc.},$$

Let a, b, c, f, g, h be the moments and products of inertia of the body about axes parallel to $O\,x\,y\,z$ passing through the centroid G. Let a', b', c', f', g', h' be similar quantities about axes $O\,x\,y\,z$.

Then
$$a' = \iiint (y^2 + z^2)\, dx\, dy\, dz,$$
$$b' = \iiint (z^2 + x^2)\, dx\, dy\, dz,$$
$$c' = \iiint (x^2 + y^2)\, dx\, dy\, dz,$$
$$f' = \iiint y z\, dx\, dy\, dz$$
$$g' = \iiint z x\, dx\, dy\, dz$$
$$h' = \iiint x y\, dx\, dy\, dz.$$

It follows at once that $\iiint x^2\, dx\, dy\, dz = \dfrac{b' + c' - a'}{2}$ etc.

Also, $a' = a + t\,(\bar{y}^2 + \bar{z}^2), \quad f' = f + t\,\bar{y}\,\bar{z}$

t being the volume of the solid.

Now, we have $L + \bar{z}\, Y - \bar{y}\, Z$

$$= \iiint \left(y\frac{\partial p}{\partial z} - z\,\frac{\partial p}{\partial y}\right)\, dx\, dy\, dz + \bar{z}\, Y - \bar{y}\, Z$$
$$= -2P \iiint [y(Gx + Fy + Cz + w) - z(Hx + By + Fz + v)]\,dx\,dy\,dz$$
$$+ 2\,\bar{z}\,(H\bar{x} + B\bar{y} + F\bar{z} + v)\,(-Pt) - 2\bar{y}\,(G\bar{x} + F\bar{y} + C\bar{z} + w)(-Pt)$$
$$= (-2P)\,\{ (Gh' - Hg') + (C - B)\,f' + F\,(c' - b') \}$$

$$+ 2Pt \{ (G\,\overline{x\,y} - H\overline{x\,z}) + (C-B)\overline{y\,z} + F(y^2 - \overline{z^2}) \}$$

$$= (-2P)[\, \{ G(h' - t\,\overline{x\,y}) - H(g' - t\overline{x\,z}) \} + (C-B)$$

$$(f' - t\,\overline{y\,z}) + F(c' - y^2 t - b' + t\,\overline{z^2})]$$

$$= -2P[(Gh - Hg) + (C-B)f + F(c-b)]$$

This depends only on A, B, C,...and a, b, c..., none of which depend on the position of the centroid. a, b, c...,depend only on the orientation of the solid. Thus the couple depends only on the orientation ot the body but not on the position of G in the liquid.

Ex. 6. A hole in the side of a ship is closed by a circular door 5 ft. in diameter hinged at the highest point and held inside against the water pressure at its lowest part by fastening. If the highest and lowest parts of the door are at a depth of 4 and 8 ft. find the least force exerted by fastening.

Ex. 7. A hemispherical body of radius a is entirely submerged in a liquid of density P so that its diametrical plane makes an angle θ with the horizontal and has its centre at a depth h. Prove that the resultant force on the curved surface is

$$\pi a^2 gP \left\{ \tfrac{5}{4}a^2 + h^2 \mp \tfrac{4}{3}\, ah\cos\theta \right\}^{\frac{1}{2}}$$

(Tripos pt. I, 1920; I. C. S. 1935)

Ex. 8   A portion of a sphere cut off by two planes through its centre inclined to each other at an angle $\dfrac{\pi}{4}$ is just immersed in a liquid with one face in the surface. Find the resultant thrust on the curved surface and show that it makes an angle

$$\tan^{-1}\left(\frac{\pi}{2} - 1\right)$$ with the horizontal·

(I. C. S. 1937)

Ex 9. In the two immersed ellipoidal surfaces

$$\text{(i)} \frac{x^2}{a^2} + \frac{y^2}{b^2} + \frac{z^2}{c^2} = 1 \quad \text{and (ii)} \frac{x^2}{a'^2} + \frac{y^2}{b'^2} + \frac{z^2}{c'^2} = 1,$$

$a > a'$, $b < b'$, $c < c'$, z-axis is vertical and the surface of the water is at a height h ($> c$) above the plane of xy. Prove that the resultant horizontal pressure on that part of (i) which lies on the positive side of yz and without the surface (ii) is

$$\tfrac{3}{4} W \frac{h}{a} \cdot \frac{b'c' (a^2 - a'^2)}{\sqrt{(a^2 b'^2 - a'^2 b^2)(a^2 c'^2 - a'^2 c^2)}}$$

W, being the weight of water displaced by volume of (i)

(I. C. S. 1935)

Ex. 10. A plane area bounded by the arcs of the four parabolas $y^2 = 4ax$, $y^2 = 4bx$, $x^2 = 4cy$ and $x^2 = 4dy$ is placed vertically in a homogeneous liquid with x-axis in the liquid line. Show that depth of centre pressure is

$$\frac{18}{7} \cdot \frac{b^{\frac{7}{3}} - a^{\frac{7}{3}})(d^{\frac{5}{3}} - c^{\frac{5}{3}})}{(d^{\frac{4}{3}} - c^{\frac{4}{3}})(b^{\frac{4}{3}} - c^{\frac{5}{3}})}$$

Ex. 11. A heavy heterogeneous liquid fills a semi-ellipsoid whose equation is $\frac{x^2}{a^2} + \frac{y^2}{b^2} + \frac{z^2}{c^2} = 1$. Show that in order that the liquid be in equilibrium the fluid arranges itself in such a way that density of any element is a function of 'z' coordinate only i. e. of its depth below the horizontal surface.

Assuming that $P = \mu r z^{r-1}$, prove that the resultant action on one of the octants into which it is divided by the vertical planes viz $x = o$ and $y = o$ is a single force acting in the line

$$ax - \frac{a^2 \Gamma(\frac{r+4}{2})}{\Gamma(\frac{1}{2}) \Gamma(\frac{r+5}{2})} = by - \frac{b^2 \Gamma(\frac{r+4}{2})}{\Gamma(\frac{1}{2}) \Gamma(\frac{r+5}{2})}$$

$$= \frac{c\,\Gamma\left(\frac{r+1}{2}\right)}{\sqrt{\pi}\,\Gamma\left(\frac{r+2}{2}\right)}\, z - \frac{c^2\,\Gamma\left(\frac{r+4}{2}\right)}{\Gamma\left(\frac{1}{2}\right)\Gamma\left(\frac{r+5}{2}\right)}$$

Ex. 12. A cubical box of side a has a heavy lid of weight W .movable about one edge. It is filled with water, and held with the diagonal through one extremity of this edge vertical. If it be now made to rotate with uniform angular velocity w show that in order that no water be spilled, W must not be less than

$$\left(\frac{7}{6} + \frac{1}{2\sqrt{3}}\,\frac{w^2 a}{g}\right) W'$$

where W' is the weight of the water in the box.

Ex. 13. A liquid of depth $2a$ and uniform density P is superposed on a liquid of density $2P$ and depth greater than a. A circular lamina of radius a is placed with its plane vertical and its centre in the surface common to the two liquids. Determine the depth of the centre of pressure neglecting atmospheric pressure.

(Tripos part I 1937)

Ex. 14. A vessel in the form of a right circular cylinder of radius a is held with its axis inclined at an angle α to the vertical and contains a volume of water which is such that the circular base of the vessel is just covered. Show that the resultant of the pressures exerted by the water on the curved surface of the cylinder is a single force of the magnitude

$$\pi\, g P\, a^2\,(\text{Sec } \alpha - \text{Cos } \alpha),$$

where P is the density of the water, and atmospheric pressure is neglected.

Ex. 15. A thin glass flask consists of a portion of a sphere of radius a on a plane circular base of radius $a \cos \alpha$, and a neck in the form of a circular cylinder of radius $a \cos \alpha$. The flask is symmetrical about a vertical line. Water is poured in until the horizontal thrusts on half of the neck and on half of the spherical portion bounded by a vertical plane are equal. Obtain an equation giving the depth of water in the neck and deduce that whatever the value of α the ratio of the depth of water in the neck to the depth in the spherical portion must exceed

$$1 + \sqrt{2}.$$

Ex. 16. A rectangular block whose edges are of lengths $2a$, $2b$, $2c$ is divided by a plane through the centre perpendicular to the edge of length $2c$, and the two halves are hinged together along edges parallel to those of length $2a$. The whole is then immersed in a liquid with the line of hinges inclined at an angle θ to the horizon and the dividing plane vertical, the hinges being in the upper face. Prove that the two halves will not separate unleess

$$\left\{ \left(1 - \frac{\sigma}{\rho} \right) c^2 - \tfrac{2}{3} b^2 \right\} Cos\, \theta > 2\, bd,$$

where d is the depth of the centre of gravity of the block, σ the density of the block and ρ that of the liquid.

Ex. 17. A cone, whose vertical angle is 2α, has its lowest generator horizontal and is filled with liquid ; prove that the resultant pressure on the curved surface is $\sqrt{(1 + 15 Sin^2 \alpha)}$ times the weight of the liquid.

CHAPTER IV.

Equilibrium of Floating Bodies.

4. 1.   The Principle of Buoyancy:— We shall first consider the case of a fluid,–liquid or gas, homogeneous or heterogeneous, at rest under the action of gravity only.   If any curved closed surface be traced out in imagination in such a fluid, the pressures exerted on all the elements of this surface by the surrounding fluid have a single resultant, which is equal and opposite to the the weight of the fluid enclosed by the surface.   This follows at once from the fact that the fluid inside the surface is in equilibrium under the action of

(i)   its own weight acting vertically through its C. G. and

(ii)   the fluid pressures acting normally on the surface

The resultant of (ii) is accordingly equal and opposite to (i).   If the curved surface is not one merely traced out in imagination in the fluid but the surface of a solid body placed in the fluid, result is the same.   Hence the resultant pressure of a heavy fluid on the surface of any solid body placed in it is a vertically upward force equal to the weight of the fluid displaced by the solid, acting through the C. G. of the displaced fluid.   If the solid is in equilibrium solely under the action of its own weight and the fluid pressures on its surface, the weight of the solid must be equal to the weight of the displaced fluid and the centres of gravity of the solid and the displaced fluid must be in the same vertical line.

Ex. 1.   A uniform rod A B, of small normal cross section and weight W has a mass of metal of small volume and weight $\frac{W}{n}$ attached to extremity B. Find the condition that the rod shall float at all angles in a given homogeneous liquid.

Let A B be the rod, its lenght being 2a. Let G be the C. G. of the rod and the piece of metal attached at B, so that $BG = \dfrac{a}{1 + \frac{1}{n}}$

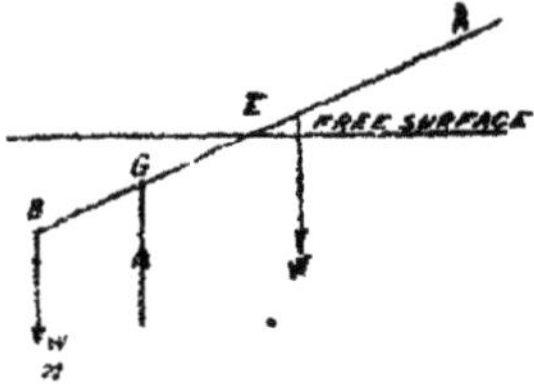

If P and s be the density of the liquid and the rod respectively, we have $W = 2\,acgs$, and by the first condition of equilibrium, weight of the solid must be equal to the weight of the fluid displaced, — we have

$$gP\, c\, BE = \left(\frac{1}{n} + 1\right) W,\ c \text{ being the cross section of the rod.}$$

Also the C. G. of the fluid displaced viz. the mid-point of BE must be identical with the point G, by the second condition of equilibrium

$$\text{Thus} \qquad BE = 2\, BG = \frac{2a}{1 + \frac{1}{n}}$$

$$\therefore\ W\left(1 + \frac{1}{n}\right) = gP\, c\, \frac{(2a)}{1 + \frac{1}{n}} = \frac{W}{1 + \frac{1}{n}} \frac{P}{s}$$

or, $(n+1)^2 s = P n^2$, which is the required condition.

Ex 2   A solid ellptic paraboloid whose equation is

$$\frac{x^2}{a^2} + \frac{y^2}{b^2} = \frac{z}{c},$$

and of height h is floating with its axis vertical and vertex downward. If the horizontal surface of fluid is at a height k above the vertex, prove

$$\frac{h^2}{k^2} = \frac{P}{\sigma}\,;\ P \text{ and } \sigma \text{ being the density of the liquid and the}$$

solid respectively.

The volume of the solid bounded by the plane $z = h$ is $\pi \int_0^h \dfrac{ab}{c} \, z \, dz$ for the section by any plane $Z = z$ is an ellipse of axes $\dfrac{a}{c}\sqrt{z}$ and $\dfrac{b}{c}\sqrt{z}$ respectively so

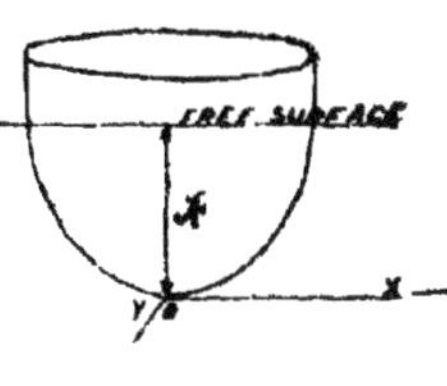

that the volume of a thin element of thickness dz is $\pi \dfrac{ab}{c} z \, dz$.

Hence if σ is the density of the solid, the weight of the solid is $\pi g \sigma \dfrac{ab}{c} \dfrac{h^2}{2}$.

Similarly the weight of the fluid displaced is

$$\frac{\pi a b g \rho}{c} \int_0^k z \, dz = \frac{\pi ab}{2c} \rho g k^2,$$ ρ being the density of the liquid.

Hence by the first condition of flotation $\sigma h^2 = \rho k^2$.

Ex. 3. A hollow hemispherical shell has a heavy particle fixed to its rim, and floats in water with the particle just above the surface, and with the plane of the rim at an angle of $45°$ to the surface; shew that the weight of the hemisphere: the weight of the water it would contain

$$:: 4\sqrt{2}-5; \; 6\sqrt{2}.$$

Let a be the radius of the hollow hemisphere, G' its C. G. so that

$$O\ G' = \frac{a}{2}.$$

Let W be its weight and W' that of the heavy particle at B. The hemisphere floats under the action of

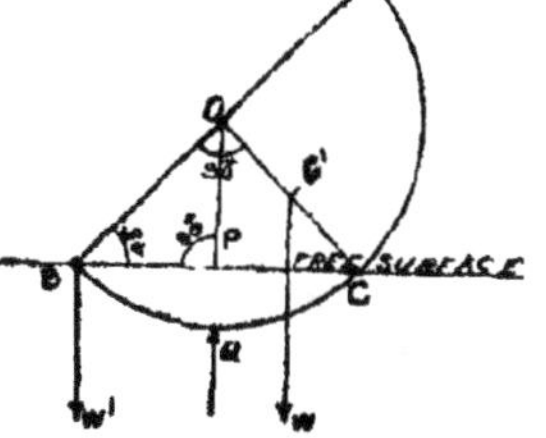

(i) a force W acting vertically downwards through G',

(ii) a force W' „   „   „   B.

(iii) the resultant of fluid pressures acting on the surface BC of the hemisphere, which by the principle of buoyancy is equal to the weight of the fluid displaced i.e. the fluid that can be contained in the segment bounded by the horizontal plane

Taking any plane at right angles to O P, the vertical through O at a distance x from O, we see that the volume of a small element of thickness dx is $\pi(a^2-x^2)\,dx$. Thus the volume of the spherical segment BC is $\pi \int_{oP}^{OQ} (a^2-x^2)dx.$

Taking moments about B, we have

$$W\left(\frac{a}{\sqrt{2}} + \frac{a}{2\sqrt{2}}\right) = \frac{\pi g \rho a}{\sqrt{2}} \int_{OP}^{a} (a^2-x^2)dx$$

$$= \frac{\pi g \rho a}{\sqrt{2}} \int_{\frac{a}{\sqrt{2}}}^{a} (a^2-x^2)dx$$

$$\therefore \frac{W}{\frac{2}{3}\pi g \rho a^3} = \frac{4\sqrt{2}-5}{6\sqrt{2}}.$$

Ex. 4. If the height of a right circular cone be equal to the diameter of the base it will float with its slant side horizontal in any liquid of greater density.

Ex. 5. An elliptic cylinder of major and minor axes $(2a, 2b)$ floats in a homogeneous liquid with vertex of the elliptic section at the top just above the liquid. If the angle that the axis makes with the vertical be θ, prove that the ratio of the height h of the cylinder to its semi axis a is

$$\frac{5\tan^2\theta + 2}{4\tan\theta}$$

Let the plane of the paper represent the vertical plane through the major axis AB. Let AE represent thet race of the horizontal plane of flotation. Since the angle between the vertical and the axis is θ, the angle between AB and AE is also θ.

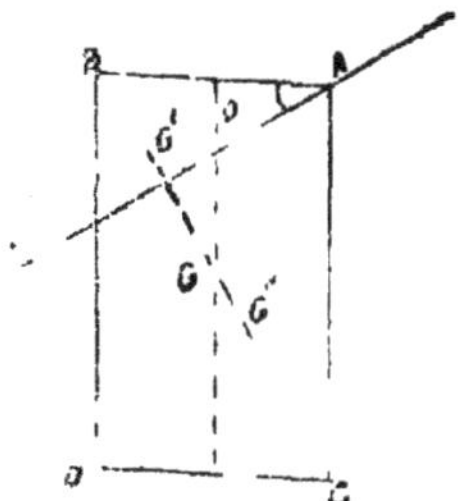

Hence taking AB, AC and a line through A perpendicular to the plane of the paper as axes of x, z and y respectively the equation of the cylinder is

$$\frac{(x-a)^2}{a^2}+\frac{y^2}{b^2}=1$$

and of the plane AE, $z = x\tan\theta$.

Now by the principle of buoyancy the C. G. of the cylinder i.e. G and the C.G. of the fluid displaced by the cylinder i.e. of the portion ACDE viz G'' must be on the same vertical line. It is obvious that C.G., G, of the portion AEB must lie on the line GG'' so that $GG''G'$ is a vertical st. line and therefore at right angles to AE.

Now the coordinates of G' are easily computed. If we take any element $dx\,dy$ of the section of the cylinder by the plane xy, the volume below the plane AE is $x\tan\theta\,dx\,dy$, the C. G. of the element being $(x,\ y,\ \tfrac{1}{2}x\tan\theta)$.

Hence if $(\bar{x},\ \bar{y},\ \bar{z})$ be the coordinates of G'

$$\bar{x}=\frac{\iint x.\,x\tan\theta\,dx\,dy}{\iint x\tan\theta\,dx\,dy},$$

$$\bar{z}=\frac{\iint\tfrac{1}{2}(x\tan\theta)^2\,dx\,dy}{\iint x\tan\theta\,dx\,dy},$$

and $\bar{y}=0$ from symmety.

$$\therefore \bar{x} = \frac{\displaystyle\int_{0}^{2a} dx \int_{-b\sqrt{1-\left(\frac{x-a}{a}\right)^2}}^{b\sqrt{1-\left(\frac{x-a}{a}\right)^2}} x^2 \tan\theta \, dy}{\displaystyle\int_{0}^{2a} dx \int_{-b\sqrt{1-\left(\frac{x-a}{a}\right)^2}}^{b\sqrt{1-\left(\frac{x-a}{a}\right)^2}} x \tan\theta \, dy}$$

$$= \frac{5a}{4}.$$

Similarly $\bar{z} = \dfrac{5a}{8} \tan\theta$.

Also clearly coordinates of G are $\left(a, o, \dfrac{h}{2}\right)$.

Since $G\,G'$ is at rt. angles to AE whose direction cosines are $(cos\,\theta,\, o,\, sin\,\theta)$, we have

$$\left(\frac{5a}{4} - a\right)cos\,\theta + \left(\frac{5a}{8}\tan\theta - \frac{h}{2}\right) sin\,\theta = o$$

$$\text{or, } \frac{h}{a} = \frac{5 \tan^2\theta + 2}{4 \tan\theta}$$

Ex. 6. Prove that the ratio of the densities of the cylinder and liquid in the above example is

$$\frac{\sigma}{\rho} = \frac{1 + Sec^2\theta}{2 + 5\tan^2\theta}.$$

Ex. 7. Prove that a triangular prism floating with its edges horizontal has in general three positions of equilibrium.

Ex. 8. A solid cone whose height is h and vertical angle $2\,\alpha$ has its vertex fixed at a distance p beneath the surface of a homogeneous liquid. The cone is in equilibrium with its axis inclined at an angle θ to the vertical and its base above thesurface prove that

$$P\,p^{4}\cos\theta\cos^{3}\alpha = a\,h^{4}[\cos(\theta-\alpha,\cos(\theta+\alpha)]^{\frac{5}{2}}$$

Let the plane of the paper represent a vertical plane through the axis VZ of the cone. Let VX be $\perp$ to VZ in this plane and VY be $\perp$ to the plane XVZ. With VX,VY,VZ as rectangular axes the equation of the right circular cone is

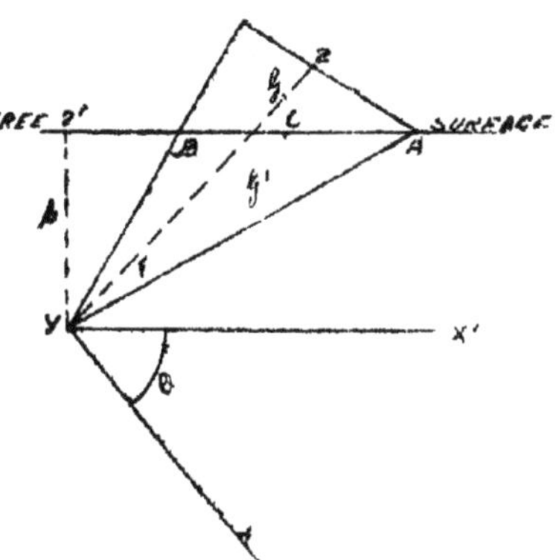

$$(x^{2}+y^{2})=z^{2}\tan^{2}\alpha,$$

α being the semi vertical angle.

Let the trace of the horizontal plane of flotation on the vertical plane XVZ be AB. Draw VX' parallel to AB. In order to find the equations of the section of the cone by the plane of flotation, let us transform axes to VX', VY and VZ', where VZ' is $\perp$ to VX' in the plane of the paper.

Let $<$X V X$'=\theta$, then if (x',y',z') be the coordinates of any point P (x,y,z) in the new system

$$x = x'\cos\theta - z'\sin\theta$$
$$y = y'$$
$$z = x'\sin\theta + z'\cos\theta.$$

Hence the equation of the cone in the new coordinates is

$$(x'\cos\theta - z'\sin\theta)^{2}+y'^{2}=(x'\sin\theta + z'\cos\theta)^{2}\tan^{2}\alpha.$$

Equation of the horizontal plane AB is clearly

$$z'=p, \text{ where } VZ'=p.$$

Hence the equation of the elliptic section by the plane of flotation is

$$(x' \cos \theta - p \sin \theta)^2 + y'^2 = (x' \sin \theta + p \cos \theta)^2 \tan^2 \alpha$$

$$\text{and } z' = p.$$

$$\text{or } \frac{\left(x' - \dfrac{p \, \mathrm{Cos}\, \theta \, \mathrm{Sin}\, \theta \, \mathrm{Sec}^2 \alpha}{\mathrm{Cos}^2 \theta - \mathrm{Sin}^2 \theta \, \tan^2 \alpha}\right)^2}{\dfrac{p^2 \tan^2 \alpha}{(\mathrm{Cos}^2\theta - \mathrm{Sin}^2\theta \, \tan^2\alpha)^2}} + \frac{y'^2}{\dfrac{p^2 \tan^2 \alpha}{(\mathrm{Cos}^2\theta - \mathrm{Sin}^2\theta \, \tan^2\alpha)}} = 1$$

$$\text{and } z' = p.$$

Hence if C be the centre of the elliptic section

$$Z'C = \frac{p \cos \theta \, \mathrm{Sin}\, \theta \, \mathrm{Sec}^2 \alpha}{\mathrm{Cos}^2 \theta - \mathrm{Sin}^2 \theta \tan^2 \alpha}.$$

Also, the volume of the fluid displaced

$$= \text{volume of the cone VAB}$$

$$= \tfrac{1}{3} \, p \, (\text{area of the elliptic section } AB)$$

$$= \tfrac{1}{3} \, p \, \frac{\pi p^2 \tan^2 \alpha}{(\mathrm{Cos}^2\theta - \mathrm{Sin}^2\theta \tan^2\alpha)^{\frac{3}{2}}}$$

Let C. G. of the cone V A B be G'. Evidently it must lie on the line joining V to the centre C of the ellipse cut out by the plane of flotation.

Also V G' = $\tfrac{3}{4}$VC.

Hence the resultant fluid pressure on the cone is an upward vertical force of magnitude

$$\frac{\pi \, g\rho}{3} \, \frac{p \, \tan^2 \alpha}{(\mathrm{Cos}^2\theta - \mathrm{Sin}^2 \theta \, \tan\alpha)^{\frac{3}{2}}}$$

acting through G'.

The cone is in equilibrium under the action of this force, its weight viz. $\tfrac{1}{3}g\sigma h^2 \tan^2 \alpha$, acting at G where VG = $\tfrac{3}{4}$ V Z, and the action of the hinge at V.

Taking moments about V, we therefore have

$$\frac{\pi g P p^3 \tan^2\alpha}{3(\cos^2\theta - \sin^2\theta \tan^2\alpha)})^{\frac{3}{2}} \; (\tfrac{3}{4}VC \, \text{Sin } CVZ')$$

$$= \tfrac{1}{3}\pi g\sigma \, h^3 \tan^2\alpha \; (V \, G \, \text{Sin } Z \, V \, Z')$$

$$\text{or,} \; \frac{p^3 P \tan^2\alpha}{(\cos^2\theta - \sin^2\theta\tan^2\alpha)^{\frac{3}{2}}} \cdots \quad \tfrac{3}{4}Z'C = \sigma h^3\tan^2\alpha(\tfrac{3}{4}h\text{Sin}\theta)$$

$$\text{or,} \; \frac{P p^4 \tan^2\alpha \cos\theta \sin\theta \sec^2\alpha}{(\cos^2\theta - \sin^2\theta \tan^2\alpha)^{5/2}} = \sigma h^4 \tan^2\alpha \sin\theta$$

$$P p^4 \cos\theta \cos^2\alpha = \sigma h^4[\cos^2\theta \, \cos^2\alpha - \sin^2\theta \sin^2\alpha]^{5/2}$$

$$= \sigma h^4[\cos(\theta - \alpha)\cos(\theta + \alpha)]^{5/2}$$

Ex. 9. If in the above example the density of the liquid varies with depth according to the law μz^r, find the corresponding relation.

Ans. $\mu \, p^x \cos\theta \cos^3\alpha = (r+4) \, \sigma \, h^4[\cos(\theta-\alpha)\cos(\theta+\alpha)]^{\frac{5}{2}}.$

Ex. 10. A solid is formed by revolving a symmetrical curve $y = f(x)$, about its axis of symmetry which is O X, (vertex being the origin O). It is divided by a plane through its axis and the parts connected by a hinge at the vertex. The system is now placed in a liquid with its axis vertical and vertex downward. If it float without separation and k be the length of the axis immersed and h the height of the solid, shew that

$$\frac{\displaystyle\int_0^k \left\{ f^3 + 3\,x(k-x)\,f \right\} dx}{\displaystyle\int_0^h f^3 \, dx} > \frac{\displaystyle\int_0^k f^2 \, dx}{\displaystyle\int_0^h f^2 \, dx}.$$

Let P O Q be the solid of revolution and let A B be the level up to which it is immersed in the liquid. Let it be divided by the plane L O M at right angles to the plane of the paper. Let O X be the axis of

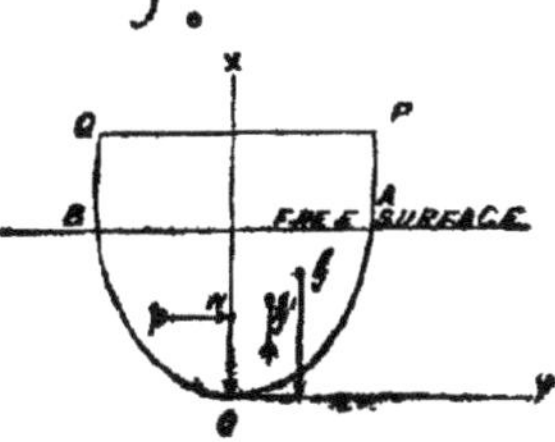

symmetry and O Y be ⊥ to OX in the plane of the paper and O Z ⊥ to OX in the plane L O M. Consider first the entire solid. Since it is in equilibrium we have by the principle of buoyancy.

$$g\sigma \int_{0}^{h} \pi y^2 dx = g P \int_{0}^{k} \pi y^2 dx,$$

where σ is the denity of the solid and P that of the liquid.

$$\therefore \quad \frac{\sigma}{P} = \frac{\int_{0}^{k} f^2 dx}{\int_{0}^{h} f^2 dx}. \qquad \ldots \qquad \ldots \qquad (1)$$

Now consider one half of the solid divided by the plane O L M. The forces acting on it are:—

(i) the weight of the half solid acting at its C. G. viz G;

(ii) the weight of the fluid displaced by this half of the solid acting at the point G', the centroid of the fluid displaced;

(iii) the pressure p on the plane O L M acting at its centre of pressure N; and

(iv) the action of the hinge at O.

Now (i) is evidently

$$g\sigma \frac{\pi}{2} \int_{0}^{h} y^2 dx$$ acting at G, where $\bar{y}$ the distance of G from the

O X is

$$\frac{\frac{\pi}{2} g\sigma \int_{0}^{h} y^2 dx \left(\frac{4}{3} y\right) \frac{1}{\pi}}{\frac{\pi}{2} g\sigma \int_{0}^{h} y^2 dx}$$

Similarly (ii) is

$$g\rho \; \frac{\pi}{2} \int_0^k y^2 \, dx \quad \text{acting at } G', \text{ where } \overline{y}' \text{ the distance of } G'$$

from O X is

$$\frac{\dfrac{\pi}{2} g\rho \int_0^k y^2 \, dx \left(\dfrac{4}{3}\dfrac{y}{\pi}\right)}{\dfrac{\pi}{2} g\rho \int_0^k y^2 \, dx}$$

Evidently (iii) is

$$\int_0^k 2p \, y \, dx \text{ acting at N where}$$

$$O\,N = \frac{\displaystyle\int_0^k 2pyx \, dx}{\displaystyle\int_0^k 2py \, dx} \quad , p \text{ being } g\,\rho\,(k-x)$$

Hence taking moments about O

$$g\rho\frac{\pi}{2} \int_0^k y^2 \, dx \times \frac{\dfrac{\pi}{2}\rho g \int_0^k y^2 \, dx\left(\dfrac{4y}{3\pi}\right)}{\dfrac{\pi}{2}g\rho \int_0^k y^2 \, dx} >$$

$$g\sigma\frac{\pi}{2} \int_0^h y^2 \, dx \times \frac{\dfrac{\pi}{2}g\sigma \int_0^h y^2 \, dx\left(\dfrac{4y}{3\pi}\right)}{\dfrac{\pi}{2}g\sigma \int_0^h y^2 \, dx} - \int_0^k 2py \, dx \; \frac{\displaystyle\int_0^k 2\,p\,x\,y\,dx}{\displaystyle\int_0^k 2\,p\,y\,dx}$$

$$\text{or } \tfrac{4}{3}\int_0^k y^3\,dx > \frac{2\sigma}{3P}\int_0^h y^3\,dx - 2\int_0^k x(k-x)\,y\,dx$$

$$\text{or }\int_0^k y^3\,dx + 3\int_0^k xy(k-x)\,dx > \frac{\sigma}{P}\int_0^h y^3\,dx$$

$$\frac{\displaystyle\int_0^k \left\{ y^3 + 3x(k-x)y \right\}dx}{\displaystyle\int_0^h y^3\,dx} > \frac{\sigma}{P} = \frac{\displaystyle\int_0^k y^3\,dx}{\displaystyle\int_0^h y^2\,dx}$$

Ex 11. A hemisphere is just completely immersed with its centre fixed and is kept at rest with its base vertical by means of a couple G, determine for any values of P and σ the reaction at the centre and the couple ⟨Tripos pt. 1, 1915⟩.

Ans. Horizontal component of Reaction $= \pi a^2 gP$

$$\text{Vertical } \qquad \text{,,} \qquad \text{,,} \; = \frac{2\pi}{3}a^3(\sigma - P)$$

$$G = \frac{\pi a^4}{4}g(\sigma - 2P).$$

4. 2. Body floating in a heterogeneous liquid:—

If the body is floating under the influence of gravity alone in a heterogeneous liquid the positions of equilibrium are still given by the principle of buoyancy proved in § 4. 1. For the resultant pressure on the floating body is still equal and opposite to the weight of the liquid displaced by it. Only in filling up the gap the law of density must be maintained i. e. the surfaces of equal density must be continuous with those of the surrounding liquid.

4. 3. General Principle of Buoyancy:— The resultant fluid pressure on a solid body wholly or partially immersed in a fluid, which is at rest under the action of given forces, is equal and opposite to the resultant of the external forces which would act on the displaced fluid. For imagine the solid abolished and its place occupied by the fluid   This fluid is in equilibrium under the action of

(i)   external forces acting at each point of the enclosed fluid.

(ii)   fluid pressures acting normally on the surface (S) enclosing the fluid.

Hence the resultant of (ii) is equal and opposite to that of (i). Now clearly the system (ii) is the same whether the space inside S is occupied by the solid or by the fluid   It follows then that the resultant of the fluid pressures acting on the boundary of the solid is equal and opposite to the resultant of the external forces acting at each point of the displaced fluid. It should be noted that this resultant may not reduce to a single force.

Hence if a solid is in equilibrium under the action of the fluid pressures and external forces which act equally both on the solid and the fluid, the resultant of the external forces acting on the solid must be equal and opposite to the resultant of the external forces acting on the displaced fluid.

Ex 1.   A homogeneous liquid of density ρ surrounds completely a solid mass M of any shape whatever.   The solid and the liquid attract one another according to the law of direct distance.   Prove that free surface of the liquid is a sphere.

A small cylinder, which is also attracted by the solid according to the same law floats in the liquid.   Show that it must float with its axis oriented towards the centre of mass of M and

$$2 d (\rho\, h' - \sigma\, h) = (\sigma\, h^2 - \rho\, h'^2)$$

P,σ being the densities of the
liquid and cylinder, h the height
of the cylinder, h' the length of the
axis immersed and d the distance of
the centre of the face nearest to the
centre of mass of the solid from it.

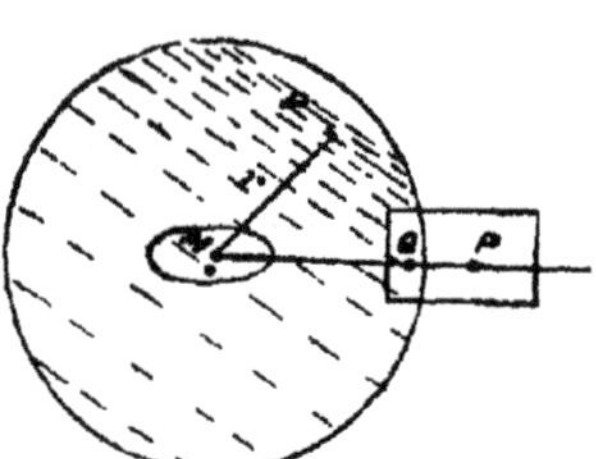

Since the law of force is that
of direct distance, the resultant attraction of the solid mass on any
particle is in the direction of and proportional to the distance of
the particle from the centre of mass O of the solid. Taking O
as the origin, the equation of equilibrium is

$$dp = -\mathrm{P}\mu M r\, dr$$

so that $$p = \tfrac{1}{2}\mu M \,\mathrm{P}\, (A^2 - r^2)^{\frac{1}{2}}$$

where the radius of the free surface where $p = o$ is A.

Again the resultant attraction of the mass M on another
mass M' is μ $MM'O$ P, P being the centre of mass of the second
body. Now the cylinder is subject to two forces

    (i)   the resultant pressure of the surrounding fluid, and

    (ii)   the resultant attraction of M

Force (ii) is evidently $M\mu$ ($\pi\, a^2 h\, \sigma$) O P, and acts along OP,
where a is the radius and P is the mid point of its axis.

Force (i) is the force which is equal and opposite to the force
acting on the fluid displaced. It is, therefore, $M\mu$ ($\pi a^2 h'\, \mathrm{P}$) OQ,
along OQ, h' being the length of axis immersed in the liquid and
Q is the mid point of immersed portion of the axis, assuming
that a is very small compared with A.

In order that the cylinder be in equilibrium O Q and O P
must be in the same line so that P,Q,O are collinear. As P,Q are
two points on the axis, it is therefore oriented towards O.

Also $M\mu$ $\pi a^2 h$ σ (OP) $= M\mu$ $\pi a^2 h'$ P (OQ)

(106)

$$\text{or } \sigma\, h\left(d + \frac{h}{2}\right) = P\, h'\left(d + \frac{h'}{2}\right)$$

$$2\, d\left(P\, h' - \sigma h\right) = (\sigma\, h^2 - P\, h'^2).$$

Ex. 2. A right circular cone floats with its vertex downward in a rectangular tank moving horizontally with acceleration f. Show that the axis of the cone makes an angle $\tan^{-1}\dfrac{g}{f}$ with the horizontal.

Find also the nature of free surface.

Ex. 3. A circular cylinder of radius a floats in a rotating liquid, itself remaining at rest with its axis vertical and a length h unimmersed. Shew that if the cylinder is sufficiently long, it will float in equilibrium with its upper rim in the surface provided the liquid is made to rotate with angular velocity $2\dfrac{\sqrt{gh}}{a}$.

(Triops Pt.I, 1924)

44. Surfaces of Flotation.

In order to specify the orientation in space of a floating body take a point of the body say its C. G., G and draw out lines GA, GB, . in all directions fixed in the body. These lines may be called axes of orientation We may then specify the orientation of the body by saying that GA for example is vertical and directed downwards towards the base. For our present purposes all positions of the body obtained by rotating it round vertical G A must be regarded as equivalent

Plane of flotation is a plane (AB) which cuts off a volume V such that the weight of volume V of the liquid is equal to that of the body (W) so that $W = gPV$, P being the density of the liquid. Volume V is called displacement.

The section of the body by a plane of flotation is a plane area, which is called the the Area of Flotation. In all possible positions of equilibrium of a given body floating freely in a given liquid the displacement is constant. For if we orient the body in s ich a way that the axis of orientation $\perp$ to a particular plane of flotation is vertical, the plane of flotation itself being made to coincide with the surface of the liquid, then by the first condition of flotation weight of the body must be equal to the weight of fluid displaced so that $V = \dfrac{W}{g\rho} = \text{const}$

' Hence without any reference to second condition (which may or may not be fulfilled all possible conditions of equilibrium are exhausted by describing planes which cut off a constant volume $\dfrac{W}{g\rho}$ 'from the body. All such planes are possible planes of flotation for we have only to make the axis of orientation at right angles to this plane vertical and the intersecting plane coincident with the free surface of the liquid in order to make it a plane of flotation.

Let us now consider the envelope of all the planes of flotation cutting off equal volume. Such a surface is called the surface of flotation and is characterised by the fact that every tangent plane is a possible plane of flotation.

Ex. Prove that in all cases two and only two tangent planes can be drawn to a surface of flotation parallel to a given plane

4·5. A Theorem of Bouguer and Dupin:—

The point of contact of each plane of flotation A B with the envelope surface S is the centre of gravity of the corresponding area of flotation.

To prove this we use the lemma: —

If we consider a tangent plane to a surface, the point of contact of this plane is found to lie on the line of intersection of this plane and any other tangent plane infinitely close to it. Thus the common point of the

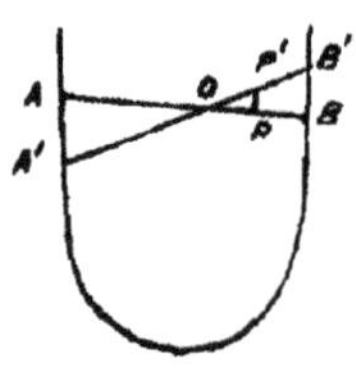

lines of intersection of this plane with neighbouring tangent planes is the point of contact

Now let A B and A′B′ be two planes of flotation inclined at an θ and infinitely close to each other. Let us take a system of rectangular axes, the line of intersection of AB and A′B′ as OX, OY in the plane A B at right angles to OX, and O Z normal to the plane A B. The equation of the plane A′B′ is accordingly $z = y \tan \theta$. Since the volumes displaced by the two planes are equal, the volume enclosed in the angles A O A′, and B O B′ are equal. Let $dx\,dy$ be an element of the plane xy at a point P (x, y) and let z be the height of the point P′, which is the intersection of the perpendicular from P on the plane AB, and the plane A′B′.

$$\text{Thus } z = y \tan \theta.$$

The total volume enclosed in the wedge B O B′ will be $\iint z\,dx\,dy$, z being $+$ive and that in the wedge AOA′ will be $\iint z\,dx\,dy$, z being $-$ive. Volumes in the two wedges being equal numerically

$$\iint z\,dx\,dy = 0,$$

integration being now extended over the whole area of flotation in the plane AB.

$$\text{or, } \iint y\,dx\,dy = 0, \text{ as } z = y \tan \theta.$$

$$\text{or } \bar{y} = 0.$$

Thus the C. G. of the area AB lies on OX i.e. on the intersection of the plane of flotation (A B) with any other plane infinitely close to it. Thus the C. G. is the point of contact of the plane with the surface of flotation.

Centre of gravity, C, of the mass of the liquid displaced is called the centre of buoyancy. The locus of C for various positions of the plane of flotation is called the surface of buoyancy.

Ex. 1. Prove that the tangent plane at any point C to the surface of buoyancy is parallel to the corresponding plane of flotation.

Ex. 2. Prove that so long as no part of the base of a right circular cone floating in a homogeneous liquid with vertex down-wards is submerged, surfaces of flotation and buoyancy are hyperbloids of revolution

Let VP be the perpendicular from V on any plane (AB) cutting the cone and θ be the angle between VP and the axis of the cone. The plane through VP and the axis of the cone will cut the cone in two lines VA and VB which intersect the given plane in the points A and B which are the extremities of the major axis of the ellipse.

Then
$$VA = \frac{p}{\cos(\theta+\alpha)}, \quad VB = \frac{p}{\cos(\theta-\alpha)}$$

$$VA \cdot VB = \frac{p^2}{\cos(\theta+\alpha)\cos(\theta'-\alpha)}$$

If V is the volume of the displaced liquid,
$$V = \tfrac{1}{3}\, p \ (\text{area of the ellipse})$$

$$= \frac{\pi\, p^3 \tan^2\alpha}{3\,(\cos^2\theta - \sin^2\theta\tan^2\alpha)^{\frac{3}{2}}}$$

(See Ex. 8 § 4 1)

so that
$$\frac{p^3}{[\cos(\theta+\alpha)\cos(\theta-\alpha)]^{\frac{3}{2}}} = \text{Cons.}$$

or VA . VB = Cons.

Since C the centre of the ellipse is the mid-point of the line AB, the locus of C will be a hyperbola with VA, VB as its asymptotes, for varying porstions of A B. Hence for all possible positions of the cutting plane the locus of the centre of gravity, of the area of flotation is a hyperbloid generated by the revolution of this curve about the axis of the cone. It follows then from the theorem of Bouguer and Dupin that this is the surface of flotation.

If H be the centre of buoyancy in any position, then H lies on the line V C such that $VH = \frac{3}{4}VC$; so that the locus of H,—surface of buoyancy, is a similar hyperbloid.

Ex. 3. Find the surfaces of buoyancy and flotation for an ellipsoid and deduce from this those of an elliptic cylinder.

Ex. 4. Find the surfaces of flotation and of buoyancy in the case of a cylinder of any cross section.

Let O be the centroid of the base and OZ, normal to the base, the line of centroids. The centroid of the cross section by any plane of flotation is the point where O Z intersects it. Thus all possible planes of flotation meet in one point, which is accordingly by the theorem Bouguer and Dupin, the surface of flotation.

If Ox, Oz, Oz be taken as rectangular axes and the equation of the cutting plane as $z = lx + my + c$, the coordinates (x, y, z) of the centre of buoyancy are given by

$$x = \frac{\int\int x\,z\,dx\,dy}{\int\int z\,dx\,dy}, \qquad \text{field of integration being the base.}$$

$$= \frac{1}{V}\left\{ \int\int x\,(l\,x + my + c)\,dx\,dy \right\}$$

$$\therefore \quad V\bar{x} = al + hm,$$

where $a = \int\int x^2\,dx\,dy \quad h = \int\int xy\,da\,dy,$
$$\int\int x\,dx\,dy = \int\int y\,dx\,dy = 0.$$

Similarly

$$V\bar{y} = \int\int yz\,dx\,dy = \int\int y\,(lx + my + c)\,dx\,dy$$
$$= (hl + bm),$$

where $b = \int\int y^2\,dx\,dy$

Also $\quad Vz = \tfrac{1}{2} \int\int z^2 \, dx \, dy$

$$= \tfrac{1}{2}(al^2 + 2h\,lm + bm^2) + \tfrac{1}{2}c^3 A.$$

Also $\quad A\,c = V.$

Eliminating l, m from these we have

$$\frac{(2\bar{z}-c)}{V} = \frac{(b\,\bar{x}^2 - 2h\,\bar{x}\,\bar{y} + a\,\bar{y}^2)}{ab - h^2}$$

Thus in the case of a solid box bounded by planes $x = \mp d$, $y = \mp e$, $z = k$ floating with the base $z = o$ wholly immersed, we have

$$\int\int x^2 \, dx \, dy = \frac{d^2}{3}(4\,de), \quad \int\int y^2 \, dx \, dy = \frac{e^2}{3}(4de)$$

$$\int\int x\,y \, dx \, dy = o \; ;$$

so that the surface of buoyancy is

$$\frac{2\bar{z} - c}{V} = \frac{3\bar{x}^2}{d^2(4\,de)} + \frac{3\bar{y}^2}{e^2(4\,de)}$$

or $\quad \dfrac{x^2}{d^2} + \dfrac{y^2}{e^2} = \dfrac{8\,de\,z}{3V} - \tfrac{1}{3},$

as $V = 4\,d\,e\,c.$

Ex. 5. Prove that the curve of buoyancy in the case of a rectangular lamina is a parabola.

4.6. Metacentre:—

Let $C\,N$, $C'\,N'$ be normals to the surface of buoyancy at C and C'. Draw $\mu\mu'$, the shortest distance line between the two normals, then μ is called the meta-centre corresponding to the line of intersection of the adjacent planes of flotation $A\,B$, $A'\,B'$, —called the axis of inclination $O\,x$.

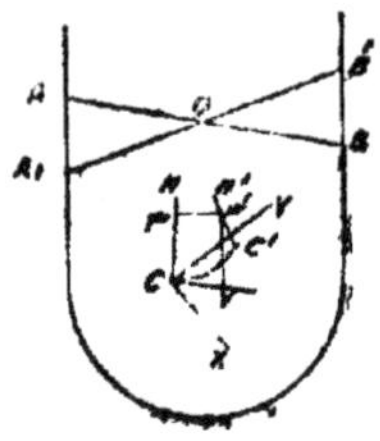

It is obvious that $\mu\mu'$ is parallel to $O\,x$ for $C\,N$ and $C'\,N'$ are respectively perpendicular to planes $A\,B$ and to $A'\,B'$.

The metacentre μ is situated in general between the two centres of principal curvature M and m of the surface of buoyancy (C) at the point C. It coincides with one of the centres of curvature M or m when the axis of inclination Ox is parallel to one of the principal directions of the surface (C) at the point C.

This theorem is really a general theorem applicable to curved surfaces and therefore also in particular to a surface of buoyancy; we proceed to prove this theorem.

Take the point C as origin, CN the normal at C as Z-axis, and CX, CY in the direction of principal radii as axes of X and Y. The equation of the surface in this system of axes with the usual notation may be written as

$$z = \tfrac{1}{2}\left(r_0 x^2 + t_0 y^2 \right) + \ldots, \text{ for small values of } x \text{ and}$$

y; $\dfrac{1}{r_0}$, $\dfrac{1}{t_0}$ being the principal radii of curvature at C

Thus $C M = \dfrac{1}{r_0}$, $C m = \dfrac{1}{t_0}$.

The equation of the normal $C'N'$ is

$$\frac{X-x}{p} = \frac{Y-y}{q} = \frac{Z-z}{-1} = \frac{r}{\sqrt{1+p^2+q^2}} = \lambda.$$

Let CV be the projection of $\mu\mu'$ on XOY plane. Clearly since $\mu\mu'$ is normal to Cμ, $\mu\mu'$ will be parallel to CV and Vμ' =Cμ i.e. the Z—coordinate of μ is equal to Z—coordinate of μ' Now let the direction cosines of $\mu\mu'$ be (L, M, N) then since $\mu\mu'$ is perpendicular to C μ and $C'\mu,'$

$$N = 0 \text{ , and } L\,p + M\,q = o \,.$$

Hence the direction cosines of CV are are (L, M, o) where $L\,p + Mq = o$. The equation of the plane CV $\mu'\mu$ is accordingly $Xp + Yq = o$. We now require the z— coordinate of μ', the point of intersection of $C'\mu'$ with the plane $Xp + Yq = o$.

Any point on the line being given by $(x + p\lambda,\, y + q\lambda,\, -z\lambda)$ we have

$$p\,(x+p\lambda)+q'y+q\lambda)=0,$$

so that $\lambda = -\dfrac{px+qy}{p^2+q^2}$

Hence $V\mu' = C\mu = z+\dfrac{px+qy}{p^2+q^2}$

$$= z+\dfrac{(r_o.r)x+\,t_.y)y}{r_o{}^2x^2+t_o{}^2y^2}$$

substituting for p and q from the equation to the surface.

Now in the limit when C' tends to C, x, y,z tend to zero in such a way that the ratio $\dfrac{y}{x}$ tends to the limit $\tan\alpha$ where α is the angle made by the limiting direction of CC' with CX.

$$\therefore \operatorname{Lim} z = C\mu = \dfrac{r_o+t_o\tan^2\alpha}{r_o{}^2+t_o{}^2\tan^2\alpha}$$

The limiting value of $C\mu$ lies therefore, between $\dfrac{1}{r_o}$ and $\dfrac{1}{t_o}$, i.e μ lies between CM and Cm. In the particular case when $\alpha=0$ or $\dfrac{\pi}{2}$, i.e. when the direction of CC' coincides with one of the principal directions of the surface at C,— $C\mu=CM$ or Cm. The centres of curvatures M and m correspond to the maximum and minimum of $C\mu$ and may be called the 'major' and 'minor' meta-centres respectively relative to the point C.

4. 7 If I be the moment of inertia of the area of flotation having an axis of intersection Ox, about this line, the meta-centre μ corresponding to the axis is at a distance I/V from G i. e. $C\mu = $ I/V.

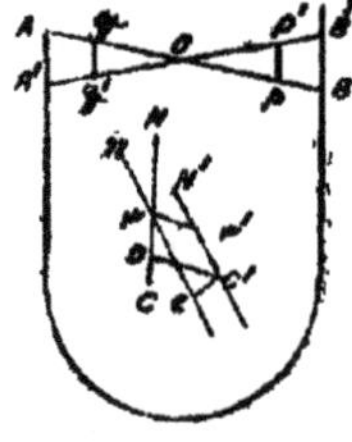

Fig. (i)

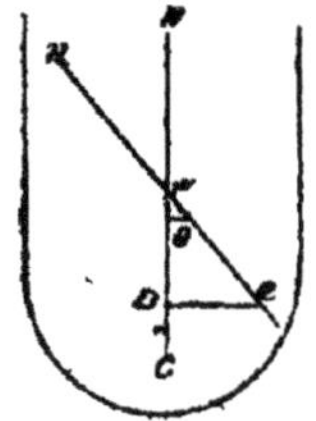

Fig. (ii)

Figure (i) shows the infinitely close normals CN and C′ N′ with μμ′, the shortest distance line between them. Draw e μn parallel to C′N′ and let e be the projection of C′ on the plane containing CμN and e μn. Fig. (ii) represents the section of the body by the plane eμN and C μn. Since μμ′ is parallel to the axis of intersection (See §4.5) and μμ′ is normal to the plane containing CμN and e μn, it follows that the axis of inter section is also normal to this plane (the plane of the section shown in Fig. ii).

Let Nμ$n=\theta$

Take as before for y—axis a line perpendicular to Ox in the plane AB, and Oz as vertical. Let (x, y, z) be the coordinates of a point $p′$ or $q′$ of the plane of flotation A′B′ relative to these axes, we have then

$$z = y \tan \theta.$$

Let $dx\, dy$ be an element of area of the plane of flotation AB placed at p or q, the moment of intertia about Ox is there fore, $1 = \int\int y^2\, dx\, dy$, integration being over the area of flotation. Let us apply to all the elements of the volume displaced in the 1st case limited by the horizontal plane AB fictitious forces in the vertically *upward* direction equal to the volume of the element. These forces then have a resultant equal to their sum viz. V acting at their centre of gravity C along the direction CN.

Similarly let us apply at each element of the volume displaced in the second case and limited by A′B′ forces equal to the volume of the element but acting vertically *downwards*. The resultant is again a force V acting at C′ vertically downwards.

The resultant of these fictitious forces is a couple whose arm is C′D, being the distance of C′ from the normal CN The result may be calculated in another way as follows: The forces acting at the common elements of the two volumes cancel each other being equal and opposite; there remain therefore only the forces applied to the elements of volume in the wedges AA′ and BB′ An elementary cylinder pp' based on $dx\,dy$ and of height z in the 1st wedge is acted by a vertically downwards force of magnitude $z\,dx\,dy$, the volume of the elementery cylinder. The moment of this force about Ox is $yz\,dx\,dy$ Similarly the volume of the cylinder qq' in the second wedge is acted upon by a vertically upward force, whose moment about Ox is $yz\,dx\,dy$. The resultant of the forces in the two wedges being known to be a couple, the sum of the moments of these forces about Ox is equal to the component of the moment of the couple in a plane normal to Ox. Thus $\int\int yz\,dx\,dy =$ V (projection of the arm of the couple, C′D in Fig (i) on a plane normal to Ox i. e. the plane of the section in Fig. (ii). $=$ V. eD.

But for every given z, whether of pp' or of qq', z is equal to $y\tan\theta$

$$\text{so that } \tan\theta \int\int y^2\,dx\,dy = \text{V.}e\,D.$$

$$\text{or, } \frac{I}{V} = \text{Lim } \frac{eD}{\tan\theta}.$$

Also, from the $\triangle\,\mu\,D\,e$, whose angle at μ is θ, we have

$$\frac{eD}{\tan\theta} = D\,\mu$$

The point D is infinitely close to C, in the limit, therefore, $D\mu = C\mu$.

Hence $\quad C\,\mu = I/V$.

4 8. Positions of equilibrium:—

The conditions of equilibrium according to the principle of buoyancy are

(i) the volume V of the immersed part is equal to $\dfrac{W}{g\rho}$, W being the weight of the body, and ρ the density of the liquid. The free surface is a tangent to the surface of flotation.

(ii)   The line GC must be vertical i.e. normal to the surface
of flotation AB.   But as the surface of flotation AB
is parallel to the tangent plane to the surface of
buoyancy at C (Ex. 1 § 4.5), GC is also normal to the
surface of buoyancy.   The centre of buoyancy corresponding to a position of equilibrium is therefore the
foot of a normal from the centre of gravity G to the
surface of buoyancy.

Conversely every normal GC dropped from G to the surface
of buoyancy will correspond to a position of equilibrium obtained
by immersing the solid up to a volume whose centre of gravity
is the foot of the normal considered.   In this position G can be
above or below C.

It follows then that the orientation of the flaoting body in the
position of equilibrium as well as the nature of equilibrium
(stable, unstable or neutral) is the same as those of a heavy body
bounded by the surface of buoyancy resting on a horizontal plane.
From this theorem it is easy to deduce the necessary and sufficient
conditions of stability of equilibrium.

4.9.   Equilibrium of a heavy solid on a horizontal surface. We
shall employ the well-known theorem of Statics that when a heavy
system is in equilibrium, the necessary and sufficient condition
of stable equilibrium is that its centre of gravity be as low as
possible i.e. lower than when it is in any of the neighbouring
positions.

Consider now a heavy solid bounded by a surface Σ convex
at a all points and resting on a horizontal plane

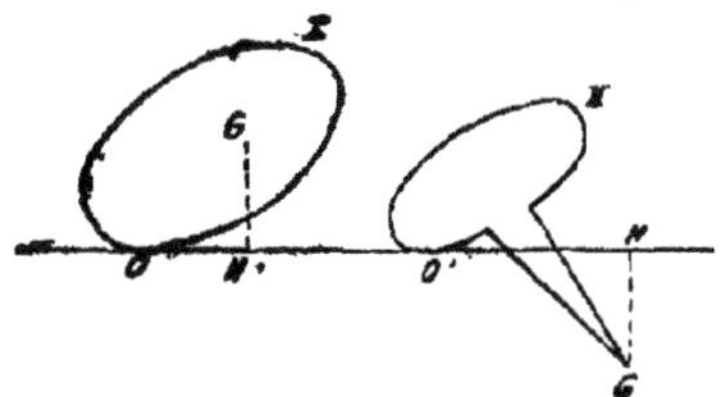

Let G be the C. G. of the body, GH its distance from the fixed plane. The positions of equilibrium are obtained by determining the positions in which GH is maximum or minimum the positions in which GH is minimum being stable and those in which it is maximum being unstable. (The segment GH must be regarded as positive or negative according as G is above or below the horizontal plane. The C G can be below the horizontal if it is external to the body as in fig II.)

Let O be the point of contact of the body with the horizontal plane, then the necessary and sufficient conditions of stable equilibrium are:—

(i)   The C. G must be on the normal at O;

(ii) It must be below the two centres of the principal curvature of the surface relative to the point O.

The first condition is evident, for if there is equilibrium it is necessary that the weight of the body acting at G must balance the reaction of the plane acting at O. The reaction at O therefore must pass through G, so that GO must be the common normal to the plane and the surface at O.

The first condition being fulfilled; for equilibrium to be stable it is necessary and sufficient that in the position of the body considered, the distance of G from the horizontal plane be less than in all other positions infinitely near to this. Instead of leaving the tangent plane fixed and displacing the body it is more convenient to regard the body as fixed in its equilibrium position and move the tangent plane. It is necessary and sufficient for equilibrium to be stable that the distance GO of G from the tangent plane at O is less than the distance of G from other tangent planes at points O' infinitely close to O.

Take O as origin, the tangent plane at O as xoy plane, and the principal directions of the surface at O as axes of x and y, and let Oz be on the same side as the surface.

Let O' (x,y,z) be any point close to O.

Let the equation of the surface be

$$z = \tfrac{1}{2}(r_o x^2 + t_o y^2)$$

$OM = \dfrac{1}{r_c}$ $Om = \dfrac{1}{t_o}$ being the principal radii of curvature.

The equation of the tangent plane at O' is

$$(Z - z) = p(X - x) + q(Y - y)$$

The distance of G (o,o,ζ) from the plane is

$$GH = (\zeta - z + px + qy)\, |\,\sqrt{1 + p^2 + q^2}.$$

Now at the point O, $p = q = x = y = z = o$, so that at O' a point infinitely near O, these quantities are very smalll. Hence the expression for G H has the same sign as ζ.

$$G\ H = [\zeta + \tfrac{1}{2}(r_o x^2 + t_o y^2) + \ldots](1 + r_o^2 x^2 + t_o^2 y_2)^{-\frac{1}{2}},$$

substituting for p,q and z from the equation of the surface.

Expanding in series of x^2 and y^2 the expression on the R.H.S. we have up to terms of the 2nd order

$$G\ H = \zeta - \tfrac{1}{2}\zeta(r_o^2 x^2 + t_o^2 y^2) + \tfrac{1}{2}(r_o x^2 + t_o y^2) + \ldots$$

$$= \zeta + \tfrac{1}{2}r_o^2\, x^2\,(\tfrac{1}{r_o} - \zeta) + \tfrac{1}{2}t_o^2 y^2(\tfrac{1}{t_o} - \zeta) + \ldots$$

For the value of G H to be minimum it is necessary and sufficient that the coefficients of x^2 and y^2 be positive.

$$\text{or, } \zeta < \frac{1}{r_o} \text{ and } \zeta < \frac{1}{t_o}$$

$i\ e.\ \zeta < OM$, and $\zeta < Om$.

Hence G must be below the 'minor' meta-centre.

Remark I: In this we can indifferently suppose the point G to be interior to the surface, regard being had to the proper sign of G H.

Remark II: The necessary and sufficient condition that the equilibrium of a floating body be stable is that G must be below m, the minor metacentre.

We have already seen that the distance

$Cm = \dfrac{I_o}{V}$, where I_o = the minimum moment of inertia of the plane of flotation with respect to an axis passing through its centre.

Hence for stability of equilibrium

$$CG \angle \dfrac{I_o}{V}$$

4. 10. We shall now prove the necessary and sufficient condition of stability of equilibrium by another method.

In § 4. 6 it has been pointed out that when the direction of CC' coincides with one of the principal directions of the surface of buoyancy at C, $C\mu = CM$ or $C\,m$.

In this case the normal at C' to the surface intersects the normal at C and μ, μ' coincide with the point of intersection. The axis of intersection in the area of flotation is a line parallel to the line of intersection of the tangent planes at C and C so that the axis of intersection is a line through the centre of gravity of the area of flotation parallel to one of the principal directions of the surface of buoyancy at C. There are accordingly two such axes of intersection corresponding to the two principal directions of the surface of buoyancy at C. If I_1, I_2 be the moments of inertia of the area of flotation about these axes then by §4-6 $CM = \dfrac{I_1}{V}$, $C\,m = \dfrac{I_2}{V}$.

Since CM and Cm are the maximum and minimum value of $C\mu(= \dfrac{I}{V})$, I, being the moment of inertia about any line through the centre of the area of flotation, it follows that I_2

$\angle$ I $\angle$ I$_1$, so that I$_1$ and I$_2$ are the greatest and least moments of interia of the area of flotation. Consequently the corresponding axes are principal axes of inertia Consider now a rotation of the body about any one of these two axes through a small angle θ. In the displaced position, a vertical force $W = (g\rho V)$ acts through G parallel to C'M, which is the vertical in the displaced position and the fluid pressure $g\rho V$ acts vertically upwards (i e along C'M) through the new centre of buoyancy C'. Hence assuming G to be below M, the moment of the restoring couple is G M Sin θ $(g\rho V)$ and is about the same axis about which the body is rotated.

$$g\rho \text{ V. } \text{ G M Sin}\theta = g\rho V \text{ (CM} - \text{CG)}\theta, \text{ } \theta \text{ being small,}$$

$$= g\rho V(\frac{I_1}{V} - h)\theta$$

$$= g\rho \text{ I}_1 - Vh) \theta.$$

If on the other hand the body be rotated through a small angle θ' about the second principal axis of inertia of the area of flotation the moment of the restoring couple about the axis of rotation is $g\rho \text{ (I}_2 - Vh)\theta'$.

If the body is rotated through a small angle about any axis through the C. G. of the area of flotation, it may be resolved into two small rotations θ, θ' about the principal axes of inertia. The restoring couples set up, therefore, will have moments $g\rho(\text{I}_1 - Vh) \theta$ and $g\rho(\text{I}_2 - Vh)\theta'$.

In order that the equilibrium be stable it is necessary that these moments be positive, so that $h = \text{CG} < \frac{I_1}{V}$ and $h = \text{C G} < \frac{I_2}{V}$.

Conversely if $h = C \text{ G} < \frac{I_2}{V}$ (where I$_2$ $<$ I$_1$) the two couples have positive moments and tend to restore the body to its equilibrium position.

Ex. 1 A solid cylinder of radius a and length h floats with its axis vertical. Find the condition of stable equilibrium.

If the length immersed is h', we have

$$g\pi a^2 h'\rho = \pi a^2 hg\sigma$$

$$\therefore h' = \frac{h\sigma}{\rho}.$$

$$OC = \frac{h'}{2}, OG = \frac{h}{2}, \text{ so that } CG = \frac{h-h'}{2}$$

For stability

$$CG < \frac{I}{V} = \frac{(\pi a^2)\frac{a^2}{4}}{\pi a^2 h'} = \frac{a^2}{4h'}$$

or, $\quad \frac{h-h'}{2} < \frac{a^2}{4h'}$

Ex.2. A uniform right circular cone of specific gravity σ, whose base is an ellipse of semi axes a, b $(a > b)$ and whose height is h floats freely in water with its axis vertical and vertex downwards If the equilibrium is completely stable, shew that

$$\sigma > \left(\frac{h^2}{h^2+b^2}\right)^3$$

If h' be the height immersed, then by the principle of buoyancy

$$\frac{h}{3}g\rho\,\sigma A = \frac{h'}{3}g\rho\,A' = \frac{h'}{3}g\rho\left(\frac{h'^2}{h^2}A\right)$$

or, $h\,\sigma^{\frac{1}{3}} = h'$ $\quad$ .. ..(1)

A being the area of the base and A′ of the plane of flotation.

The plane of flotation is an ellipse whose axes are $\left(\frac{ah'}{h}, \frac{bh'}{h}\right)$

hence I_1, the moment of inertia about major axis is $\dfrac{b^2 h'^2}{4\,h^2}\left(\dfrac{\pi ab h'^2}{h^2}\right)$

Also $OG = \frac{3}{4}h$ and $OC = \frac{3}{4}h'$, C being the centre of buoyancy

For stability $CG = \frac{3}{4}(h-h') < \dfrac{I_1}{V}$

$$\text{or, } \tfrac{3}{4}(h-h') < \frac{b^2 h'^2 (\pi a b h'^2)}{4 h^4 \left(\dfrac{\pi a b}{3} \dfrac{'^2 h}{h^2} \right)}$$

$$\text{or, } \tfrac{3}{4}(h-h') < \frac{3 b^2 h'}{4 h^2}$$

$$\text{or, } h^3 < (h^2 + b^2) h' = (h^2 + b^2)\, h\, \sigma^{\frac{1}{3}}$$

$$\text{so that } \sigma > \left(\frac{h^2}{h^2 + b^2} \right)^3.$$

Ex.3. If a solid cone of density σ floats in a liquid of density P show that the equilibrium is stable if

$$\text{(i) } \frac{r}{h} > \sqrt{\left(\frac{P}{\sigma} \right)^{\frac{1}{3}} - 1}, \text{ vertex downwards}$$

$$\text{(ii) } \frac{r}{h} > \sqrt{\left(\frac{P}{P - \sigma} \right)^{\frac{1}{3}} - 1}, \text{ vertex upwards,}$$

r, h being the radius and height of the cone

Ex. 4. A thin rectangular strip of uniform material having sides of length l and πa is bent into a channel of semi circular section (radius a and length l, with open ends and immersed in water. The specific density of the material is $\tfrac{1}{2}$.

Confining attention to positions in which the straight edges of the channel are horizontal, show that there are two configurations of stable equilibrium. Are there any configurations of unstable equilibrium ? (Tripos pt. 1 1927)

Ex. 5. The radius of gyration of the section of a ship at the water level is 20 ft., and the volume of water displaced is 24 A cubic ft. where A is the area of the water line. Assuming the curve of buoyancy to be a parabola show that if the C. G. of the ship is $\tfrac{3}{4}''$ above the meta-centre, the ship will heel over through about 5° into a position of stable of equilibrium.

(Only rolling displacements are to be considered)

Let the centre of gravity G be on the axis of the parabola of buoyancy and let m be the corresponding meta-centre.

Then
$$Cm = \frac{Ak^2}{V} = \frac{A(20)^2}{24\,A} = \frac{50}{3}\ \text{ft.}$$

$$\therefore\ CG = Cm + \frac{3''}{4} = \left(\frac{50}{3} + \frac{1}{16}\right)\ \text{ft.}$$

Also since $Cm =$ radius of curvature of the parabola at the vertex $= 2a$, $2a$ being its semi latus rectum.

Thus
$$2a = \frac{50}{3}\ \text{ft.}$$

Other positions of equilibrium are obtained by drawing normals from G to the parabola,

If μ be the slope of a normal, its equation is
$$y = \mu\,x - 2a\,\mu - a\mu^3.$$

Since it passes through G $\left(\frac{50}{3} + \frac{1}{16},\ o\right)$

we have
$$\mu\left(\frac{50}{3} + \frac{1}{16}\right) - 2a\mu - a\,\mu^3 = o$$

The solution $\mu = o$ corresponds to the position in which the axis is vertical.

The other two solutions give the oblique positions of equilibrium.

We have then
$$a\,\mu^2 = \left(\frac{50}{3} + \frac{1}{16}\right) - 2a$$

$$= \frac{50}{3} + \frac{1}{16} - \frac{50}{3} = \frac{1}{16}$$

$$\therefore \mu = \pm\frac{1}{4\sqrt{a}} = \pm\frac{\sqrt{3}}{4\times 5} = \pm\frac{\sqrt{3}}{20}$$

$$= \pm\,.0866$$

$$(\ 124 \ )$$

Thus if the angle between the normal through G and the axis of the parabola is θ, $tan\ \theta = .0866$

$$\text{or } \theta = 5° \text{ approx.}$$

Thus if the ship be rolled through 5° on either side of the position in which O G is vertical, the oblique positions will be positions of equilibrium. Since the intermediate position is of unstable equilibrium (G being above the metacentre) these positions will be stable as positions of stable and unstable equilibrium occur alternately.

Ex. 6. A beam of length l and density σ has a square section ABCD of side a and floats in a liquid of density $P(>\sigma)$ with the side l horizontal and A B above the surface of the liquid.

Prove that a beam of the same dimensions but of density $P—\sigma$ will float in the inverted position with the same plane section in the free surface.

If $\dfrac{\sigma}{\rho}\left(1-\dfrac{\sigma}{\rho}\right) < \dfrac{1}{6}$ shew that the only position of equilibrium is horizontal and that it is stable for small displacements about the length l.

$$\text{(I. C. S. 1934)}$$

Ex. 7. A uniform solid cone of semi vertical angle 30° and specific gravity $\frac{1}{2}$ floats with vertex downwards in water with the axis vertical. The vertex is loaded with a particle whose mass is n times the mass of the cone. Show that the equilibrium is neutral if

$$1+n = \frac{3\sqrt{2}}{4}$$

$$\text{(I. C. S. 1921)}$$

(Hint . Here CG=CM.)

Ex. 8. Prove that an isosceles triangular prism or wedge floating with its base not immersed and its edges horizontal has three or only one positions of equilibrium.

In the former case the position with base horzontal is unstable, while in the latter case it is stable.

Let the wedge float with its edges horizontal and let $b\ d$ be any plane of flotation. Taking oblique axes AB and AD as axes of X and Y we find that the coordinates of the centre of gravity of the triangle A $b\ d$ are $\left(\dfrac{X}{3}, \dfrac{Y}{3}\right)$ where A $b = X$, A$d = Y$.

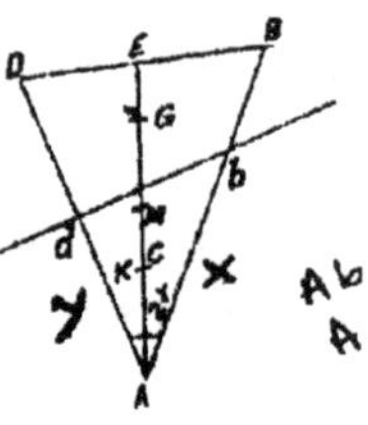

Since the weight of the wedge ABD is equal to the weight of the volume of fluid displaced by it, we have

$$\tfrac{1}{2}(AB)\,(AD)\,\text{Sin } 2\alpha.\ g\sigma l = \tfrac{1}{2}XY\ \text{Sin } 2\alpha.g\rho l$$

l being the length of the horizontal edge.

$$\therefore XY = p^2\frac{\sigma}{\rho}, \text{ where } AB = AD = p.$$

The locus of the centre of gravity C of the triangle Abd is therefore the hyperbola

$$XY = \frac{p^2\sigma}{\rho} \qquad \ldots \qquad \ldots \qquad (1)$$

Clearly AB, AD are the asymptotes of this hyperbola. The surface of buoyancy is therefore a hyperbolic cylinder whose asymptotic planes are the sides of the wedge.

The positions of equilibrium are given by drawing normals from G to this surface. Since G is on AE, the bisector of the angle BAC, G is a point on the major axis of the hyperbola.

Now it is easily proved that from a point G on the axis of a hyperbola, either three normals can be drawn or only one according as

$$A\,G \quad \gtrless \quad \frac{a^2 + b^2}{a}\ , \ a, b \text{ being the major and minor}$$

axes.

Also if 2α be the angle between the asymptotes of the hyperbola, we have

$$\tan \alpha = \frac{b}{a};$$

and $\quad \dfrac{a^2+b^2}{4} = \dfrac{p^2\sigma}{9\rho}$, since the equation of the hyper-

bola with asymptotes as axes is $XY = \dfrac{a^2+b^2}{4} = \dfrac{p^2\sigma}{9\rho}$ by (1)

Thus there are three positions of equilibrium or only one accccording as $A\,G = \dfrac{2}{3}p\cos\alpha \gtrless a(1+\tan^2\alpha) = \dfrac{2}{3}p\sqrt{\dfrac{\sigma}{\rho}}\cos\alpha\,\sec^2\alpha,$

or according as,
$$\cos^2\alpha \gtrless \sqrt{\dfrac{\sigma}{\rho}}.$$

If $\cos^2\alpha > \sqrt{\dfrac{\sigma}{\rho}}$, there is only one position of equilibrium which is the position with its base horizontal.

One of the principal sections of the surface of buoyancy is the section by the vertical plane perpendicular to the edges of the wedge, the 2nd being normal to this. If K be the vertex of the hyperbola, K M, the height of the minor meta-centre,

$$= \text{(radius of curvature of the hyperbola at its vertex K)}$$

$$= b^2/a = a\,\tan^2\alpha = \frac{2}{3}p\sqrt{\frac{\sigma}{\rho}}\cos\alpha\,\tan^2\alpha$$

Hence $A\,M = A\,K + K\,M = \dfrac{2}{3}p\sqrt{\dfrac{\sigma}{\rho}}\cos\alpha\,(1+\tan^2\alpha)$

$$= \frac{2}{3}p\sqrt{\frac{\sigma}{\rho}}\sec\alpha.$$

The necessary and sufficient condition of stability, as we have seen, is that G be below M so that

$$A\,G < A\,M$$

$$\text{or, } \frac{2}{3}p\cos\alpha < \frac{2}{3}\sqrt{\frac{\sigma}{\rho}}\sec\alpha$$

Or, $cos^2\alpha < \sqrt{\dfrac{\sigma}{\rho}}$, which is also the condition that there is only one position of equilibrium.

Thus if there is only one position of equilibrium the position is also stable. On the other hand if $cos^2\alpha > \sqrt{\dfrac{\sigma}{\rho}}$, there are three positions of equilibrium, but the intermediate one viz. horizontal position, is unstable. The other two must therefore be stable in accordance with the well-known principle that positions of stable and unstable equilibrium occur alternately.

Ex. 9. Find a solid of revolution such that when a segment of it is immersed in a liquid, the distance between the centre of buoyancy and the metacentre may be constant, whatever be the height of the segment immersed.

(Tripos part I 1939)

Take the origin, O of the coordinates at its lowest point, the axis of x being vertically upwards and that of y horizontal. Then if (x,y) are the coordinates which determine the surface of flotation in the *axially* vertical position and (x',y') those belonging to another parallel plane, we have at once

$$CM = J/V = \frac{\pi y^2 \left(\frac{y^2}{4}\right)}{\pi \int_0^x y'^2 dx'}$$

$$= \frac{y^4}{4 \int_0^x y'^2 dx'}$$

$\therefore$ if CM is constant and equal to m, whatever x may be, we have

$$\frac{1}{4} y^4 = m \int_0^x y'^2 dx'$$

Differentiating $y^3 \; \dfrac{dy}{dx} = m\, y^2$

$$\therefore \; y^2 = 2m\, x.$$

The generating curve is, therefore, a parabola, and the solid of revolution is the paraboloid generated by the revolution of the parabola about O x.

Ex. 10. Find the solid of revolution such that when a segment of it is immersed in a liquid, the height of meta-centre above its lowest point is independent of the segment immersed.

(Ans. Anchor-ring, formed by the revolution of a circle about a tangent).

Ex.11 If the height in the above example were a function $\phi\,(x, y)$, x, y being the coordinates characterising the plane of flotation, show that the differential equation of the generating curve is

$$\frac{d}{dx} \left\{ \frac{y^3\,\dfrac{dy}{dx} + (x-\phi)y^2}{\dfrac{a\phi}{dx} + \dfrac{dy}{dx}\,\dfrac{d\phi}{dy}} \right\} = y^2.$$

Ex. 12. The cross section of a cylinderical ship is two equal arcs of equal parabolas of latus rectum l, which touch at the keel, the common vertex of the two parabolas so that the sides of the ship are concave to the water. The ship is floating upright with its keel at a depth h. Prove that the height of the metacentre above the keel is

$$h \left(\frac{3}{4} + \frac{h^2}{l^2} \right).$$

Ex. 13. A solid of uniform density σ floats partly immersed in a homogeneous liquid of density P. Show that a solid of the same size and shape and of uniform density $(P - \sigma)$ can float inverted with the same plane of flotation in the same liquid; and that if the equilibrium is stable in one case it is also stable in the other case for like displacements.

4. 11. Equilibrium of a vessel containing a liquid:—

Suppose a vessel containing a given volume of liquid of density ρ floats in a liquid of density ρ'. If the vessel receives a small angular displacement there will be a force of buoyancy due to the external fluid acting upwards through its metacentre M; the line of action of the contained liquid acts along the vertical through its new centre of gravity and it 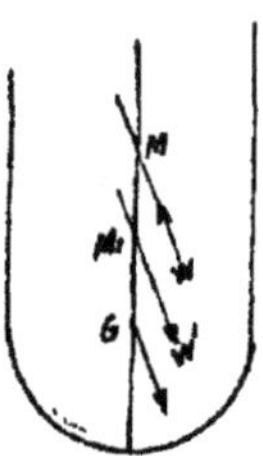 intersects the line G M in M_1, the meta-centre of the contained liquid. This force acts downwards. (It is assumed that the body is symmetrical about the plane of displacement through its centre of mass and that the centres of mass of the body and of the liquid are in the same vertical line). Taking moments about G, the resultant fluid pressures will tend to restore equilibrium or reverse it according as

$$W\ G\ M - W'\ G\ M_1 \gtrless .$$

$$\text{or,} \quad \frac{W}{W'} \gtrless \frac{GM_1}{GM} .$$

Ex. 1. Consider a cylinder containing water floating in a liquid of specific gravity w with its axis vertical.

Let $h =$ height of the cylinder,

h', the height of the contained water

Let d be the depth of the cylinder in the given liquid, and a be the radius of the cylinder.

Than $W' = \pi a^2 g h' \, \rho$

$$W = \pi a^2 g d\, \rho w$$

Again $GM = OM - OG = OC + CM - OG$

$$= \frac{d}{2} + \frac{a^2/4}{d} - \frac{h}{2} .$$

$$GM_1 = OM_1 - OG = OC' + C'M_1 - OG$$

$$= \frac{h'}{2} + \frac{a^2/4}{h'} - \frac{h}{2} \, .$$

$\therefore$ For stable equilibrium

$$-\frac{GM_1}{GM} = \frac{2h'^2 + a^2 - 2hh'}{2d^2 + a^2 - 2\,dh} \cdot \frac{d}{h'} < \frac{W}{W'} = \frac{d\,w}{h'}$$

or, $\qquad \dfrac{2h'^2 + a^2 - 2hh'}{2d'^2 + a^2 - 2\,dh} \cdot \; < w.$

Ex. 2. Establish a similar relation for a right circular cone floating with its axis vertical and containing some liquid.

$$\text{Ans.} \quad \left(\frac{z}{h'}\right)^3 > \frac{9\,h'\,sec^2\alpha - 8h}{9\,z\,sec^2\alpha \quad 8h} \, ,$$

where $h =$ the length of the axis of the cone,

$\qquad h' = \qquad$ „ $\qquad$ „ $\qquad$ in the contained liquid,

$\qquad z =$ the length beneath the surface of the external fluid,

and $\alpha =$ the semi vertical angle.

Ex. 3. A paraboloidal cup, the weight of which is w, standing on a horizontal table, contains a quantity of water, whose weight is $n\,w$. If h be the height of C. G. of the cup and the contained water, the equilibrium is stable if the latus rectum of the parabola is

$$> 2\,(n+1)\,h.$$

Let the equation of the parabola generating the paraboloid be $y^2 = 4\,ax$, axis being $O\,x$ and tangent at the vertex being y-axis.

Let z be the height of the water in the cup, then $O\,C$, C being the C.G. of the contained water,

$$= \frac{\pi \int_0^z y^2\,x\,dx}{\pi \int_0^z y^2\,dx} = \frac{\int_0^z x^2\,dx}{\int_0^z x\,dx} = \tfrac{2}{3}\,z \, .$$

Let the height of C.G. of the cup above O be k

then $h = \dfrac{kw + nw\left(\frac{2}{3}z\right)}{w + nw} = \dfrac{k + \frac{2}{3}nz}{n + 1}$.

Height of meta-centre above C.

$$= C\,M = \frac{\pi\,y^2\left(\frac{y^2}{4}\right)}{\pi\int_0^z y^2\,dx} = \frac{4\,a\,z(az)}{2az^2} = 2\,a.$$

Thus in the subsequent displacement the weight of the contained water must be imagined to act at M i.e. at height $\frac{2}{3}z + 2a$.

$\therefore$ M the metacentre of the system is given by

$$O\,M = \frac{wk + nw\left(\frac{2}{3}z + 2a\right)}{w(n+1)} = h + \frac{2an}{n+1}.$$

Also the radius of curvature R, of the paraboloid at the vertex $= 2a$.

Hence from a well known result in Statics we have for stable equilibrium

$$\frac{1}{OM} > \frac{1}{R} = \frac{1}{2a}$$

or, $\dfrac{1}{h + \dfrac{2an}{n+1}} > \dfrac{1}{2a}$, which leads to

$$4\,a > 2\,(n+1)\,h.$$

Ex. 4. A cylinderical vessel, the weight of which may be neglected, contains water, and the vessel is placed on the vertex of a fixed rough sphere with the centre of its base in contact with the sphere. Find the condition of stability for infinitesimal displacements. Prove also that if the equilibrium be neutral for such displacements, it is really unstable.

Ex. 6. A hemispherical shell, containing liquid is placed on the vertex of a fixed rough sphere of twice its diameter; prove that the equilibrium will be stable or unstable according as the weight

of the shell is greater or less than twice the weight of the
liquid.

Ex 6. A thin vessel in the form of a surface of revolution
contains a given quantity (volume V) of homogeneous liquid of
specific weight w. It rests with its vertex at the highest point
of a rough curved surface, prove that the equilibrium is stable
or unstable for lateral displacements according as

$$(Vw+W)R > \text{ or } <(1+\frac{R}{R'})(Vwk + Iw + Wh) ,$$

where W is the weight of the vessel without the liquid, I the
moment of inertia of the free surface of the liquid and h, k the
heights of the centres of gravity above the vertex of the vessel
and the liquid respectively, R,R' being the radii of curvature of the
vessel and the fixed surface in the plane of the displacement

4. 12. Stability of a body floating in two liquids.

Let a solid float in two liquids of densities P and $P + P'$,
the former being above the latter. Let V be the volume of the
solid immersed and V' only that part of the volume which is
immersed in the second liquid only. Let A,A' be the areas of
flotation of the two liquids.

We may evidently suppose the volume V to be immersed
in a liquid of density P and V' to be immersed in a liquid of
density P'. The forces which support the weight of the body are
$gP V$ and $(gP'V')$ acting upwards at H and H', the centres of
gravity of the volumes V and V' supposed to be homogeneously
filled. Let G be the C.G. of the body. We shall consider only
the simple case in which the body is symmetrical with respect
to a vertical plane perpendicular to the plane of displacem nt so
that G,H,H' are in the same vertical line.

Let the body be displaced through ϕ about any horizontal
axis in the plane of symmetry, the moment of the restorative
couple will be

(133)

$$g\rho \, (I_1 - V. \, HG) \, \theta + g\rho' \, (I_2 - V'. \, H'G) \, \theta,$$

I_1, I_2 being the moments of inertia of the areas of flotation about axis through the centres of gravity of these areas.

For stability of equilibrium

$$\rho \, (I_1 - V. \, HG) > \rho' \, (V' \, H'G - I_2).$$

Ex. 1. A uniform liquid of density σ_2 overlies another of greater density σ_1 and a body with a plane of symmetry floats with its plane vertical so as to be in contact with both liquids. Prove that the meta centric height from the bottom of the body is

$$\frac{(z_1 V_1 + K_1{}^2 A_1)(\sigma_1 - \sigma_2) + (z_2 V_2 + K_2{}^2 A_2)\,\sigma_2}{V_1(\sigma_1 - \sigma_2) + V_2\,\sigma_2}$$

where V_1 is the volume submerged in the lower liquid, Z_1 the height of the centre of buoyancy of this volume above the lowest point of the body, A_1, K_1 the area and radius of gyration of the lower "water line"; and V_2 is the whole volume below the upper "water line", z_2 is the height of the centre of buoyancy which this volume would have if it were submerged in a single liquid, and A_2, K_2 refer to upper water line.

(Tripos Pt. II, 1921)

4. 13. Stability of a body floating in a heterogeneous liquid.

It should be noted that when a body floats in a heterogneeous liquid, which is subject to the action of gravity, horizontal planes are surfaces of equal density.

Consider now a heterogeneous liquid arranged in horizontal layers of equal density viz. the topmost layer of density ρ_1, next of $\rho_1 + \rho_2$, next of $\rho_1 + \rho_1 + \rho_3$, etc. Let the volume of the solid cut off by these layers be $v_1, v_2, v_3 \ldots$ etc. and let H_1 H_2, $H_3 \ldots$ be the centres of gravity of these volumes when homogeneously filled. Let A_1, A_2, $A_3 \ldots$ and k_1, k_2, $k_3 \ldots$ be the areas and radii of gyration of the sections of the body by the layers of equal density.

The forces called into play by the immersion of the body in such a system are the same if the volume v_1 of the body were immersed in a homogeneous liquid of density P_1, v_2 in that of density P_2, v_3 in that of density P_3 etc.

Now if the body be displaced through a small angle θ about any horizontal axis in the plane of symmetry (assuming that it had one), the moment about G, the C. G. of the body, of forces tending to restore equilibrium are

$$g P_1 (A\, k_1{}^2 - v_1 . H_1 G)\theta,\; g P_2 (A_2\, k_2{}^2 - v_2\, H_2 G)\, \theta,\dots$$

$\therefore$ Total moment

$$= g \left\{ \sum_1^n P_m\, A_m\, k_m{}^2 - (P_1\, v_1 . H_1 G + P_2 v_2\, H_2 G + \dots) \right\}$$

Now if masses $P_1\, v_1$, $P_2{'}\, v_2$, . act at H_1, H_2, ...

$$\text{then } (P_1\, v_1 + P_2\, v_2 + \dots)\, HG = \sum_1^n P_m\, v_m\, H_m\, G,$$

where H is the centroid of the liquids displaced by the body.

$$\therefore \sum_1^n P_m\, v_m\, H_m\, G = (HG)\, M_o$$

M_o being the mass of the liquids displaced by the body.

Hence the total moment of the couple is

$$g \left\{ \sum_1^n P_m\, A_m\, k_m{}^2 - M_o\, (HG) \right\} \theta.$$

The case of a heterogeneous liquid whose density varies continuously is immediately deduced from this by dividing the liquid into an infinite member of infinitely thin layers.

Let the functional relation between P at any point and its depth z below the horizontal surface of flotation be given by

$$P = f(z).$$

Considering two consecutive layers of density $P_1 + P_2 + \ldots P_{n-1}$, and $P_1 + P_2 + \ldots P_r$ at depths z and z and $z+dz$ we see that P_r, thedifference between their densities,

$$= f(z+dz) - f(z)$$
$$= \frac{df}{dz} dz$$

Hence in the limit the expression

$$\sum_1^n P_m A_m k^2_m = P_1 A_1 k_1{}^2 + \sum_2^m P_m A_m k_m{}^2$$

$$= P_1 A_1 k_1{}^2 + \int_0^h (A k^2) \frac{df}{dz} \, dz,$$

where h is the depth of the lower most layer.

Moment of the restoring couple is

$$g\theta \left\{ P_1 A_1 k_1{}^2 + \int_0^h A k^2 \frac{df}{dz} dz - M_0 HG \right\}$$

For stability of equilibrium, we must have

$$P_1 A_1 k_1{}^2 + \int_0^h A k^2 \frac{df}{dz} dz > M_0 HG$$

or, $HG < \dfrac{P_1 A_1 k_1{}^2 + \int_0^h A\, k^2 \frac{df}{dz}\, dz}{M_0}$

$\therefore$ Metacentric height $\quad HM = \left\{ P_1 A_1 k_1{}^2 + \int_0^h A k^2 \frac{df}{dz} dz \right\} \dfrac{1}{M_0}$

Remark : $P_1 A_1 k_1{}^2 + \int_0^h A k^2 \frac{df}{dz} dz$

$$= P_1 A_1 k_1{}^2 + [A k^2 f]_0^h - \int_0^h f\, d(A k^2)$$

$$= A_h k_h{}^2 P_h - \int_o^h P d(A k^2).$$

$$= - \int_o^h P d (A k^2) = \int_h^o P d (A k^2)$$

if the solid does not have a flat bottom.

Hence for solids without a flat bottom, metacentric height

$$H\ M = \frac{1}{M_o} \int_h^o P d(A k^2)$$ the limits o and h refer to the top and

and bottom sections.

Ex. 1. Show that in order that the equilibrium of a right circular cone of semi vertical angle α floating in a liquid whose density is directly proportional to the depth, be stable $\cos^2 \alpha$

$$< \frac{4h'}{5h}$$ where h' is the length of the axis immersed and h is the

height of the cone.

Here sections by horizontal planes are circles. Consider a section by a plane distant z from the vertex. Then.

$$A = \pi (z \tan \alpha)^2, \quad k^2 = \frac{z^2 \tan^2 \alpha}{4}$$

$$\therefore A k^2 = \frac{\pi}{4} z^4 \tan^4 \alpha.$$

The required condition of stable equilibrium is

$$H\,G < \frac{\int_o^{h'} P d \left(\frac{\pi}{4} z^4 \tan^4 \alpha\right)}{\int_o^{h'} P (\pi z^2 \tan^2 \alpha)\, dz}$$

$$< \tan^2 \alpha \frac{\int_o^{h'} P z^3 dz}{\int_o^{h'} P z^2 dz}$$

$$< \frac{3}{5} h' \tan^2 \alpha.\ \text{since } P = \mu (h' - z)$$

$$\text{Also } H\,G = \tfrac{3}{4}\,h - \frac{\int_{0}^{h'} z\,(\pi \rho z^{2}\,\tan^{2}\alpha)\,dz}{\int_{0}^{h'} \pi\,z^{2}\,\tan^{2}\alpha\,\rho\,dz}$$

$$= \frac{3}{4}\,h - \frac{3h'}{5}.$$

Hence the required condition is

$$\frac{3}{4}\,h < \frac{3}{5}\,(1+\tan^{2}\alpha)h' = \frac{3}{5}\,h'\,\sec^{2}\alpha$$

$$\text{or, } \cos^{2}\alpha < \frac{4}{5}\,\frac{h'}{h},$$

Ex. 2. Determine the condition of stability of a solid homogeneous cylinder of radius a under the same circumstances.

$$[\text{Ans. } a^{2} \gg h'(h - \tfrac{2}{3}\,h')].$$

Ex. 3. A heavy homogeneous cube is completely immersed with two faces horizontal in a fluid whose density $=k$ times the cube of the depth. Prove that the meta-centric height is $k\,\dfrac{a^{7}}{120M}$, where M is the mass and a the length of an edge of the cube.

Ex. 4. Find the metacentric height in the case of a solid of a revolution formed by the revolution of a curve $y = f(x)$ about x — axis, floating with vertex downwards in a liquid whose density at depth z is $\phi(z)$. The length of the axis immersed is h'.

$$\text{Ans } \frac{\int_{0}^{h'} \phi(h'-x)\,f^{3}\,f'\,dx}{\int_{0}^{h'} \phi(h'-x)\,f^{2}\,dx}$$

Ex. 5. If the meta-centric height in the above example is constant whatever be the law of density of the liquid show that the solid is a paraboloid of revolution.

Ex. 6. A paraboloid of revolution floats with its axis vertical and vertex downwards in a liquid whose density varies as the depth; the equilibrium will be stable or unstable according as $4\,h <$ or $> 3\,(4\,a + h')$, where h is the length of the axis, $4\,a$ the latus rectum of the generating parabola, and h' the length of the axis immersed.

Ex. 7. An oblate spheroid floats half immersed with its axis vertical, in a liquid whose density varies as the square of the depth. Prove that the height of the meta-centre above the surface is $\dfrac{5}{8}\dfrac{a^2 - b^2}{b}$.

(Apply Ex. 4.)

Miscellaneous Examples.

Ex. 1. A uniform right circular cone of weight W floats with its axis vertical and vertex downwards in a homogeneous liquid which is contained in a circular cylinder of radius r with vertical axis; the cone in equilibrium displaces a volume $\pi\, r^2\, h$ of the liquid and its vertex is at a depth h below the surface. The cone is slowly lifted just clear of the liquid, its axis being kept vertical; prove that work done is

$$\tfrac{1}{4}\,W\,(3\,h - 2\,h').$$

(M. A. Punjab Univ. 1935

Ex. 2. If W be the weight of a body and V the volume of the part immersed in a liquid contained in a fixed vase. Prove that if the floating body be lowered vertically a small distance $\delta\,S$, the centre of gravity of the liquid contained in the vase rises by the quantity $\dfrac{g\rho\, V\delta S}{W'}$

W', being the weight of the contained liquid and ρ its density.

Ex. 3. Deduce by means of the above result the principle of Archimedes from the theorem that the height of the common centre of gravity of the solid and liquid must be a maximum or minimum.

Ex. 4. A life belt in the form of an anchor-ring generated by a circle of radius a floats in water with its equatorial plane horizontal; shew that, z the depth immersed, is given by

$$z = a (1 - \cos \alpha)$$

$$2 \pi s = (2 \alpha - \sin 2 \alpha),$$

s being the specific gravity of the material of the belt.

Ex 5. An isosceles triangular lamina ABC right angled at C floats with its plane vertical and the angle C immersed in a liquid of which the density varies as depth. Prove that if $\frac{\pi}{4} + \theta$ be the angle which AB makes with the vertical in either of the positions in which AB is not horizontal, the value of θ is given by

$$m \sin^2 \theta \cos^2 \theta = (\sin \theta + \cos \theta)^3.$$

(I. C. S. Higher Mathematics 1933)

Ex. 6. A homogeneous solid body consisting of a hemisphere of radius a with its plane face attached to one end of a circular cylinder of radius a and length a floats in equilibrium in a homogeneous liquid. The axis of symmetry of the body is vertical and the cylindrical portion is uppermost. The length of the cylindrical portion immersed is $\frac{3}{4} a$. Find the position of the metacentre and determine whether the equilibrium is stable or unstable

(Tripos Part 1 1938)

(Ans. $\dfrac{27a}{190}$ from the centre of the hemisphere.)

Ex 7. Prove that if the equilibrium of a solid cone floating with its vertex downwards and axis vertical is neutral for an infinitesimal displacement, it is really stable for any finite displacement

CHAPTER V.

Gases.

5. 1. We have seen that what distinguishes a liquid from a gas is its compressibility. A perfect fluid which is absolutely in practice nearly) incompressible is called a liquid. A perfect fluid which is compressible is called a gas. We shall now describe some of the more important properties of compressible fluids or gases.

5 2. Torricelli's Experiment. Take a glass tube about 3 ft. long open at one end and closed at the other. Fill it with mercury and invert it in a vessel of mercury so as to immerse its open end. It will be noticed that mercury in the tube will fall until the height of the column is about 30 inches If A be any point on the level surface of the mercury in the vessel and Q be

a point in the same level inside the tube, we know that pressures at A and Q must be equal. Now pressure at A is the pressure of atmosphere π and the pressure at Q is that of a column of mercury of height PQ, i. e. $g\sigma$ PQ, σ being the density of mercury. since the pressure at P is zero.

Hence $\pi = g\sigma$ (PQ).

This simple apparatus was first devised by Torricelli and is known as barometer. Clearly we may take the height PQ of the column of mercury as a measure of atmospheric pressure. We may also use any other liquid such as water. Since the density of mercury is about 13. 5 times that of water, the height of a water barometer will be about $13\frac{1}{2} \times 30$ inches, or $33\frac{3}{4}$ ft.

Ex. Prove that the barometeric heights to which liquids rise are inversely proportional to their densities.

5.3 Laws of Boyle and Dalton

Consider a given mass of gas enclosed in a volume. If we neglect the weight of the gas its pressure at any point of the enclosure is given by $dp = o$.

It is, therefore, the same at all points and is equal to whatever value it has at the surface. Whenever a given mass of gas in an enclosure is said to be at pressure p, it is this constant pressure that is referred to.

Now the volume of the gas may be altered by compression or dilation i. e. change of pressure, keeping temperature constant, or by a change of temperature keeping pressure constant, or by a change of pressure and temperature simultaneously. The law governing the change of volume and pressure when temperature remains constant was first discoverd by Robert Boyle. He showed that the pressure of the gas varies inversely as the volume of the enclosure provided the temperature remains constant.

Thus $pv = $ const.

Since density ρ of of the gas varies inversely as the volume, it follows that pressure varies directly as the density so that

$$\frac{p}{\rho} = \text{const.}$$

The law relating to the change of volume consequent upon a change of temparature, (pressure remaining constant), was discovered independently by Charles, Dalton and Gay Lussac. They found that:—

" If pressure remain constant, an increase of temperature of $1°C$ produces in a mass of gas an expansion $\frac{1}{273}$ of its volume at $0C$."

Thus let v_o be the volume of the gas at $o°C$ and let v_t be its volume at $t°C$, then

$$v_t = v_o\left(1 + \frac{t}{273}\right) = v_o\,\frac{(273+t)}{273}$$

pressure p remaining constant

Similarly, $v_t' = v_o\left(\frac{273+t'}{273}\right)$

so that $\dfrac{v_t}{273+t} = \dfrac{v_t'}{273+t'}$.

If we define 'absolute temperature' of the gas by the relation

$$T = 273 + t, \qquad\qquad (1)$$

it follows that if pressure remain constant, the volume of the gas varies directly as its absolute temperature,

i. e. $\dfrac{v}{T} = $ const.

We shall now deduce the law of change of volume, when both temperature and pressure vary. Let $(p,\ v,\ T)$ be the pressure, volume, and 'absolute temperature' of the gas. Let us keep T constant and change pressure to p', so that by Boyle's law, the volume changes to $\dfrac{pv}{p'}$

If we now alter the temperature T to T' we have by Dalton's law

$$\frac{v'}{T'} = \frac{p\,v}{p'\,T},$$

where v' is the new volume.

$$\therefore \frac{pv}{T} = \frac{p'v'}{T'} = \text{cons.}$$

The equation

$$\frac{pv}{T} = \text{const.}$$

satisfied by the pressure, temperature, and volume of the gas is known as its *equation of state.*

Experiment, however, shows that not all gases obey this equation accurately and even those which do, do so only approximately for certain ranges of temperature and pressure, beyond which the relation is no longer satisfied   A gas which obeys the equation of state

$$\frac{pv}{T} = \text{const.}$$

is known as an 'ideal' or 'perfect' gas.   Various equations of state for imperfect gases have been formulared but the best known is that given by Van der Waal

$$\frac{1}{T} \left(p + \frac{a}{v^2} \right) (v - b) = const,$$

where a, b are constants for the same mass of gas, but depend on the amount of gas as well as on its nature.

5 4   Nature of Gas Pressure.

The nature of this pressure is best understood on the basis of Kinetic Theory of Gases.   According to this theory the molecules of a gas are in a state of incessant motion describing rectilinear paths with uniform velocity except when they encounter other molecules or the walls of the enclosure- The pressure of the gas on a small element of a wall of the enclosure is due to the continual impacts of the molecules on it. So also the pressure at any other point of the volume is the result of molecular impacts on a small area imagined to be placed at the point.   With the help of certain appropriate assumptions it can be shown that when the gas is in a steady state, the pressure due to molecular impacts on any element of the wall of the enclosure or on any plane element imagined elsewhere is the same, being equal to

$$\frac{1}{3} \frac{Nm\,\overline{c^2}}{v},$$

where N is the number of molecules of the gas in the enclosure, m the mass of a molecule, $\bar{c}^2$ the mean square velocity ie the mean value of c^2, where c is the velocity of a molecule, and v is the volume of the enclosure. Now according to the fundamental hypothesis of Kinetic Theory the temperature of the gas depends only on its mean square velocity, so that if temperature remains constant, so would $\bar{c}^2$. Hence if temperature of the gas remains constant, its pressure varies inversely as the volume. Thus Kinetic Theory gives a simple explanation of Boyle's Law. Indeed Kinetic Theory postulates the relation

$$\tfrac{1}{3} m \ c^2 = RT, \qquad \ldots \qquad .. \qquad (1)$$

where R is a universal gas constant, the same for all gases, and T is its absolute temperature.

We have therefore,

$$p = \frac{NRT}{v}$$

$$\text{or,} \quad \frac{pv}{T} = NR = const \quad .. \qquad . \qquad (2)$$

It will be seen that we have tacitly assumed the identity of 'absolute temperature' as defined by equation (1) of § 5.3, with the 'absolute temperature' of the Kinetic Theory as defined by relation (1) of this article. This identification is justifi d in works on Kinetic Theory of Gases.

In establishing the formula quoted above for the pressure exerted on the walls of an enclosure Kinetic Theory assumes the molecules to. be spherical points devoid of size and shape. It further assumes that the forces of cohesion between the molecules are non-existent. In any real gas, however, the molecules must have size and shape. Nor will the forces of cohesion be entirely negligible. Hence it comes about that the equation of state (2) which is accurately satisfied in the case of an ideal gas will only be approximately satisfied when applied to a real gas. It can be shown that the equation of state, which takes into account the size of the molecules and the cohesive forces between them is Van der Waal's Equation

$$\left(p + \frac{a}{v^2} \right)(v - b) = RNT,$$

where a, b are constants for the same mass of gas, but depend on its nature and amount, R is a universal gas constant, and N is the number of molecules of the gas in the enclosure.

5. 5. Mixture of Ideal Gases.

If two enclosures containing two gases at the same pressure and temperature are connected together, the molecules of one gas diffuse into those of the other until they are completely mixed provided there is no chemical action between the gases. The volume of the mixture is the sum of the volumes of the enclosures, its pressure and temperature being the same as those of the constituent gases. It is easy to deduce from this experimental fact that

"If two volumes V_1, V_2 of different ideal gases at pressures p_1, p_2 and absolute temperatures T_1, T_2 are mixed together, the volume V, the pressure p, and absolute temperature T, of the mixture are connected by the relation.

$$\frac{pV}{T} = \frac{p_1 V_1}{T_1} + \frac{p_2 V_2}{T_2}.$$

If the temeprature T_1 and pressure p_1 of the first gas be changed to T and p respectively, its volume will become

$$\frac{p_1 V_1}{T_1} \frac{T}{p};$$

similarly the volume of the second gas at temperature T and pressure p will be

$$\frac{p_2 V_2}{T_2} \frac{T}{p}.$$

Now if two gases of volumes $\dfrac{p_1 V_1}{T_1} \dfrac{T}{p}$ and $\dfrac{T}{p} \dfrac{p_2 V_2}{T_2}$

respectively at the same temperature and pressure be mixed, the volume V of the mixture at the temperature T and pressure p will be

$$\left(\frac{p_1 V_1}{T_1} + \frac{p_2 V_2}{T_2}\right)\frac{T}{p}$$

Hence $\dfrac{pV}{T} = \dfrac{p_1 V_1}{T_1} + \dfrac{p_2 V_2}{T_2}$

The result can obviously be extended to a mixture of any number of gases.

5. 6. Isothermals.

For an ideal gas the relation between pressure, volume and temperature is expressed by the equation

$$pv = RNT \qquad \ldots \qquad (1)$$

If we take p, v as rectangular axes and draw the various curves by giving to T different constant values in the above equation, these curves are known as the isothermals of an ideal gas. The isothermals of an ideal gas are plainly rectangular hyperbolas.

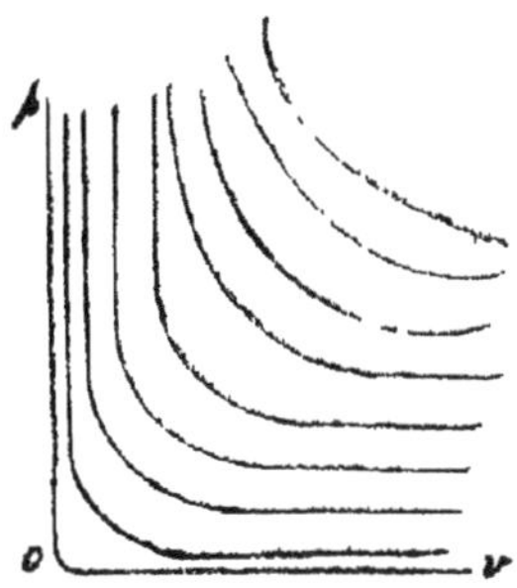

For a real gas, the isothermals are the system of curves obtained by assigning constant value to T in Van der Waal's equation

$$\left(p + \frac{a}{v^2}\right)(v - b) = RNT \qquad \ldots \qquad \ldots \qquad (2)$$

These isothermals have been traced in the figure below.

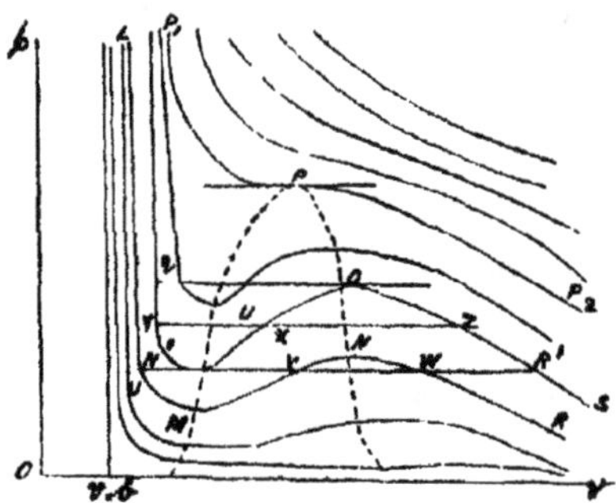

Differentiating (2) with respect to v, we have

$$\left(\frac{dp}{dv}-\frac{2a}{v^3}\right)(v-b)+\left(p+\frac{a}{v^2}\right)=0.$$

Hence the locus of the points of the isothermals at which $\frac{dp}{dv}=0,$—i. e. the points of the isothermals where the tangents are parallel to v—axis,—is a curve

$$p=\frac{a(v-2b)}{v^3} \qquad \cdots \qquad \cdots \qquad (3)$$

This curve MPN is traced in the figure. It is easy to see that the curve MPN has the maximum ordinate at the point P whose coordinates are $\left(3b,\ \frac{a}{27b^2}\right)$. The isothermal through P clearly corresponds to a value of T which is given by

$$NRT=\frac{8}{27}\ \frac{a}{b} \qquad \cdots \qquad \cdots \qquad (4)$$

This isothermal is repesented by P_1PP_2 in the figure. The curve M P N intersects an isothermal corresponding to a value of T which is less than that given by equation (4) in two points M, N. Thus there are two points of the isothermal at which curve MPN cuts it. As we move closer towards the isothermal

P_1PP_2 the two points M and N come closer and closer till they coincide with the point P. The curve MPN, therefore, meets the isothermal P_1PP_2 in two coincident points. Since at every common point of this isothermal and the curve M P N

$$\frac{dp}{dv} = 0, \quad \frac{d^2p}{dv^2} = o \text{ at P for the isothermal.}$$

The isothermal therefore has a point of inflexion at P, the tangent at which is horizontal.

The curve MPN, however, does not intersect any isothermal which corressponds to a value of T exceeding that given by equation (4). All such isothermals are therefore everywhere convex to the axis of v. Consider now again an isothermal lying below P_1PP_2 such as L MNR. The curve MPN interesects

it in two points M and N, at which therefore $\frac{dp}{dv} = o$.

Take any point V on the isothermal lying between M and N. Draw through it a line parallel to v-axis. It meets the isothermal in two other points U and W. It is then clear that the points U, V, W represent the states of the substance having the same pressure and temperature We shall now show that the state represented by the point V is unstable, and therefore

incapable of actual realization. At the point V, $\frac{dp}{dv}$ is positive,

it accordingly represents a state such that a decrease in volume, keeping temperature constant, is accompanied by a decrease in pressure. When therefore a slight *increase* in external pressure decreases the volume of the gas in the state represented by V the pressure of the gas also decreases. There is therefore an unbalanced external pressure which tends to decrease the volume still further. The state represented by V is, therefore, unstable. Since V was taken arbitrarily anywhere between points M and N of the isothermal LMNR, every point of the isothermal lying between M and N represents an unstable state. At points

U and W, $\frac{dp}{dv}$ is negative, so that the states represented by them are stable. The point W obviously represents the gaseous state and the point U corresponding to lesser volume is believed to represent the liquid state. With this interpretation it follows immediately that a gas, whose temperature is kept above that of the isothermal P_1PP_2 cannot be liquefied by any amount of compression. The temperature of the isothermal $P_1 P P_2$ is known as the critical temperature of the subs'ance

"So long as the temperature is above the critical temperature, no pressure, however great, can liquefy the gas."

A substance in the gaseous state whose temperature exceeds its 'critical temperature' is a 'gas', whereas if it is below its critical temperature it is called a vapour.

The laws enunciated in the preceding articles are equally true of vapours.

Point P of the isothermal $P_1 P P_2$ is known as the critical point of the gas. The values v_c, p_c, and T_c corresponding to this point are known as critical volume, critical pressure and critical temperature. We have already seen that

$$v_c = 3b, \; p_c = \frac{a}{27b^2}, \; R \, N \, T_c = \frac{8a}{27b}.$$

If we adopt critical volume, critical pressure and critical temprature as the units of volume, pressure, and temperature the equation of state assumes a simple form, which is known as the "reduced equation of state". Denoting volume, pressure, and temperature by $\bar{v}$, $\bar{p}$, $\bar{T}$ respectively we have

$$\bar{v} = \frac{v}{v_c}, \; \bar{p} = \frac{p}{p_c}, \; \bar{T} = \frac{T}{T_c}.$$

so that $v = 3 \, b \; \bar{v}$, $p = \frac{a}{27b^2} \, \bar{p}$, $R \, N \, T = \frac{8a}{27b} \bar{T}$

Substituting these values in (2) the equation of state reduces to

$$\left(\bar{p} + \frac{3}{\bar{v}^2} \right) \left(v - 1 \right) = \frac{8}{3} \bar{T}$$

This equation is the same for all gases, for the quantities a and b which vary from one gas to another, have entirely disappeared. It is known as the reduced equation of State of Van der Waal.

Ex 1. The tube of a barometer rises to $34''$ above the mercury in the trough, and the mercury column is $30''$ high. Find what changes are produced in the height of the column by the following operations successively performed : —

(i As much air is allowed to rise through the mercury as would at atmospheric pressure occupy $2''$ of the tube.

(ii) A rod of iron whose volume equals $5''$ of the tube is allowed to float at the top of the mercury column.

(Take the specific gravities of mercury and iron as 13.5 and 7.5 respectively .

Let the height of the mercury column be x'' after the operation (i). The volume of air enclosed in the tube above the mercury column is therefore $A(34-x)''$, A being the cross section of the tube. If the pressure of the the air is p, we have by Boyle's law, since its volume at atmospheric pressure Π is 2 A, $A(34-x)p = 2\,A\,\Pi$

$$\text{or, } p = \frac{2\Pi}{34-x} \qquad \ldots \qquad \ldots \qquad (1)$$

But the pressure p and the pressure of the column x of mercury must be equal to the atmospheric pressure.

$$\therefore\ p + g P x = \Pi,$$

where P is the density of mercury.

Now $\Pi = g P (30)$, since the length of the column under atmospheric pressure is $30''$, whe have from (1)

$$\frac{2(30)\,gP}{34-x} + gP\ x = gP(30)$$

$$\text{or, } x^2 - 64x + 960 = 0$$

Hence $x = 24''$, $40''/$.

Clearly the second solution $40''$ is inadmissible.

Hence the mercury column will fall by $6''$.

Let the length of the column after the operation (ii) as well be x_1.

Let α be the coss section of the iron rod and l its total length. Then

$$l\,\alpha = 5A \qquad \ldots \qquad \ldots \qquad \ldots \qquad (2)$$

The volume of iron immersed in mercury

$$= \frac{7\cdot 5}{13.5}\, l\alpha = \frac{5}{9}\, l\alpha$$

$\therefore$ Volume of iron unimmersed $= \dfrac{4}{9}\, l\alpha$

Now if the height of the mercury column be x_1 inches, the volume occupied by air

$$= (34 - x_1)\, A - \frac{4}{9}\, l\alpha$$

$$= (34 - x_1)\, A - \frac{20}{9}\, A \qquad \ldots \qquad \ldots\text{by}(2)$$

The pressure of the air is by Boyle's law

$$\frac{\pi 2A}{(34 - x_1)\, A - \dfrac{20}{9}\, A} = \frac{2\pi}{34 - x_1 - \dfrac{20}{9}}$$

Now the pressure at the top of the trough is

$$g^{\rho}x + \frac{2\pi}{34 - x_1 - \dfrac{20}{9}} = \pi$$

or, $g\,(13.5)\,x_1 + \dfrac{2\,(30g)\,(13\cdot5)}{34 - x_1 - \dfrac{20}{9}} = 30g\,(13\cdot15)$

or, $x_1 + \dfrac{540}{286 - 9x_1} = 30$

or, $(9x_1 - 286)(30 - x_1) + 540 = o$

$$\therefore x_1 = 23 \frac{1}{9} \text{ inches appro } x.$$

There is accordingly a further fall of approximately $\frac{3}{8}''$ in the mercury column.

Ex. 2. A diving bell is suspended in water at a fixed depth below the upper surface of water. The area of the surface of water within the bell is A. There is in the bell a volume pA of air under a pressure h as measured on the water barometer scale. A small object of volume A a and of specific gravity σ falls from a shelf inside the bell and floats on the enclosed water. Show that x the resulting rise in the level of the enclosed water satisfies the equation

$$x^2 - x(h + p + o\sigma) + ha\sigma = o.$$

Will the bell contain less or more water than before?

(I. C. S. 1927)

Ex. 3. A canister of weight W without a lid, made of uniform thin material in the form of a right circular cylinder of radius a and height h is inverted and sunk in water, the whole of air originally in it being imprisoned. Shew that when the canister is in equilibrium with its axis vertical, the height of the air column is $\dfrac{h\,H}{H + \sigma h}$, and that the water level inside is at a depth σh below the level outside, where $\sigma = \dfrac{W}{\pi a^2 hw}$, w being the weight of unit volume of water and H, the height of water barometer.

Show that the canister is stable in this position only if the centre of gravity is below the centre of gravity of the displaced water, that is, if

$$\frac{a}{2h} < \frac{\sigma h (1 + \sigma) - H(1 - \sigma)}{H(2 - \sigma) - \sigma^2 h}$$

(Tripos, 1932).

Ex. 4. A circular cone, hollow but of great weight is lowered into the sea by a rope attached to its vertex; prove that the depth of the level of water inside the cone when the vertex is at a given depth c below the surface is given by

$$x^4 + (k+c)\, x^3 - k\, h^3 = o,$$

where h is the height of the cone and k is the height of water barometer.

Ex. 5. A cylinderical diving bell sinks in water until a certain portion V remains occupied by air and in this position a quantity of air, whose volume under atmospheric pressure was $2\,V$ is forced into it. Show how far the bell must sink in order that the air may occupy the same space as in the first position.

(I. C. S. Lower 1932)

(Ans. Twice the height of water barometer).

Ex. 6. Two bulbs containing air are connected by a horizoutal glass tube of uniform bore, and a bubble of liquid in this tube separates the air into two equal quantities. The bubble is then displaced by heating the bulbs to absolute temperatures T and T'; prove that if the temperature of each bulb be decreased t degrees the bubble will receive an additional displacement which bears to the original displacement the ratio of

$$2\,t : (T + T' - 2t).$$

Let V be the volume of any one of the bulbs, and v the volume of the tube AO, when the bubble is at the middle point of the tube so that air on both sides of the bubble is at the same pressure and

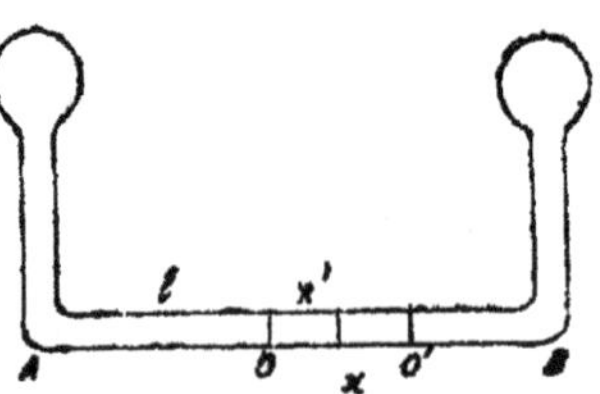

volume and consequently also at the same temperature (T).

Let the bubble move from O to O', when the temperature of one of the bulbs is changed to T'. Let $OO' = x$. Since the bubble is in equilibrium the pressure p on the two sides must be equal.

The volume, pressure and absolute temperature of air to the left of the bubble are $V + \alpha\,(l+x)$, p, T, where α is the cross section of the tube.

Corresponding quantities for air to the right of the bubble are $V - \alpha\,'l - x)$, p, T'

Hence by Boyle's and Gay Lussac's Laws

$$p\frac{V+\alpha\,(l+x}{\mathsf{T}} = p\frac{V+\alpha\,(l-x)}{\mathsf{T}'}$$

or, $V(T-T') + l\alpha\,(T-T') = \alpha x\,(T+T')$ .. (1)

If the temperature be now changed to $T-t$ and $T'-t$, respectively, the displacement OO'' will be x' given by

$$V(T-T') + l\alpha\,(T-T') = \alpha x'\,(T+T'-2t) \quad ... \quad (2)$$

Substracting 2) from (1)

$$2\,tx = (x'-r)(T+T'-2t)$$

$$\therefore \frac{x'-x}{x} = \frac{2t}{T+T'-2t}$$

Ex. 7. A pressure guage consists of a U—tube of uniform bore containing mercury, one arm of the tube being closed at the top and containing 15 c. c of air at atmospheric pressure, and the other arm being connected to the receiver of a condenser Initially the pressure of the receiver is atmospheric and by working of the condenser, the volume of the air in the guage is reduced to $3\cdot5$ c c. and the mercury is 15 cm. Find the pressure in the receiver Assume that the height of a mercury barometer is 760 mm. and that the temperature in the guage is unaltered.

(Ans. Approximately 4.68 atmosphere)

Ex. 8. The lengths of the arms of a siphon measured vertically are h, k ($h > k$). The siphon is filled with liquid of density σ greater than the density ρ of the liquid in the v-ssel. Prove that the siphon will begin to work with the end of the longer arm immersed in the liquid in the vessel provided the depth of that end below the surface of the liquid in the vessel exceeds $(h-k)\ \dfrac{\sigma}{\rho}$.

Let A B O O' C be the siphon filled with a liquid of density σ. Let the arm O B A $= k$ be immersed in the liquid of density ρ contained in a vessel.

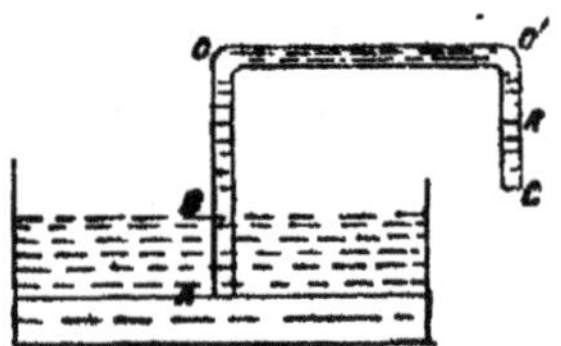

Pressure at A of the liquid in the vessel is

$g\rho\ d + \pi$, where $d = $AB, and π is atmospheric pressure.

Plainly pressure at A of the liquid in the siphon is $g\sigma h$

$$\therefore \pi = g(\sigma h - \rho d) \qquad \ldots \qquad \ldots \qquad \ldots \quad (1)$$

Pressure at C is $g\sigma k$. The siphon will work only if $g\sigma k > \pi$

or $g\sigma k > g(\sigma h - \rho d)$

or, $d > \dfrac{\sigma}{\rho}(h - k)$,

Ex. 9. The figure illustrates a siphon for drawing water from a cask. The lengths of pipe DB, B A are 40 and 160 inches respectively. The end A is initially closed and the pipe from A to C filled with water, the air enclosed being at atmospheric pressure. The end A is then opened and as water level in C A decreases the level in D B rises. If a balance is obtained just before the water has risen to B. what length of water will

Show that the siphon cannot be started by the process descibed above if the initial length of water in the arm A C is less than 120 inches.

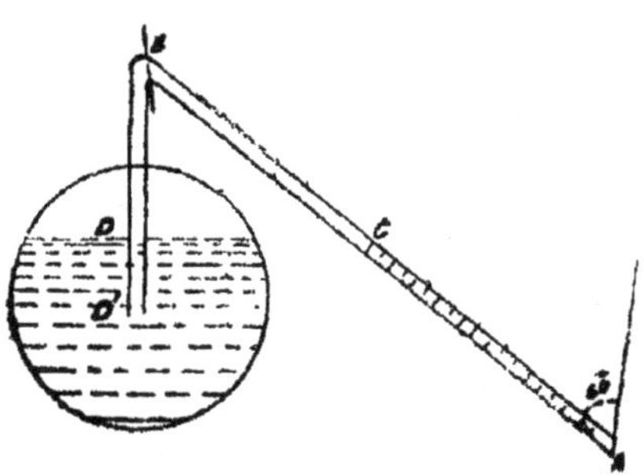

Let A C $= y$ and let x be the length of water that runs out by the time water in D B rises up to B when equilibium is reached.

If p be the pressure of the air in the equilibrium position, pressure at A would be

$$p + g\rho\,(y - x)\,\cos 60^\circ = \Pi,$$

for otherwise the liquid at A will not be in equilibrium.

Here Π is atmospheric pressure.

Likewise pressure at D will be $p + g\rho\ (DB) = p + g\rho\ (36) = \Pi.$

$$p + g\rho\,(y - x)\,\cos 60^\circ = p + g\rho\,(36)$$

or, $y - x = 72''.$

Thus length of water that will remain in the arm is 72".

Also by Boyle's Law

$$p (160-y+x)a = \pi (160+40-y) \alpha,$$

α being the cross section of the tube

$$\text{But } p = \pi - g P \text{ (DB)}$$
$$= g P (12) (33) - g P (36)$$
$$= g P (12) (30).$$

Substituting for p and $y-x$ in the above

$$g P (12) (30) (160-72) = g P (12) (33' (200-y)$$

or, $y = 120"$.

Ex. 10. One end of a siphon is immersed in a liquid whose density at any point is proportional to the nth power of the depth below the surface, the highest point of the siphon being at the level of the free surface of the liquid, and the siphon is filled with homogeneous liquid whose density is equal to that at the immersed end. Prove that liquid will flow at the free end of the siphon even if it be above the level of the immersed end provided

(i) that the vertical distance of the free end above the immersed be less than $\dfrac{1}{n}$ th of the vertical distance of the former below the surface of the liquid; and

(ii) that the atmospheric pressure exceeds $\left(\dfrac{n}{n+1}\right)$ of the pressure at the immersed end.

5. 7. Work done by the pressure of a gas in expansion:

Let us consider a gas enclosed in an expansible envelope. Its pressure on each element, $d S$ of the envelope is continually pushing the element $d S$ outwards along

the normal to it. Hence when the volume of the gas increases, a certain amount of work is done by the pressure on the various elements. Taking the element $d\,S$ at P, the work done by pressure p will be $pdS.\,\delta n$, where δn is the small length PP′ taken along the normal at P. Hence the total work done in the small displace ment produced by the movement of every small elem ent of the surface a distance δn normally outwards is.

$$\Sigma\, pdS.\,\delta n$$

Since the pressure p is the same at every point of the surface of the enclosure, we have

$$\Sigma\, pdS.\ \delta n = p\,\Sigma\, dS\,(\delta n)$$
$$= pdr,$$

where dv is the total change in volume by the displacement δn of every element of the envelope.

Hence work dW done by the pressure of the gas in expanding from A BC to A B′C′ is given by

$$d\,W = pdr.$$

Total work done by the pressure of a gas on its envelope in expanding from an initial volume v_0 to v, is, therefore, given by

$$W = \int_{v_0}^{v_1} pdv.$$

In the particular case of isothermal expansion of an ideal gas we have

$$pv = \text{const.}$$

$$\therefore\, W = \int_{v_0}^{v_1} \frac{c}{v}\,dv = c\,\log\,\frac{v_1}{v_2} = pv\,\log\frac{v_1}{v_0}$$

In the case of an actual gas, where the pressure and volume in an isothermal expansion are connected together by Van der Waal's relation

$$(p + \frac{a}{v^2})(v-b) = c,$$

we have

$$W = \int \left[\frac{c}{v-b} - \frac{a}{v^2} \right] dv$$

$$= \left[c \log (v-b) + \frac{a}{v} \right]_{v_0}^{v^1}$$

$$= c \log \frac{v_1-b}{v_0-b} + a(\frac{1}{v_1} - \frac{1}{v_0})$$

$$= (p + \frac{a}{v^2})(v-b) \log \frac{v_1-b}{v_0-b} + a(\frac{1}{v_1} - \frac{1}{v_0})$$

Ex. 1. A piston of weight w rests in a vertical cylinder of transverse section k, being supported by a depth a of air. The rod receives a vertical blow p, which forces the piston down through a distance h; prove tha'

$$(w + \pi k) \left\{ h + a \log \frac{a-h}{a} \right\} + \frac{gp^2}{2w} = 0'$$

π being atmospheric pressure. The temperature of air is assumed to remain constant.

When a blow p is imparted to the piston, it starts moving at once with a velocity u given by

$$\frac{w}{g} u = p$$

Hence the Kinetic energy generated is $\frac{1}{2} (\frac{w}{g}) u^2 = \frac{1}{2} \frac{gp^2}{w}$

Further a force $(\pi k + w)$ acts on the piston downwards and if it moves a distance h before coming to rest, work done by this force is $(\pi k + w) h$.

(160)

Hence the work done in compressing air in the cylinder must be equal to $\frac{1}{2}\ \dfrac{g\mathrm{P}^2}{w}+(\Pi k+w)h.$

Now the initial volume of the air in the cylinder is ka, final being $k\,(a-h)$. Since the piston is at rest originally thrust of the atmospheric pressure on the piston and the weight of the piston must balance the thrust of the pressure of the air below, so that $\Pi\,k+w=pk$,

p being the pressure of the air in the cylinder. As the gas is compressed isothermally work done on it is given by

$$-\int_{ka}^{k(a-h)}pdv$$

$$=-\int_{ka}^{k(a-h)}\frac{cdv}{v}=-\frac{(\Pi k+w)}{k}\,ak\,\log\frac{a-h}{a}$$

$$=-(\Pi k+w)\,a\,\log\frac{a-h}{a}.$$

Hence we have

$$\frac{g\mathrm{P}^2}{2w}+(\Pi k+w)\,l=-(\Pi k+w)\,a\,\log\left(\frac{a-h}{a}\right)$$

which gives the required result.

Ex. 2. A piston without weight fits into a vertical cylinder, closed at its base and filled with air, and is initially at the top of the cylinder; if water be slowly poured on the top of the piston, show that the upper surface of the water will be lowest when the depth of the water is $(\sqrt{ah}-h)$, where h is the height of the water barometer and a the height of the cylinder.

Ex. 3. An ideal gas is compressed to $\dfrac{1}{n}$th of its original volume and in this process the relation of pressure to volume is expressed by $pv^\gamma = $ const., where γ has a constant value. It is then cooled at constant volume to its original temperature. Finally it is expanded at this constant temperature to its original volume. Show that the net energy expended on the gas in this cycle (i. e. work done on the gas) is k times the work done in compression, where

$$k = 1 - \frac{(\gamma - 1) \log n}{n^{\gamma - 1} - 1}$$

Let the initial volume, pressure and absolute temperature of the gas be v_1, p_1, T_1 respectively. Work done on the gas in compressing it to the volume $\frac{v_1}{n}$ is given by

$$W = - \int_{v_1}^{v_1/n} p\, dv.$$

Since during the compression

$$pv^\gamma = c = p_1 v_1^\gamma$$

$$W = - \int \frac{c}{v^\gamma}\, dv = \frac{p_1 v_1}{\gamma - 1} \left[n^{\gamma - 1} - 1 \right]$$

Let the temperature of the gas in the new condition be T_1'. Now pressure p_1' in the new state is given by

$$p_1' \left(\frac{v_1}{n} \right)^\gamma = p_1 v_1^\gamma$$

$$\text{or, } p_1' = n^\gamma p_1$$

Since $\frac{pv}{T}$ is constant for an ideal gas, it follows that

$$\frac{p_1'(v_1)}{T_1' \, n} = \frac{p_1 v_1}{T_1}$$

so that $T_1' = n^{\gamma-1} T_1$.

The gas is, therefore, at pressure, $n^\gamma p_1$ temperature $n^{\gamma-1} T_1$ and volume $\dfrac{v_1}{n}$. If we keep volume constant and alter the temperature $n^{\gamma-1} T_1$ to T_1 pressure becomes $n p_1$.

We now have the gas at temperature T_1, pressure $n\, p_1$ and volume $\dfrac{v_1}{n}$. If the gas be allowed to expand isothermally to its original volume v_1, work done by the gas is given by

$$W' = p_1 v_1 \int_{\frac{v_1}{n}}^{v_1} \frac{dv}{v} = p_1 v_1 \log n$$

Hence total work done on the gas

$$- W - W'$$

$$= \frac{p_1 v_1}{\gamma - 1} (n^{\gamma-1} - 1) - p_1 v_1 \log n$$

$$= k W \quad \text{where } k = 1 - \frac{(\gamma - 1) \log n}{n^{\gamma-1} - 1}$$

5.8. Thermodynamics. It is now an accepted physical principle that a quantity of heat is the same thing as a quantity of mechanical energy. This equivalence was first established by Joule's experiments. Joule showed that a unit of heat viz a calorie was equivalent to 41.8×10^6 ergs. This constant is known as Joule's mechanical equivalent of heat. With its help we could express any quantity of heat in terms of units of mechanical energy.

If we now consider a gas as a system of molecules between which there act forces which have a potential, the gas will possess energy, which will consist of the kinetic energy of molecular motion and the potential energy of intermolecular forces. This energy, which will of course, depend on the configuration and motion of the molecules is known as internal energy of the gas. Let U be the internal energy of a gas, so that we may write

$$U = N \left(\tfrac{1}{2} m \, \bar{c}^{\,2} \right) + \bar{\phi}$$

where $\left(\tfrac{1}{2} m \, \bar{c}^{\,2} \right)$ is the mean energy of the N molecules, and ϕ is the potential energy of the intermolecular forces.

It is clear that the difference between the energies in two given states depends only on those states and not upon the mode of change from the one to the other.

Let us suppose that a quantity dQ of heat expressed in mechanical units is absorbed by the gas from some external source so that as a consequence its pressure, volume and temperature change. Let us suppose that after this absorption the gas again assumes a steady state and that in this state its internal energy is $u + du$. Now the work done by the gas in expanding from volume v to $v + dv$ is pdv. Hence by the principle of conservation of energy change in the energy of the gas must be equal to the energy supplied minus the work done by the gas in expansion

$$i.\ e.\ du = dQ - pdv$$

$$\text{or, } dQ = du + pdv.$$

This equation expresses the First Law of Thermodynamics.

5. 9. Internal energy of an ideal gas. The State of an ideal gas is defined by its pressure, temperature and volume. Since these three quantities are not independent being connected by the relation $\dfrac{pv}{T} = const$, the state of the gas is given by any two of the quantities p, v, and T. Hence internal energy

u is a function of two indepeldent variables only. We can easily show that in the case of an ideal gas it depends only on its temperature. If a gas initially in steady state be allowed to suddenlyexpand by the opening of a stop cock which establishes communication with a previously exhausted vessel, a number of intricate mechanical and thermal changes will at first occur. Let the walls of the enclosures be absolutely rigid and non conducting. Let u_I be the internal energy of the gas in the initial state and u_2 in the final state. Neither thermal nor mechanical energy has been added to the gas from without. The walls of the enclosure being non conducting as well as rigid, it follows from the first law of Thermodynamics

$$u_2 - u_\mathrm{I} = o.$$

If we wait long enough to allow thermal equilibrium to be established, we shall find that temperature of the gas remains unaltered. But the volume of the gas changes. The change of volume, therefore, has no effect on the internal energy provided its temperature remains constant,

$$\text{or} \quad \left(\frac{\partial u}{\partial v} \right)_\mathrm{T} = o.$$

Hence taking v,T as independent variables

$$du = \left(\frac{\partial u}{\partial \mathrm{T}} \right) . d\mathrm{T}.$$

$$\therefore \ dQ = \left(\frac{\partial u}{\partial \mathrm{T}} \right) . d\mathrm{T} + pdv \qquad .. \qquad \dots (1)$$

5. 10. **Specific Heat** -- Specific heat of a substance is the ratio of the amount of heat required to raise by $1°c$ the temperature of the body to the amount of heat required to increase by $1°c$ the temperature of an equal weight of water. If an amount of heat dQ produces in unit mass a change of temperature $d\mathrm{T}$, the specific heat is $\dfrac{dQ}{d\mathrm{T}}$.

At a given temperature any number of specific heats might be defined according to the conditions under which heating takes place. For the quantity of heat absorbed in a given change of state depends partly on the manner in which that change is brought about. In the case of a gas we shall consider only two cases:—

(i) when the pressure remains constant, the gas being allowed to expand,

(ii) when the volume remains constant.

The specific heat in the former case is called the specific heat at constant pressure and is denoted by c_p, whereas that in the latter case is known as specific heat at constant volume and is denoted by c_v.

From equation (1) of § 5.9 it is easy to see that

$$c_v = \frac{dQ}{dT} = \left(\frac{\partial u}{\partial T} \right)$$

$\therefore$ we have $dQ = c_v\, dT + pdv$.

But for an ideal gas $\dfrac{pv}{T} = const = c$

$$\therefore\ p\, dv + v\, dp = c\, d\,T.$$

so that, $dQ = cdT + c_v\, dT - vdp,$

$$\therefore\ c_p = \left(\frac{dQ}{dT} \right)_p = c_v + c$$

or, $c_p - c_v = c = const.$

Thus $c_p > c_v$ since c is positive.

Now it is found that c_p is constant within a considerable range of temperature. Hence c_v is also a constant within the same range. We have,

$$u = c_v\, T + const \qquad \dots \qquad \dots \qquad (1)$$

For a perfect gas $\frac{c_p}{c_v}$ is found to be 1.41.

Remark: In 5.8 we found that

$$u = N(\tfrac{1}{2}m\,\overline{c^2}) + \overline{\varphi}.$$

But as pointed out in § 5.4, $\dfrac{N}{2}m\,\overline{c^2} = \tfrac{3}{2}R\,T$

$$u = \tfrac{3}{2}R\,T + \overline{\varphi}$$

If $\overline{\varphi}$ the contribution from the potential energy of the molecules be ignored, this expression coincides with that given in (1). It is thus seen that the internal energy of an ideal gas consists entirely of the kinetic energy of its molecules, the potential energy due to the molecular forces being zero.

5.10. **Adiabatic Expansion**—An adiabatic expansion or compression is one which takes place without any heat being imparted to or lost from the gas. For an adiabatic change therefore, we have $dQ = o$,

so that $du + p\,dv = o$

or, $c_v d\,T + p\,dv = o.$

But $pv = cT$, $\therefore p\,dv + v\,dp = cdT.$

Eliminating dT, we have

$$\frac{c_v}{c}(p\,dv + v\,dp) + p\,dv = o.$$

But $c_p - c_v = c$

$\therefore c_v(p\,dv + v\,dp) + (c_p - c_v)\,p\,dv = o$

or, $dp + \dfrac{c_p}{c_v}\,p\,dv = o$

or, $pv^{\gamma} = \text{const.}$, where $\dfrac{c_p}{c_v} = \gamma$

This equation is the equation of adiabatic change, i.e., a change during which no heat is lost or gained.

The relation holds in the case of a sudden dilatation or compression which occurs so rapidly that there is no time for any sensible loss of heat, or for any addition of heat from external sources.

Ex. A certain volume of a perfect gas at absolute temperature T_o is compressed adiabatically till the temperature becomes T_1 and volume v_1. It is then allowed to expand isothermally till its volume is v_2, after which it again expands adiabatically till its temperature is T_o. If the gas is again compressed isothermally till it is restored to its initial state, prove that the work done by the gas in the cycle of transformations is

$$R (T_1 - T_o) \log \frac{v_2}{v_1}$$

where R is the gas constant defined by the relation $\frac{vp}{T} = R$.

Let p_o, v_o, T_o denote the initial state of the gas, and let p_1, v_1, T_1 be the state after the first adiabatic transformation. In the figure A denotes the initial state and B, the final state. Work by the gas during the compression is

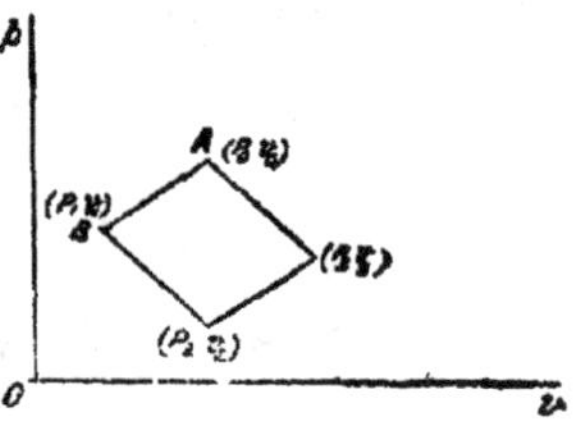

$$W_1 = \int_{v_o}^{v_1} p\,dv = \int_{v_o}^{v_1} \frac{c\,dv}{v^\gamma} = \frac{c}{1-\gamma} \left[\frac{1}{v_1^{\gamma-1}} - \frac{1}{v_o^{\gamma-1}} \right]$$

where $p_o v_o^\gamma = p_1 v_1^\gamma = c$.

$$\therefore W_1 = \frac{p_1 v_1 - p_o v_o}{1-\gamma}$$

But since $\frac{p_1 v_1}{T_1} = \frac{p_o v_o}{T_o} = R$

$$\therefore W_1 = \frac{R}{1-\gamma}\ (T_1 - T_o) \qquad ' \quad \ldots \qquad \ldots \quad (1)$$

The gas is now allowed to expand isothermally from volume v_1 to volume v_2, its temperature remaining T_I, work done by the gas is

$$W_2 = \int_{v_1}^{v_2} pdv = R\ T_I\ \log\frac{v_2}{1} \qquad \ldots(2)$$

During the next adiabatic transformation, work done by the gas is

$$W_3 = \frac{p_3\ v_3 - p_2\ v_{2,}}{1-\gamma}$$

where $p_3\ v_3$, are the pressure and volume in the state at which the temperature of the gas is T_o.

$$\text{But } \frac{p_3\ v_3}{T_o} = \frac{p_2\ v_2}{T_I} = R$$

$$\therefore W_3 = R\ \frac{T_o - T_I}{1-\gamma} \qquad \ldots \qquad \ldots \qquad (3)$$

Work done by the gas during the final isothermal transformation

$$\text{is } W_4 = R\ T_o\ \log\frac{v_o}{v_3} \qquad \ldots \qquad \ldots \qquad (4)$$

$$\text{But } p_2\ v_2^\gamma = p_3\ v_3, ^\gamma\ p_2 v_2 = R\ T_1;$$

$$\text{also } p_3\ v_3 = p_o\ v_o = R\ T_o.$$

$$\therefore p_3\ v_3^\gamma = R\ T_o v_3^{\gamma - 1}$$

$$p_2\ v_2^\gamma = R\ T_I\ v_2^{\gamma - 1}$$

$$\text{or,}\left(\frac{v_2}{v_3}\right)^{\gamma - 1} = \frac{T_o}{T_I}.$$

Similarly it may be shown that

$$\left(\frac{v_1}{v_0} \right)^{\gamma-1} = \frac{T_0}{T_1}.$$

It follows then $\dfrac{v_1}{v_0} = \dfrac{v_2}{v_3}$

Equation (4) gives

$$W_4 = R\,T_0\,log\,\frac{v_1}{v_2} \qquad \ldots \qquad \ldots \qquad (5)$$

From (1), (2), (3) and (5) we see that total work done *by* the gas is

$$R\,(T_1 - T_0)\,log\,\frac{v_2}{v_1}.$$

Remark: The cycle of transformations which the gas is supposed to undergo is known as Carnot's cycle.

5 12   Atmosphere in isothermal (conductive) equilibrium,

It the temperature of the air be assumed to be uniform, throughout, the relation between pressure and density is

$$p = k\,\rho \qquad \ldots \qquad \ldots \qquad \ldots(1)$$

The equation of hydrostatical equilibrium under the action of gravity, which may be assumed to be uniform, is

$$dp = -\,g\,\rho\,d\,z \qquad \ldots \qquad \ldots \qquad (2)$$

z-axis being the vertical oriented upwards.

From (1) and (2) we have

$$log\,\frac{p}{p_0} = -\frac{g}{k}\,(z - z_0)\,;$$

p_0 being the value of p at height z_0.

If $z_0 = o$ and H be the height of the homogeneous atmosphere of density ρ_0, that could produce the pressure p_0, we have

$$p_0 = g\,\rho_0\,H,$$

$$\therefore k = g\,\mathrm{H};$$

Hence $p = p_o e^{-z/\mathrm{H}}$

or, $\rho = \rho_o e^{-z/\mathrm{H}}$

Thus the density of the atmosphere falls off exponentially with the height above the earth's surface.

Ex·1 In an atmosphere at rest under gravity, the height H of the equivalent homogeneous atmosphere above any point at height h, measured in terms of air of the density at height h is given as a function of h. Show that the pressure p at height h is given by

$$p = p_o\, e^{-\int_o^h \frac{dh}{\mathrm{H}}}$$

where p_o is the pressure at $h = o$.

Show that in an isothermal atmosphere H is a constant independent of h, and deduce that an isothermal atmosphere extends to infinity

Ex. 2. A large spherical balloon of radius r and total weight W floats with its centre at a height h above the surface of the earth. Show that h is given by

$$e^{\frac{gh}{k}} = \frac{4\pi\,p_o k}{g\,\mathrm{W}}\left\{ r\cosh\frac{gr}{k} - \frac{k}{g}\sinh\frac{gr}{k} \right\}$$

where p_o is the pressure at the surface of the earth and k is a certain constant.

Let O be the centre of the balloon and P be any point so that angle between OP and the vertical through O is θ. Consider now an area of the spherical surface formed by the revolution of the small element PP' ($= r\,d\theta$) round the vertical through O. Every point of this area is at the same height ($h - r\cos\theta$) above the earth, so that pressure at any point P is

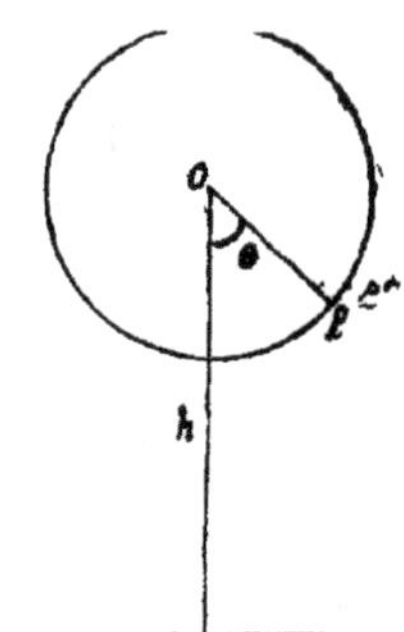

$$p_0\, e^{-\frac{g}{k}(h - r\cos\theta)}$$

acting normally along the radius PO

Hence the component of the pressure along the upward vertical through O is

$$p_0\, e^{-\frac{gh}{k}} \cdot e^{\frac{gr}{k}\cos\theta}\cos\theta.$$

Vertical component of total pressure acting on the belt considered above is

$$2\pi\, r^2 \sin\theta\, d\theta\, p_0\, e^{-\frac{gh}{k}}\, e^{\frac{gr}{k}\cos\theta}\cos\theta.$$

Hence total upward thrust of the atmospheric pressure is

$$2\pi r^2\, p_0 e^{-\frac{gh}{k}} \int_0^{\pi} \sin\theta\cos\theta\, e^{\frac{gr}{k}\cos\theta}\, d\theta$$

$$= 2\pi r^2 p_0\, e^{-\frac{gh}{k}} \int_{-1}^{+1} x\, e^{\frac{gr}{k}x}\, dx$$

$$= 4\,\pi\,r^2\,\mathrm{p_o}\,e^{-\frac{gh}{k}}\left\{\frac{k}{gr}\cosh\frac{gr}{k}-\frac{k^2}{g^2r^2}\sinh\frac{gr}{k}\right\}$$

Since the balloon is in equilibrium, this must be equal to its weigh W.

$$\therefore\ e^{\frac{gh}{k}}=\frac{4\,\pi\,p_o k}{g\,\mathrm{W}}\left\{r\cosh\frac{gr}{k}-\frac{k}{g}\sinh\frac{gr}{k}\right\}$$

Ex. 3. Taking into account the variation of gravity with height and assuming that the temperature of the air is constant at all heights prove that at a height x the pressure p of the air is given by

$$\log\frac{p}{p_o}=-\frac{g_o\,ax}{k\,(a+x)},$$

where a is the earth's radius, $k=p_o/\,\mathrm{P_o}$, and p_o, $\mathrm{P_o}$, $g_\bullet$ are the values of the pressure, density and gravity at the earth's surface.

A balloon carrying a self registering barometer records pressures equivalent to h and h_1 inches of mercury when it ascends to heights equal to fractions a and a_1 of the earth's radius respectively. Prove that

$$\frac{a\,g_o}{k}\cdot\frac{a_1-a}{(1+a)(1+a_1)}=\log\frac{h}{h_1}+2\log\frac{1+a_1}{1+a}$$

Ex. 4 A small hollow gas tight sphere containing hydrogen requires a force mg to prevent it from rising when the lowest point touches the ground. The total mass of sphere and hydrogen is M. Show that the sphere can float in equilibrium with its lowest point at a height h above the ground where

$$h=\frac{p_o}{g\mathrm{P_o}}\log\frac{\mathrm{M}+m}{\mathrm{M}}$$

$\mathrm{P_o}$, p_o being the density and pressure at the ground.

5. 13. Atmosphere in adiabatic (convective) equilibrium.

The law of variation of atmospheric density investigated in the preceeding article is the law which would undoubtedly become established if the earth's atmosphere were left at rest for a sufficient time. This is, however, far from being the case, for under actual conditions the earth's atmosphere is continually being agitated by currents and storms, so that there is an incessant mechanical transference of air from one part of the atmosphere to another. Besides, conduction of heat in gases is very slow. It, therefore, results that the atmosphere is never permitted to assume the equilibrium density which has been investigated on the hypothesis that the atmosphere is at a uniform temperature. As an element of atmosphere moves from one layer to another, its density changes and consequently also its temperature. But before its temperature has adjusted itself to that of its new surroundings it moves again to some other layer. Hence the density of the atmosphere is determined not by the equalisation of temperature necessary to a permanent state, but by the condition "that an element of atmosphere on being moved from one place to another shall take up the requisite pressure and volume without any loss or gain of heat by conduction taking place." That is, the law connecting the pressure and volume in the atmosphere is the adiabatic law found in § 5·11.

We thus have for the equilibrium of atmosphere

$$dp = -g\rho\, dz.$$

Also the adiabatic law connecting p and ρ is

$$p = k\rho^{\gamma}$$

$$k\gamma\rho^{\gamma-1}\frac{d\rho}{dz} = -g\rho$$

Integrating, $\dfrac{k\gamma}{\gamma-1}(\rho_0^{\gamma-1} - \rho^{\gamma-1}) = gz,$ $\qquad\qquad$ ·· (1)

where P_0 is the density at $z=o$.

Since $p = R\rho T$, $\dfrac{p}{\rho} = k\rho^{\gamma-1} = RT$

$$\therefore \frac{\gamma}{\gamma-1}\,R\,(T_0 - T) = gz$$

or, $\dfrac{T_0 - T}{z} = \text{const},$

where T_0 is the temperature at $z=o$.

Thus the temperature decreases as we move upwards, the amount of decrease being proportional to the height.

Ex. 1. Show that there is a superior limit to the height of an atmosphere in convective equilibrium. This limit is

$$\frac{p_0}{g\rho_0(\gamma-1)}\,\gamma$$

where p_0 and P_0 are the pressure and density at the earth's surface.

Ex. 2. If the absolute temperature T at a height z is a given function $\phi(z)$ of the height, show that the ratio of the pressures at two heights z_1, z_2 is given by

$$\log \frac{p_2}{p_1} = \frac{g}{k}\int_{z_1}^{z_2}\frac{dz}{\phi(z)}.$$

k being a constant defined by the equation $p = k\rho T$.

As an aeroplane ascends the temperature and pressure are simultaneously recorded and a curve is drawn plotting the absolute temperature against the logarithm of the pressure, prove that height ascended between two readings is

$$-\frac{k}{g}\int_{x_1}^{x_2} T\,dx,$$

where $x = \log p$.

Ex. 3. In a vertical column of perfect gas the pressure and absolute temperature at any height z are p and T. Prove that

$$z = \frac{p_0}{g P_0 T_0} \int_p^{p_0} \frac{T dp}{p}$$

where p_0, P_0, T_0 are pressure, density and absolute temperature at the bottom.

Height is measured in an aeroplane by means of a specially graduated aneroid barometer. The graduations are such that the true height would be read direct if the temperature of atmosphere were uniformly at $10°c$. Show that the instrument will read differences of height correctly whatever the barometric pressure at ground level.

To find the true height when the temperature is not uniform it is necessary to read the temperature during ascent. Show that the true height corresponding to a recorded height z is $\int_{z_0}^{z} \frac{T}{283} dz_1$, where z_0 is the reading at ground level and T the absolute temperature when the reading is z_1.

(Tripos Pt. II, 1921).

Ex. 4. Assuming the temperature of the air to diminish uniformly with the height prove that the difference of level of two stations is

$$H \frac{T_0 - T_1}{273} \frac{\log \dfrac{h_0}{h_1}}{\log \dfrac{T_0}{T_1}}$$

where H is the height of the homogeneous atmosphere at $0°$ centigrade, T_0, T_1, are the absolute temperatures of the stations,

h_0, h_1 are the barometeric heights reduced to $0°$ centigrade. Prove also that if as an approximation the temperature were taken to be constant and equal to $\frac{1}{2}(T_0+T_1)$ the calculated height would be too great by a fraction of its true value equal roughly to $\frac{1}{3}[\frac{T_0-T_1}{T_0+T_1}]^2$ assuming (T_0-T_1) to be small.

Ex. 5. A perfectly flexible balloon contains a light gas of total mass m. At the ground level it is at the same temperature as the surrounding air. Prove that it will exert the same lift at all heights if it remains at the same temperature as the air round it; but that if the gas inside expands adiabatically the lift at height z will be less than the lift at the ground level by the amount

$$mg\sigma\left\{1-\left(1-\frac{z}{H}\right)^{\frac{\gamma'-\gamma}{(\gamma-1)\gamma'}}\right\}$$

where σ is the ratio of the density of the air to that of gas under standard conditions, γ, γ' are the ratio of specific heats for air and the gas and H is the height of the atmosphere i. e. height at which pressure, temperature and density vanish. It is supposed that the balloon is never fully expanded.

Let ρ be the density of the air at height z and let ρ' be that of the gas inside the balloon when at this height. Then the volume of the gas inside the balloon at this height is $\frac{m}{\rho'}$. The volume of the air displaced by the balloon is accordingly $\frac{m}{\rho'}$ and therefore weight of the air displaced by the balloon is $\frac{mg}{\rho'}\rho$.

Hence the upward lift at any height z by the air outside the balloon is $mg\left(\frac{\rho}{\rho'}\right)$ where $\frac{\rho}{\rho'}$ is the ratio of the density of surrounding air at height z to that of the gas inside the balloon. Now if he temperature T outside the balloon is the same as that of the gas inside it, we have $\dfrac{p}{\rho T}=R$, for the air and $\dfrac{p'}{\rho'T'}=R'$, for the gas.

The balloon being flexible, $p=p'$ at any height and $T=T'$ by hypothesis, hence at any height z

$$\frac{\rho}{\rho'}=\frac{R'}{R}=\text{const.}$$

Hence the upward thrust of the air is the same at all heights.

If the gas inside expands adiabatically we have $p'=k'\,\rho'^{\gamma'}$, where p', ρ' are the pressure and density respectively of the gas and γ' is the ratio of specific heats.

The equation of pressure for air is $dp=-g\rho\,dz$;

$$\text{Also } p=k\rho^{\gamma}$$

$$\therefore k\rho^{\gamma-1}=-\frac{\gamma-1}{\gamma}\,gz+\text{cons.}$$

But $\rho=o$ when $z=H$

$$\therefore \rho^{\gamma-1}=\frac{g(\gamma-1)\,H}{k\gamma}\left[1-\frac{z}{H}\right]$$

$$\text{or } \rho=K'\left[1-\frac{z}{H}\right]^{\frac{1}{\gamma-1}}$$

$\therefore$ pressure p at height z is equal to

$$k\rho^{\gamma}=kK'^{\gamma}\left[1-\frac{z}{H}\right]^{\frac{\gamma}{\gamma-1}}$$

This is also the pressure of the gas inside the balloon as the bolloon is flexible. Hence if ρ' be the density of the gas at height z

$$p = k'\rho'^{\gamma'}$$

$$= k\rho^{\gamma} = kK'^{\gamma} \left[1 - \frac{z}{H}\right]^{\frac{\gamma}{\gamma-1}}$$

$$\rho' = \left(\frac{kK'^{\gamma}}{k'}\right)^{\frac{1}{\gamma'}} \left(1 - \frac{z}{H}\right)^{\frac{\gamma}{(\gamma-1)\gamma'}}$$

Hence $\dfrac{\rho'}{\rho} = \left(\dfrac{kK'^{\gamma}}{k'}\right)^{\frac{1}{\gamma'}} \dfrac{1}{K'} \left(1 - \dfrac{z}{H}\right)^{\frac{\gamma-\gamma}{(\gamma-1)\gamma'}}$

In particular if $z = 0$

$$\left(\frac{\rho'}{\rho}\right) = \frac{1}{K'}\left(\frac{kK'^{\gamma}}{k'}\right)^{\frac{1}{\gamma'}} = \frac{1}{\sigma}$$

$\therefore$ upward thrust at the ground level minus that at a height
'z' is

$$m g \left\{ \left(\frac{\rho}{\rho'}\right)_{0} - \left(\frac{\rho}{\rho'}\right)z \right\}$$

$$= mg\sigma \left\{ 1 - \left[1 - \frac{z}{H}\right]^{\frac{\gamma'-\gamma}{(\gamma-1)\gamma'}} \right\}$$

Ex. 6. A cylinderical well contains air at constant temperature, and densities at the top and bottom are ρ and ρ_0. Assuming g to be constant show that the mean density of the air in the well is $\dfrac{\rho_1 - \rho_0}{\log\left(\dfrac{\rho_1}{\rho_0}\right)}$.

(M.A. Punjab Univ. 1935)

We have for equilibrium of air

$$dp = -g\rho dz$$

where $p = k\,\rho$

$$\therefore \frac{d\rho}{\rho} = -\frac{g}{k}\,dz$$

or, $\rho = \rho_o e^{-\frac{gz}{k}}$

$$\text{Average density } \bar{\rho} = \frac{\displaystyle\int_o^h (\pi a^2)\,\rho_o e^{-\frac{gz}{k}}\,dz}{\displaystyle\int_o^h (\pi a^2)\,dz}$$

$$= \frac{(\rho_o - \rho_1)k}{hg},$$

h being the height of the cylinder.

$$\text{Since } \rho_1 = \rho_o\, e^{-\frac{gh}{k}}$$

$$\therefore h = -\frac{k}{g}\log \frac{\rho_1}{\rho_o}$$

$$\text{Hence } \bar{\rho} = \frac{\rho_1 - \rho_o}{\log\left(\frac{\rho_1}{\rho_o}\right)},$$

Ex. 7.   A bent tube of uniform bore, the arms of which are at right angles revolves with constant angular velocity w about the axis of one of its arms, which is vertical and has its extremity immersed in water.   Prove that the height to which water will rise in the vertical arm is

$$\frac{\pi}{g\bar{\rho}}\left(1 - e^{-\frac{w^2 a^2}{2k}}\right)$$

a being the length of the horizontal arm, Π the atmospheric pressure, and P the density of water, and k the ratio of the pressure of the atmosphere to its density.

Ex. 8   When the pressure of a given mass of a gas is p, its volume is v. If the gas is allowed to expand slowly from volume v_0 to volume v, show that W, the work done is $\int_{v_0}^{v} p\, dv$.

For a gas which is such that for $p > p_0$.

$$\mathrm{W} = pv + p_0\, v_0 + p_0{}^2 \frac{v}{p} + const,$$

verify that v decreases as p increases from p_0 and find v in terms of p.

(Tripos part I 1938)

$$\left[Ans.\ v = \frac{v_0}{p_0}\, pe^{-\frac{p^2 - p_0{}^2}{2p_0{}^2}} \right]$$

Ex. 9.   A hollow closed rigid vessel whose walls are of negligible thickness has volume V and contains air of density σ at atmospheric pressure Π and absolute temperature T. The vessel is held below the surface of a lake of uniform density P and temperature T.   A small hole is made at the lowest point of the vessel allowing water to enter the vessel but no air to escape. All changes take place isothermally.   When water ceases to enter the vessel, the water surface inside it is at a depth h below the surface of the lake.   If the vessel, when released, can float freely (totally immersed) in this position, determine h in terms of M, V, Π, σ, P and g where M is the mass of the vessel when empty.

Find whether the equilibrium is stable or unstable for vertical displacements.

(Tripos 1939).

(181)

$$\left[An\ h = \frac{\pi\left\{ (P - \sigma)\ V - M \right\}}{gP\ (M + \sigma V)} \right.$$

Ex. 10. Two cylindrical gasholders, of weights W_1 and W_2 and of cross sections A_1 and A_2 float in water with their tops at the same height h above the water. The combined quantity of gas in them would occupy a volume V at the atmospheric pressure π. Prove that

$$h = \frac{\pi\left\{ V - \frac{1}{g}\left(W_1 + W_2 \right) \right\} - \frac{W_1^2}{gPA_1} - \frac{W_2^2}{gPA_2}}{\left(A_1 + A_2 \right)\pi + W_1 + W_2}$$

where P is the density of water, and the buoyancy of the water displaced by the side of the gasholders is neglected.

Ex. 11 In ascending a mountain the temperature of the air is found to decrease by a quantity proportional to the height ascended and h, k are the observed heights of the barometer at two stations whose difference of altitude is z Show that z varies as $h^m - k^m$, where m is a certain constant, and where changes of density in the barometer are neglected

CHAPTER VI.

Capillarity.

6 1. When the surface of water contained in a vase is carefully examined it is found to be imperfectly level becoming considerably curved in the vicinity of the walls of the vase. Again, if the lower end of a vertical tube having a narrow bore is immersed in water, the liquid rises some distance above the level of the outer surface of water. The free surface of the liquid within the bore is curved and appears to cling to the wall of the tube at a definite angle. This angle is called the "the angle of capillarity." If a small quantity of mercury is poured on a horizontal plate, it forms a drop. If the quantity of mercury is exceedingly small it assumes a nearly spherical shape. A larger quantity spreads out into a cake-shaped mass with a nearly flat top and with rounded edges. These and other allied phenomena are explained on the hypothesis that the molecules of the liquid and the solid with which the liquid is in contact attract one another with forces,—capillary forces,—whose range of action is very small.

6·2 Historical introduction. Many of the phenomena due to capillary forces were described as early as 1670 by Borelli; but the first accurate observations of capillary action of tubes and glass plates were made by Francis Hawksbee (1713), who ascribed the action to the attraction between glass and the liquid. He observed that the effect was the same in thick tubes as in thin tubes and concluded th t only those particles of glass, which are very near the surface have any influence on the phenomena. Clairaut in his "Theorie de la figure de la Terre" (1743) attemped unsuccessfully to calculate the elevation of liquids in capillary tubes. In 1805 Thomas Young compared the free surface of a liquid to that of a membrane equally stretched in all directions. He also gave for the first time the differential equation to be satisfied by such a surface. But as Laplace and Poisson have pointed out, "the identity of the surface of a liquid with that of a stretched membrane can only be the consequence of and not the principle of the solution of the problem".

A satisfactory explanation of the capillary phenomena on the basis of a mathematical theory was not forthcoming till 1806, when Laplace formulated his theory of capillary action. The fundamental hypothesis of his theory was that any two molecules of the liquid attract one another with a force which acts along the line joining them and whose magnitude is proportional to their masses but depends on their distance according to an unknown law.   Laplace also assumed that these molecular forces become infinitely small when the distance between the molecules exceeds a small distance ε called the "radius of molecular activity."   On the basis of these simple assumptions he explained nearly all the phenomena of capillary action then known.

It had been noticed that the angle of capillarity for a given liquid and solid was constant along the curve of contact of the liquid and the solid. Laplace's theory   suffered from the defect that it was not able to explain this constancy except in the case of a cylinder.   In 1830, Gauss proved the constancy of the angle of capillarity by applying the theory of virtual work.

About the same time (1831) Poisson in his "Nouvell The'orie de 1, action Capillaire" pointed out that the theories of Laplace and Gauss had taken no account of the fact that the density of the liquid near the free surface is not constant. By means of extremely complicated but very well conducted calculations he proved the constancy of the angle of capillarity and established other results already given by Laplace and Gauss.

Poisson's analysis was simplified considerably by Mathieu & Poincare.' Hagen, Brunner and others studied with the utmost precision the elevation and depression of liquids by capillary action and showed that the theoretical results of Laplace, Poisson, Gauss etc. are completely in accord with experiment. Plateau's celebrated work,- "Sur Les Liquides Soumis aux seules forces moleculaires''—contains an elaborate account of the mathematical theory of capillarity and of his own extensive series of experiments.

6. 3.   Theory of capillarity, in its most general form, is the study of the forms assumed by the surfaces of liquids in contact with each other and with solid bodies. The curious forms of such surfaces become explicable only on the hypothesis of the existence of intense molecular forces having an extremely small range of action.

Let m_1 and m_2 be masses of two molecules of the liquid and   be the distance between them. The molecular force between them is then assumed to be

$$m_1 \, m_2 \, f \, (r_{12}),$$

f, being an unknown function, which becomes infinitely small when r_{12} exceeds ε, "the radius of molecular activity". Here it is tacitly assumed that the linear dimensions of the molecules are infinitely smaller than the length of any line from the surface of one to the other, for otherwise the quantity r_{12} would have no meaning unless, of course, the molecules are supposed to be spherical.

In order to proceed further it is now necssary to make some assumption concerning the constitution of matter. No doubt the application of Integral Calculus to the determination of the action produced on a molecule of a body by the neighbouring molecules is rigorously justifiable only on the assumption that matter is completely continuous and that there is no vacant space, however small, between the molecules. Still such an hypothesis, as remarked by Lame', is inadmissible. On the other hand the assumption that the molecules of matter are very distant from each other so that the space surrounding any molecule is comparatively void of matter, makes the application of mathematical analysis almost impossible. We, therefore, s rike a via media and assume that matter is quite closely packed, the dimensions of molecules being great compared with the distances between the surfaces of two contiguous molecules   Matter may, therefore, be regarded as sufficiently continuous so as to permit the application of Integral Calculus at any rate as a very close approximation to truth. But on this assumption, when calculating the molecular force between two very clo-e molecules m_1 and m_2, it will be necessary to imagine both the molecules as subdivided into infinitesimal parts 'm_1 and δm_2 so that the dimensions of each part are infinitely smaller than the distance between any two points on the parts cons dered. If r_{12} be the distance between these parts, the attraction between them will be $\delta m_1 \, \delta m_2$ f (r_{12}). Integrating over the two molecules we shall obtain the force acting between them. In what follows, therefore, we shall apply the Integral Calculus as though matter were continuous.

6. 4.   Consider a homogeneous liquid in contact with a solid body. Let (X, Y, Z) be the components of the external force per unit mass acting on the liquid. In order to determine the equilibrium of the liquid we shall apply the principle of virtual work.

Let m_1, m_2.   .. m_i,   ..   be the molecules of the liquid and M_1, M_2,   .. Ms, ... those of the solid. Let r_{i2} be the distance between the molecules m_i and m_2 and R_{i2} that between m_i and M_2. Let m_i $m_2 f$ (r_{12}) be the attraction between m_i and m_2, and m_i M$_2$ F (r_{i2}) be the attraction between m_i and M$_2$. Then the virtual work of two equal and opposite forces between m_1 and m_2 acting along r_{12} consequent upon a slight displacement $\delta\, r_{12}$ is

$$-m_1\, m_2 f\,(r_{12})\; \delta r_{12}$$

Similarly the virtual work of the force between m_1 and M_1 is

$$-m_1\, M\; F\,(R_{i3})\; \delta\; R_{i3}.$$

The virtual work of the external force (X, Y, Z) is

$$m_i\, [X\delta x + Y\delta y + Z\delta z].$$

Since the system is in equilibrium, the sum of the virtual works must be zero for any displacement consistent with the laisons or constraints of the system.

$$\text{Or,}\quad \Sigma\, m_i\; [X\delta x + Y\delta y + Z\delta z] - \tfrac{1}{2}\Sigma_1\Sigma_2\, m_i\quad m_2\; f\,(r_{12})\quad \delta r_{12}$$
$$-\Sigma_1\Sigma_2 m_1\, M_2\, F\,(R_{12})\delta\; R_{i3} = 0 \qquad\qquad \dots \quad (1)$$

Here the first sum extends over each molecule of the liquid, the second sum, which is double extends over every arrangement of two molecules of the liquid; and the third sum, which is also double, extends over every molecule M of the solid paired with every molecule of the liquid. We have taken the factor $\tfrac{1}{2}$ in the second sum in order to ensure that each pair of molecules of the liquid contributes towards the sum only once.

$$\text{Let}\qquad \int_r^{\varepsilon} f\,(r)\, dr = \int_r^{\infty} f\,(r)\, dr = \phi(r)$$

since $f\,(r)$ is infinitely small when $r > \varepsilon$.

$$\text{Similarly let}\quad \int_r^{\varepsilon} F\,(r)\, dr = \int_r^{\infty} F\,(r)\, dr = \Psi(r)$$

$$\therefore -f\,(r)\; \delta r = \delta\phi\,(r),\ and -F\,(r)\; \delta r = \delta\psi\,(r)$$

Accordingly equation (1) becomes

$$\Sigma\, m_1\, [X\delta x + Y\delta y + Z\delta z] + \tfrac{1}{2}\Sigma_1\Sigma_2\, m_1 m_2 \delta\phi(r_{12})$$
$$+ \Sigma_1\Sigma_2\, m_1^1 M_2 \delta\psi\,(R_{12}) = o.$$

Remark :—Since $f(r)$ *and* F (r) are negligibly small when $r\,7\,\varepsilon$ so are $\phi(r)$ an*d* $\psi(r)$.

Now, set $U = \Sigma\, \smallint (X dx + Y dy + Z dz)\, m_1$

$$+ \tfrac{1}{2}\Sigma_1 \Sigma_2\, m_1\, m_2 \phi(r_{12}) + \Sigma_1 \Sigma_2\ ^{m_1} M_2 \phi\,(R_{12}) \tag{2}$$

The condition of equilibrium is, therefore, $\delta U = o$ for every possible displacement consistent with the laisons of the system.

6. 5. We shall now evaluate the double sums encountered in the preceeding article. Consider the sum $\Sigma_1\Sigma_2\, m_1\, m_3\, \phi(r_{12})$.

Take first a molecule m_1 so situated that the sphere of radius ε round m_1 as centre is completely immersed in the liquid. The sum $m^1 \Sigma_2\, m_2\, \phi(r_{12})$, where m_2 extends to every molecule of the liquid except m_1, is clearly the same as if the sum extended only to molecules within the sphere of molecular activity, for $\phi(r_{12})$ vanishes for $r_{12} > \varepsilon$.

Accordingly $\Sigma_2\ m_2 \phi\ (r_{12}) = P \smallint (4\,\pi r^2 dr)\, \phi\,(r),$

$$= 4\pi P \int_0^{\varepsilon} r^2\, \phi\,(r)\, dr = \mathrm{cons} = L\ (say),$$ where P is the density of the liquid,

If it were possible to surround every molecule by the sphere of molecular activity in such a way that the latter remains wholly inside the liquid, the calculation of $\Sigma_1\Sigma_2\, m_1\, m_2 \phi(r_{12})$ would be a simple matter, for it would be $= \Sigma\, m_1\, L = ML$, M being the total mass of the liquid.

Actually, however, it is impossible to do so for molecules at a distance less than ε from the free surface of the liquid or the surface of contact of the liquid with the solid. We are, however, able to do so by drawing an imaginary shell of constant thickness ε surrounding the free surface and the surface of contact between the liquid and the solid. It is clear then that

$$ML = S_1 S_2 [m_1 m_2 \phi(r_{12})] + \Sigma_1 \Sigma_2 m_1 m_2 \phi (r_{12})$$

where the summation S exteds over mole of the umles imaginary shall. We now proceed to prove thet $S_1 S_2 m_1 m_2 \phi (r_{12})$ is proportional to the sum of area of the free surface and the area of the surface of the liquid in contact with the solid.

Let A B and A′ B′ be the surface of the liquid and the outer surface of the imaginary shell respectively. The two surfaces are by hypothesis parallel, the normal distance between them being ε. Consider now an element of volume at Q, whose mass is $P\,ds\,dz$ where $z = pQ$, and ds is an elementary area of the surface through Q parallel to the surface

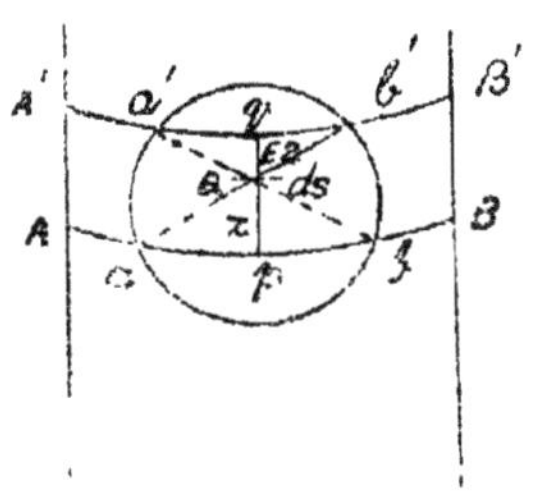

A B or A′ B′. Draw a sphere of radius ε round Q. Take polar coordinates with Q as pole, Qp as the axis of θ and any line through Q at right angles to Qp as the axis of ox.

Let us take dS so small that the distance of any point P(r, θ, Ψ) from any point of the elementary area dS at Q is the same as QP $= r$. Hence $S_1 S_2 m_1 m_s \phi (r_{12})$

$$= \int\int\int\int\int\int (P\,dS\,dz)(Pr^2 dr\,sin\,\theta\,d\theta\,d\Psi)\phi (r)$$

$$= P^2 \int\int\int [dS\,dz \int\int\int r^2 \phi (r)\,sin\,\theta d\,d\theta d\Psi]$$

The limits of the triple integral within brackets are to be such that the field of integration is the volume between the surfaces A B and A′ B′ and the sphere of molecular activity round Q. Since the radius of the sphere is infinitely small compared to the free surface of the liquid and the surface in contact with the solid, the sections of the sphere by the surfaces A B and A′ B′ may be taken to be planes

Hence $\iiint r^2 \phi(r) \sin\theta \, dr \, d\vartheta \, d\Psi$

$$= \iiint_{\text{sector } a\,Qb\,p\,a} + \iiint_{a\,Q\,a',\, b\,Q\,b'} + \iiint_{a'Qb'qa'}$$

$$= \int_0^{2\pi} d\Psi \int_0^{\cos^{-1}\frac{z}{\varepsilon}} \sin\theta \, d\theta \int_0^{z \sec\theta} r^2\phi(r) \, dr + \int_0^{2\pi} d\Psi \int_{\cos^{-1}\frac{z}{\varepsilon}}^{\cos^{-1}\frac{z-\varepsilon}{\varepsilon}} \sin\theta \, d\theta \int_0^{\varepsilon} r^2 \phi(r) \, dr$$

$$+ \int_0^{2\pi} d\Psi \int_{\cos^{-1}\frac{z-\varepsilon}{\varepsilon}}^{\pi} \sin\theta \, d\theta \int_0^{(z-\varepsilon)\sec\theta} r^2 \phi(r) \, dr$$

$$= \mu(z, \text{ (say)}.$$

Hence $S_1 S_2 \, m_1 \, m_2 \, \phi(r_{12}) = P^2 \iiint dS \, \mu(z) \, dz$

$$= P^2 \iiint dS \int_0^{\varepsilon} \mu(z) \, dz = A'P^2 S, = B\,S$$

where B is a constant and S is the sum of the area of the free sur'ace and the surface of contact of the liquid with the solid. Let the former be σ and the latter be λ, then

$$S = \sigma + \lambda$$

Hence $\Sigma_1 \, \Sigma_2 \, m_1 \, m_2 \, \phi(r_{12})$

$$= M \, L - (\lambda + \sigma) \, B$$

$$= 2 \, A - (\lambda + \sigma) \, B,$$

A, B being constants.

Similarly it is easy to establish that

$$\Sigma_1 \, \Sigma_2 \, m_1 \, M_2 \, \Psi(R_{12}) = E \, \lambda.$$

Hence by equation (2) of § 6.4

$$U = \Sigma \int (X \, dx + Y \, dy + Z \, dz) \, m_1 + A - \tfrac{1}{2}B(\lambda + \sigma) + E\lambda$$

$$= \Sigma \int (X dx + Y\, dy + Z\, dz)\, m_1 + A - \tfrac{1}{2}B\; \sigma - (\tfrac{1}{2}B - E)\lambda.$$

where A,B,E are positive numbers.

Remark:— We have assumed that the density ρ is uniform throughout the liquid. As mentioned in § 6.2, this assumption has been criticised by Poission and Mathieu. The results obtained by them on the assumption that t e density of the liquid near the free surface varies are, however, similar to those obtained above.

6.6 *Equilibrium of a liquid contained in a vase.* If the only external force acting on the liquid be that of gravity, then taking the upward vertical as z-axis, we have $X = Y = o$, $Z = -g$.

$$\text{Hence } U = - g \Sigma \int m_1\, dz + A - \tfrac{1}{2}B\; \sigma - (\tfrac{1}{2}B - E)\; \lambda$$

$$= - g \Sigma\; m_1 z + A - \tfrac{1}{2}B\sigma - (\tfrac{1}{2}B - E)\lambda$$

$$= - g\rho \int\int\int z dv + A - \tfrac{1}{2}B\; \sigma - (\tfrac{1}{2}B - E)\; \lambda$$

where dv is an element of volume of the liquid, σ is the area of the free surface and λ the area of the surface of contact of the liquid and vase.

For equilibrium we must have

$$\delta U = o$$

$$\text{or, } - g\rho \delta \int\int\int z dv - \tfrac{1}{2}B\; \delta\sigma - (\tfrac{1}{2}B - E)\delta\lambda = o \ldots\ldots(1)$$

We now proceed to calculate the variation of each of the three terms of the above equation. Let AB be the free surface of the liquid in its equilibrium position and $A_1 B_1$ its position after a virtual displacement. These two surfaces enclose a volume between themselves. We split this volume into small elements by drawing nomals M M', NN' at each point of

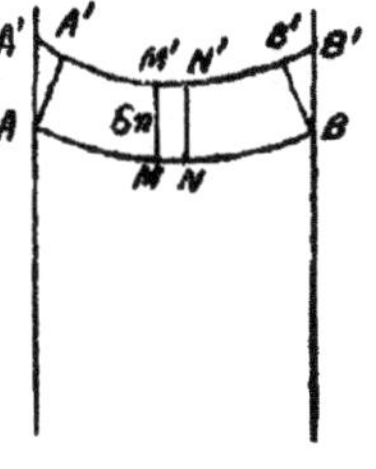

the contour of a small element dS, (MN), of the surface AB. If $MM' = \delta n$, the volume of the element is $d\tau = \delta n dS$.

Now $\int\int\int g^\rho z\, dv$ is the moment of the weight of the liquid with respect to xoy plane. Its variation is therefore clearly the moment of the weight of the liquid contained in the surfaces AB and A_1B_r.

Hence $\delta \int\int\int g^\rho z\, dv = \rho g \int\int z\, \delta n\, dS \ldots (2)$,

where the field of integration of the double integral on the right hand side is the free surface of the liquid.

To find the variation $\delta\sigma$ of the free surface area, we require the difference between σ and σ_1, the areas of A B and $A_1 B_1$.

$$\therefore\ \delta\sigma = \sigma_1 - \sigma \qquad \ldots \bullet \quad \ldots \qquad (3)$$

Let L be the curve of contact of the surface AB with the vase and L_1 the corresponding curve of $A_1 B_1$. Draw normals at each point of the curve L to the surface AB. These normals intersect the surface $A_1'B_1$ in a curve L', bounding an area σ' of the surface $A_1 B_1$.

Let σ'' be the area of the surface $A_1 B_1$ bounded by the curves L_1 and L'.

$$\therefore\ \sigma_1 = \sigma' + \sigma''$$

Accordingly,

$$\delta\sigma = \sigma' + \sigma'' - \sigma$$
$$= \sigma'' + \int\int_{L'} dS' - \int\int_{L} dS \qquad \ldots \qquad \ldots \qquad (4)$$

dS' being an element of the surface A' B' and dS of A B.

Let us now compare dS' and dS. Imagine the net work of principal lines of curvature of the surface drawn out on it.

Let MN and MP be two such lines through M, then the normals at M and N intersect at C and the normals at M and P, at C′ and MC and MC′ are the radii of principal curvature.

Since $<$ PMN is a right angle, area dS of the mesh MPQN is MN$\times$MP. The normals at the points M, N, P, etc trace a corresponding mesh M′N′Q′P′ on the surface A′B′, whose area dS =M′N′$\times$M′P′.

Now MM′ $= \delta n$. Hence from the triangle MPC′ we have

$$\frac{M'P'}{MP} = \frac{M'C'}{MC'} = \frac{MC'-MM'}{MC'} \cdot \quad 1 - \frac{\delta n}{R_1}$$

R_1 being a principal radius of curvature of the surface at M. Similarly,

$$\frac{M'N'}{MN} = 1 - \frac{\delta n}{R_2}$$

$$\therefore \frac{dS'}{dS} = (1 - \frac{\delta n}{R_1})(1 - \frac{\delta n}{R_2})$$

$$= 1 - \delta n (\frac{1}{R_1} + \frac{1}{R_2})$$

neglecting term of the second infinitesimal order.

$$\text{Hence } dS' - dS = - \delta n (\frac{1}{R_1} + \frac{1}{R_2})\, dS$$

$$\therefore \iint_{L'} dS' - \iint_{L} dS = - \iint_{L} (\frac{1}{R_1} + \frac{1}{R_2}) dS\, (\delta n) \qquad (5)$$

Let us now evaluate the annular area σ'' between the curves L_1 and L′ of the surface A_1 B Take two points A and C on the curve L infinitely near each other. The normals AA′ and CC′ at A and C respectively to the surface AB meet the curve L′ in points A′, C′ infinitely near each other.

From A′ and C′ draw lines A′A₁ & C′C₁ lying in the surface A₁ B₁ and perpendicular to AA′ and CC′ respectively.

These lines divide the area σ'' into elements A′A₁C₁C′, whose area is sensibly

$$dw = ds \times A_1 A',$$

ds being the element AC of the curve L.

Defining the 'angle of capillarity' to be the angle between the free surface and the surface of the solid at any point of the curve L, it is easy to see that angle AA₁A′ after the displacement can be identified with θ, the angle of capillarity.

Hence $A_1 A' = AA' \cot \theta = \delta n \dfrac{\cos \theta}{\sin \theta}$

$$\therefore dw = ds \frac{\cos \theta}{\sin \theta} \, \delta n,$$

so that

$$\sigma'' = \int\!\!\int dw = \int \frac{\cos \theta}{\sin \theta} \delta n \, ds.$$

it follows from (4) and (5) that

$$\delta \sigma = \int_L \frac{\cos \theta}{\sin \theta} \delta n ds - \int\!\!\int_L \left(\frac{1}{R_1} + \frac{1}{R_2}\right) \delta n \, dS \qquad (6)$$

Finally we require the variation $\delta\lambda$ of the surface of the liquid in contact with the solid vase. It is clear that $\delta\lambda$ is the area comprised between the lines L and L₁. An element of this area is AA₁ C₁C.

Hence $\delta\lambda = \displaystyle\int_L ds A A_1$

$$= \int_L \frac{\delta n}{\sin \theta} \, ds.$$

The Equation of Equilibrium (1) accordingly becomes

$$-g^P \int\int_L z\, \delta n\, dS + \frac{B}{2} \int\int_L \left(\frac{1}{R_1}+\frac{1}{R_2}\right) \delta n dS - \frac{B}{2} \int_L \frac{\cos\theta}{\sin\theta}\, \delta n ds$$

$$-\left(\frac{B}{2}-E\right)\int_L \frac{\delta n}{\sin\theta}\, ds = 0.$$

$$\int\int_L \left[-g^P z+\left(\frac{1}{R_1}+\frac{1}{R_2}\right)\frac{B}{2}\right]\delta n\, dS + \int_L \left\{ \left(E-\frac{B}{2}\right)-\frac{B}{2}\cos\theta \right\}$$

$$\frac{\delta n}{\sin\theta}\, ds = 0. \quad (7)$$

This equation must be satisfied whatever be the value of δn, provided, of course, that the value of δn is itself compatible with the laisons of the system. Now the liquid being assumed to be incompressible, the algebraic sum of the variations of the volume resulting from the virtual displacement of the bounding surfaces must be zero. We have already seen that the volume of an element comprised between the free surface and its displaced position is $\delta n\, dS$. Hence the incompressibility of the liquid imposes the contraint,

$$\int\int_E \delta n\, dS = 0 \qquad (8)$$

If we take into account this equation, equation (7) is satisfied for any arbitrary value of δn compatible with the laisons if

$$-g^P z + \frac{B}{2}\left(\frac{1}{R_1}+\frac{1}{R_2}\right) = \text{const.} = K \qquad (9)$$

and

$$\left(E-\frac{B}{2}\right)-\frac{B}{2}\cos\theta = 0 \qquad (10)$$

These conditions are obviously sufficient; for if they are satisfied, the second term of equation (7) vanishes, whereas the iirst reduces to the product $K \int\int_L \delta n\, dS$ and is therefore zero by (8).

These conditions are also necessary for if they are not satisfied, we can arrange a displacement of such a kind that although equation (8) may vanish yet equation (7) will not.

Let us first suppose that $-g\rho z + \dfrac{B}{2}\left(\dfrac{1}{R_1} + \dfrac{1}{R_2}\right)$ is not a constant. It is then a function of the coordinates of the surface and its value at any point lies between a relative maximum and minimum as the field of variation of the function is a finite region. If K be a value intermediate between this maximum and minimum, the function

$$-g\rho z + \frac{B}{2}\left(\frac{1}{R_1} + \frac{1}{R_2}\right) - K \tag{11}$$

is sometime positive and sometime negative.

Let us give to δn a value zero along the curve L and a value of the same sign as the expression (11) at other points of the surface. These values can always be found so as to satisfy (8).

We then have

$$\iint_L K\,\delta n\,dS = o$$

and therefore,

$$\iint_L\left[-g\rho z + \frac{B}{2}\left(\frac{1}{R_1} + \frac{1}{R_2}\right)\right]\delta n\,dS$$

$$= \iint_L\left[-g\rho z + \frac{B}{2}\left(\frac{1}{R_1} + \frac{1}{R_2}\right) - K\right]\delta n\,dS.$$

Now by hypothesis δn is zero along L so that the line integral of Equation (7) vanishes   Also δn is of the same sign as expression (11), so that the surface integral of (7) is not zero as each element is positive. It follows then that Equation (7) cannot be satisfied so that equilibrium is impossible. Condition (9) is therefore necessary.

Let us now suppose that condition (9) is satisfied but not (10), we can always choose values of δn satisfying (8) and such that along the line L, the sign of δn is the same as that of

$$(E - \frac{B}{2}) - \frac{B}{2} \cos \theta.$$

The first integral of Equation (7) is zero while the second is positive. Equation (7) cannot be satisfied.

It follows then that Equation (9), (10) are the necessary and sufficient condiions of equilibrium.

Equation (9) is the equation of the free surface of the liquid and Equation (10) shows that the angle of capillarity θ is constant at every point L of the curve of contact of the free surface of the liquid and the containing vase (or the adjacent solid).

6. 7. We now proceed to give the differential equation of the free surface of the liquid.

We have already seen that if R_1, R_2 be the principal radii of curvature of the free surface at any point

$$\frac{B}{2g\rho} \left(\frac{1}{R_1} + \frac{1}{R_2} \right) = z + \frac{K}{g\rho}$$

$$\text{or, } a^2 \left(\frac{1}{R_1} + \frac{1}{R_2} \right) = (z - h)$$

where $a^2 =$ the positive quantity $\dfrac{B}{2g\rho}$, and $h = \dfrac{-K}{g\rho}$.

From solid geometry we know that

$$\left(\frac{1}{R_1} + \frac{1}{R_2} \right) = \frac{(1 + p^2)\, t + (1 + q^2)\, r - 2pqs}{(1 + p^2 + q^2)^{3/2}},$$

where $p = \dfrac{\partial z}{\partial x}$, $q = \dfrac{\partial z}{\partial y}$, $r = \dfrac{\partial^2 z}{\partial x^2}$, $s = \dfrac{\partial^2 z}{\partial x \partial y}$, $t = \dfrac{\partial^2 z}{\partial y^2}$

The differential equation of the free surface becomes

$$\frac{(1 + p^2)\, t + (1 + q^2)\, r - 2pqs}{(1 + p^2 + q^2)^{3/2}} = \frac{1}{a^2}(z - h) \quad \dots \quad (1)$$

Remark I :—If the free surface is surface of revolution generated by the revolution of a curve $z = f(x)$ about the (vertical) axis of z, the principal radii of curvature at any point are known to be the radius of curvature of the meridian section and the normal intercepted between the point and the axis of revolution.

The former radius of curvature is

$$\frac{[1 + f'^2(x)]^{3/2}}{f''(x)}$$

and the latter is

$$x \sqrt{1 + \frac{1}{f'^2}}$$

Hence

$$\frac{1}{R_1} + \frac{1}{R_2} = \frac{f''(x)}{[1 + f'^2(x)]^{\frac{3}{2}}} + \frac{f'(x)}{x \sqrt{1 + f'^2(x)}}$$

$$= \frac{f''(x) + \frac{1}{x} f(x)[1 + f'^2(x)]}{(1 + f'^2(x))^{\frac{3}{2}}}$$

The differential equation of the generating curve of the free surface is

$$\frac{f''(x) + \frac{1}{x} f'(x)[1 + f'^2(x)]}{(1 + f'^2(x))^{\frac{3}{2}}} = \frac{z - h}{a^2} \quad \cdots \quad (2)$$

This result is, of course, also directly deducible from equation (1).

Remark II. The "Constant of Capillary forces" $\frac{B}{2}$ is called surface tension' of the liquid. See also § 6. 10

6. 8. Weight of liquid rising in a cylindrical tube. Consider a cylinderical tube plunged vertically in the liquid. The equation of the free surface can be written as

$$\frac{(1+q^2)\,\dfrac{dp}{dx} + (1+p^2)\,\dfrac{dq}{dy} - pq\left(\dfrac{dp}{dy} + \dfrac{dq}{dx}\right)}{(1+p^2+q^2)^{\frac{3}{2}}} = \frac{z-h}{a^2}$$

or, $\dfrac{d}{dx}\left(\dfrac{p}{\sqrt{1+p^2+q^2}}\right) + \dfrac{d}{dy}\left(\dfrac{q}{\sqrt{1+p^2+q^2}}\right) = \dfrac{z-h}{a^2}$

or, $\dfrac{dU}{dx} + \dfrac{dV}{dy} = \dfrac{z-h}{a^2}$,

where $U = \dfrac{p}{\sqrt{1+p^2+q^2}}$, $V = \dfrac{q}{\sqrt{1+p^2+q^2}}$.

Multiplying both sides of this equation by $dx\,dy$ and integrating, the field of integration being a cross section of the cylinder

$$\iint_c \left(\frac{dU}{dx} + \frac{dV}{dy}\right)dx\,dy = \frac{1}{a^2} \iint (z-h)\,dx\,dy.$$

Now the left hand side by Green's Theorem is easily transformed into a line integral.

It is equal to

$$\int_c (U \cos \varepsilon + V \sin \varepsilon)\,ds,$$

where ε is the angle between the normal to the curve of the right section of the cylinder and the x-axis.

Hence $\displaystyle\iint \left(\frac{dU}{dx} + \frac{dV}{dy}\right) dx\,dy = \int_c \frac{p \cos \varepsilon + q \sin \varepsilon}{\sqrt{1+p^2+q^2}}\,ds$

Now the direction cosines of the normal to the free surface and the normal to the wall of the cylinder are respectively,

$$\frac{p}{\sqrt{1+p^2+q^2}}, \quad \frac{q}{\sqrt{1+p^2+q^2}}, \quad \frac{-1}{\sqrt{1+p^2+q^2}}$$

$$\cos \varepsilon \quad , \quad \sin \varepsilon \quad , \quad 0 \quad .$$

Hence if θ is the angle of capillarity

(199)

$$\cos \theta = \frac{p \cos \varepsilon + q \sin \varepsilon}{\sqrt{1 + p^2 + q^2}}$$

Accordingly,

$$\int_c \frac{p \cos \varepsilon + q \sin \varepsilon \, ds}{\sqrt{1 + p^2 + q^2}} = \cos \theta \int ds = l \cos \theta.$$

since θ is constant; l being the length of the contour of a normal section of the cylinder.

Hence $\iint (z-h)\, dx dy = a^2 \, l \cos \theta.$

The quantity h represents the z-coordinate of the level surface of the liquid outside the tube. Hence $\iint_c (z-h)\, dx dy$ is the volume v of the liquid which rises in the tube above the horizontal surface outside the tube.

$$\therefore v = a^2 \, l \cos \theta.$$

If angle θ is obtuse as in the case of a glass tube dipped in mercury, the value of v is negative which indicates that the liquid is depressed in the tube.

Ex. 1. Prove that the volume of the liquid that rises in the space between two cylinderical tubes of the same material dipped in a liquid is proportional to

$$(l+l') \cos \theta,$$

where l, l' are the lengths of the contours of the normal sections of the tubes and θ is the angle of capillarity for both the tubes

Ex. 2. A cylinderical tube of any cross section is plunged in a liquid so that the angle between the generators and the vertical is α. Show that the volume of the liquid that rises in the tube is (sec α) times the volume that would rise if the tube is plunged vertically.

Ex. 3. A large drop of a liquid having a nearly flat top rests on a horizontal plane in the form of a surface of revolution.

(200)

If r is the radius of the section of the surface by the horizontal plane on which it rests and ϕ the angle of capillarity, prove that the volume V of the drop is

$$(2\,\pi r a^2\ sin\ \phi + \pi h\ r^2)$$

where h is the height of the highest point of the drop above the horizontal plane and $g^p a^2$ is the surface tension of the liquid.

Let us take the vertical axis of revolution of the solid as axis of z and the origin of coordinates in the horizontal plane.

We have seen that the equation of the surface is

$$(z-h) = a^2\ (\frac{1}{R_1} + \frac{1}{R_2})\qquad \dots \qquad \dots \qquad (1)$$

where h is a constant and $a^2 = \dfrac{B}{2g^p}$ so that $\dfrac{B}{2}$ = surface tension $= g^p a^2$.

Since the drop is very large and has a flat top the principal radii of curvature at the top must be infinite so that if z_0 be the height of the highest point above the horizontal plane, we have

$$z_0 - h = o.$$

Hence h is the height of the highest point above the horizontal plane.

Multiply both sides of Equation (1) by $dx\,dy$ and integrate over the projection of the free surface of the drop on the horizontal plane.

$$\therefore \int\int z\,dxdy - h\int\int dxdy = a^2 \int\int (\frac{1}{R_1} + \frac{1}{R_2})\,dxdy$$

$$\text{or, } V - \pi r^2 h = a^2 \int\int (\frac{1}{R_1} + \frac{1}{R_2})\,dxdy.$$

$$\text{But } \int\int (\frac{1}{R_1} + \frac{1}{R_2})\,dxdy = 2\,\pi r\ sin\ \phi \qquad (see\ \S\ 6.8)$$

Hence $V = 2\pi r a^2 \sin\phi + \pi h r^2$.

Ex. 4. A drop of mercury resting on a horizontal plane is in the from of a surface of revolution. If h be height of the topmost point of the drop above the horizontal plane and i the angle made by the surface of the drop with horizontal, prove that

$$h = 2a \cos\frac{i}{2} - \frac{2a^2}{b} + \frac{2a^2}{3r} \cdot \frac{1 - \sin\frac{i}{2}}{\cos\frac{i}{2}} \quad (appox)$$

where b is the radius of curvature of the meridian curve at the top and r is the radius of the base of the drop, and $g^p a^2$ is the surface tension of the liquid.

We know that $\dfrac{1}{R_1} + \dfrac{1}{R_2} = \dfrac{z - h'}{a^2}$

Taking a horizontal line through P as x-axis and the *downward* vertical as z-axis, we have

$$\frac{z - h'}{a^2} = \left(\frac{1}{R_1} + \frac{1}{R_2} \right)$$

Since $z = o$ at the topmost point P, where the radii of principal curvature are b, b we have

$$h' = -\frac{2a^2}{b} \qquad (2)$$

Set $\dfrac{dz}{dx} = \tan\phi$,

then $\dfrac{1}{R_1} = \dfrac{\sin\phi}{x}$, $\dfrac{1}{R_2} = \dfrac{d\phi}{ds} = \dfrac{d\phi}{dz} \dfrac{dz}{ds} = \sin\phi \dfrac{d\phi}{dz}$

Equation (1), therefore, becomes

$$\frac{d\phi}{dz} \sin\phi + \frac{\sin\phi}{x} = \frac{z - h'}{a^2}$$

Intergrating,

$$\frac{(z-h')^2}{2a^2} = -\cos\phi + \int^{z} \frac{\sin\phi}{x}dz + C.$$

Now $\phi = o$ when $z = o$, therefore,

$$\frac{(z-h')^2}{2a^2} = 1 - \cos\phi + \int_o^{z} \frac{\sin\phi}{x}dz + \frac{h'^2}{2a^2}$$

$$= (1 - \cos\phi) + \int_o^{z} \frac{\sin\phi}{x}dz + \frac{2a^2}{b^2},$$

by (2).

Assuming that b, the radius of curvature at the top is very large, the last term of the above equation is very small and may therefore be neglected.

Let the distance x of any point of the free surface from the axis be denoted by $(r+u)$ where r is the radius of the base. We have then

$$\frac{(z-h')^2}{2a^2} = (1 - \cos\phi) + \int_o^{z} \frac{\sin\phi}{u+r}dz$$

If r be large compared with a^2, we have to the first approximation,

$$\frac{(z-h')^2}{2a^2} = (1 - \cos\phi) = 2\sin^2\frac{\phi}{2}$$

or, $z - h' = 2a\sin\frac{\phi}{2}$

Substituting this value in the integral

$$\int \frac{\sin\phi}{u+r}dz = \int \frac{\sin\phi}{u+r}a\cos\frac{\phi}{2}d\phi = \int \frac{2a\sin\frac{\phi}{2}\cos^2\frac{\phi}{2}}{(u+r)}d\phi$$

$$= -\frac{4a}{3} \int \frac{1}{u+r} \, d \left(\cos^3 \frac{\phi}{2} - 1\right)$$

$$= \frac{4a}{3} \frac{1-\cos^3 \frac{\phi}{2}}{u+r} + \frac{4a}{3} \int \frac{1-\cos^3 \frac{\phi}{2}}{(u+r)^2} \, d\phi$$

Neglecting the last term as very small compared with the first, we have

$$(z-h')^2 = 4a^2 \, \mathrm{Sin}^2 \frac{\phi}{2} + \frac{8a^3}{3} \cdot \frac{1-\cos^3 \frac{\phi}{2}}{(u+r)}$$

$$\text{or } z-h' = 2a \, \mathrm{Sin} \frac{\phi}{2} + \frac{2a^2 \left(1-\cos^3 \frac{\phi}{2}\right)}{3 (u+r) \, \mathrm{Sin}\frac{\phi}{2}}$$

Now if i be the acute angle made by the surface of the drop with the horizontal plane, we have $\phi = \pi - i$, at any point of the base, where $z = h$ (say) and $u = o$.

$$\therefore \ h-h' = 2a \cos \frac{i}{2} + \frac{2a^2}{3r} \cdot \frac{1-\mathrm{Sin}^3 i/2}{\cos \ i|2}$$

$$\text{or } h = 2a \cos \frac{i}{2} - \frac{2a^2}{b} + \frac{2a^2}{3r} \cdot \frac{1-\mathrm{Sin}^3 i \ 2.}{\cos \frac{i}{2}}$$

This gives the height of the drop.

Ex 5. Prove that the formula

$$q = -\frac{2a^2}{b} + \sqrt{4a^2 \cos^2 \frac{i}{2} + \frac{8a^3}{3r} \left(1-\mathrm{Sin}^3 \frac{i}{2}\right) \left(1-\frac{a}{r} \, \mathrm{Sin} \, \frac{i}{2}\right)}$$

gives a better approximation than the formula given in the preceding example.

Ex. 6. Show that the radius of curvature 'b' at the top of the surface is given by

$$\frac{1}{b}=2\sqrt{2}\; a^{-\frac{3}{2}}\sqrt{\pi r}\,\tan\frac{\pi-i}{4}\,e^{-\frac{r}{a}}-4\,\mathrm{Sin}^{2}\,\frac{\pi-i}{4}$$

where r is the radius of the section at the base.

Ex 7. A drop of mercury rests in the form of a surface of revolution on a horizontal pla, e. Show that if r be the radius of the base and R the greatest radius of any horizontal section

$$R=r+\beta-\frac{a^{2}}{6\,(r+\beta)}\left(\frac{1}{2\cos\frac{^{2}\pi}{8}}+2-3\log\tan\frac{\pi}{8}\right)$$

$$+\frac{a^{2}}{6\,(r+\beta)}\left(\frac{1}{2\cos^{2}\frac{\pi-i}{4}}+4\,\cos^{2}\frac{i}{2}-3\log\,\tan\frac{\pi-i}{4}\right)$$

where $\beta=R-r$ and i is the angle between the tangent at the top to the meridian curve and the horizontal.

Ex. 8. A drop of a liquid whose volume is v rests in the form of a surface of revolution, show that radius r of the section of the horizontal plane on which it rests is the positive root of the quadratic equation

$$r^{2}+\left(1-\frac{1-\mathrm{Sin}^{3}\frac{i}{2}}{\mathrm{Cos}^{2}\frac{i}{2}}-2\,\mathrm{Sin}\,\frac{i}{2}\right)ar-\frac{v}{2\pi a\,\mathrm{Cos}\frac{i}{2}}=0$$

6. 9 *Rise of liquid near a plane plunged vertically in it.*

Let us take x-axis to be such as to be perpendicular to the plane, z—axis being vertical and lying in the plane. If the plane be so large that we can neglect what is happening at its extremities, the free surface of the liquid assumes the form of a cylinder whose generators are parallel to y-axis. Hence the coordinate z of any point of the free surface is independent of y. The equation (1) of § 6. 7 for the free surface becomes

$$\frac{\dfrac{d^2z}{dx^2}}{\left[1+\left(\dfrac{dz}{dx}\right)^2\right]^{\frac{3}{2}}} = \frac{z-h}{a^2}$$

or integrating

$$\frac{1}{\left[1+\left(\dfrac{dz}{dx}\right)^2\right]^{\frac{1}{2}}} = C - \frac{(z-h)^2}{2a^2}$$

If we count z from the natural leval of the liquid, the plane $z=o$ meets the free surface asymptotically and the radius of curvature is infinite. Hence for $z=o$, $\dfrac{d^2z}{dx^2} = \dfrac{dz}{dx} = o$, so that $h=o$ and $C=1$.

we, therefore, have

$$\pm \frac{dx}{dz} = \frac{(2a^2 - z^2)}{z\sqrt{4a^2 - z^2}} \qquad \dots \qquad \dots \qquad (1)$$

or, $\pm x = \sqrt{4a^2 - z^2} - a \, log \dfrac{\sqrt{4a^2 - z^2} + 2a}{z} + const \quad \dots \quad (2)$

Let θ be the angle of capillarity, then θ is the angle made by the normal at P to the free surface with x—axis. If the liquil rises to a height k against the plane, then O P $=k$ so that

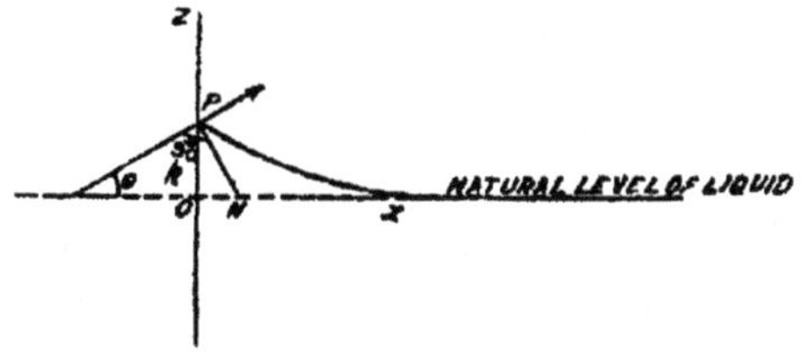

$$tan\,(90+\theta) = \left|\frac{dz}{dx}\right|_{z=k}$$

(206)

$$= \frac{k\sqrt{4a^2-k^2}}{2a^2-k^2} \qquad \ldots \qquad \text{by (1)}$$

$$\text{or, } \sin\theta = \left(1 - \frac{k^2}{2a^2}\right)$$

$$\text{or, } k = \pm a\sqrt{2(1-\sin\theta)} = \pm 2a\sin\left(\frac{\pi}{4} - \frac{\theta}{2}\right).$$

$+$ or $-$ sign being taken according as the liquid rises or is depressed.

If the liquid wets the plane, $\theta = o$ so that the height to which it rises is $a\sqrt{2}$.

Ex. 1. If a plane is inclined at an angle i to the horizontal, the height to which the liquid rises is

$$2a\sin\left(\frac{i-\theta}{2}\right)$$

where $g^\cap a^2$ is the surface tension.

Ex. 2. Two parallel planes are plunged vertically in a liquid, the angle of capillarity of both the planes being ϕ. If the distance between the planes be very small, show that the height of the liquid which rises against any plane is approximately

$$\frac{2a^2}{l}\cos\phi + \left(-\sin\phi\cos\phi + \frac{\pi}{2} - \phi\right)\frac{l}{4\cos^2\phi}$$

where l is the distance between the planes and $g\rho a^2$ is the surface tension.

Ex 3. A capillary tube of narrow bore and circular cross section is plunged in a liquid. If the angle of capillarity ϕ is acute and the radius of the tube r, shew that the free surface of the liquid in the tube is the surface obtained by the revolution of the curve

$$z = c - \sqrt{c^2-x^2} + \frac{c^3}{3a^2}\log\frac{c+\sqrt{c^2-x^2}}{2c}$$

about the z-axis, which is the vertical through the centre of a circular section.   Here

$$c = \frac{r}{\cos\phi} - \frac{r^3}{3a^2}\ \frac{1}{\cos^3\phi}\ \frac{\sin^2\phi}{(1+\sin\phi)}\ , \text{ and } g^{\rho}a^2$$

is surface tension of the liquid.

Let us take the origin in the plane of the level surface.

If x be the distance of any point on the surface from the z—axis, we have

$$\frac{\frac{d^2z}{dr^2} + \frac{1}{x}\frac{dz}{dx}\,[1+(\frac{dz}{dx})^2]}{[1+(\frac{dz}{dx})^2]^{\frac{3}{2}}} = \frac{z}{a^2} \quad \cdots \qquad (1)$$

Multiplying both sides of (1) by x and then integrating with respect to x we have

$$\frac{x\frac{dz}{dx}}{\sqrt{1+(\frac{dz}{dx})^2}} = \frac{1}{a^2}\int_0^x xz\,dx \qquad \cdots \qquad \cdots \qquad (2)$$

If r is very small, we may suppose that the surface of the meniscus differs only slightly from the portion of a sphere.

The meridian curve of the surface will,   therefore, be a circle whose equation is

$$z = l - \sqrt{c^2 - x^2},$$

l and c being constants.   Let us set

$$z = l - \sqrt{c^2 - x^2} + u,$$

where u is a small function of x.   We have then

$$\frac{dz}{dx} = \frac{x}{\sqrt{c^2 - x^2}} + \frac{du}{dx}$$

we have then

$$\sqrt{1+\left(\frac{dz}{dx}\right)^2} = \frac{c}{\sqrt{c^2-x^2}}\left(+1\frac{x\sqrt{c^2-x^2}}{c^2}\frac{du}{dx}\right)$$

$$\frac{x\frac{dz}{dx}}{\left(+\left(\frac{uz}{dx}\right)^2\right)} = \left(\frac{x^2}{c}+\frac{x\sqrt{c^2-x^2}}{c}\frac{du}{dx}\right)\left(1-\frac{x\sqrt{c^2-x^2}}{c^2}\frac{du}{dx}\right)$$

$$= \frac{x^2}{c}+x\frac{(c^2-x^2)^{\frac{3}{2}}}{c^3}\frac{du}{dx}$$

Also $\dfrac{1}{a^2}\displaystyle\int_0^x xz\, dx = \dfrac{x^2 l}{2a^2}+\dfrac{(c^2-x^2)^{\frac{3}{2}}-c^3}{3a^2}$

neglecting $\dfrac{1}{a^2}\displaystyle\int ux\, dx$.

Equation (2) then leads to

$$\frac{du}{dx}=c^2\left(\frac{cl}{2a^2}-1\right)\frac{x}{(c^2-x^2)^{\frac{3}{2}}}+\frac{c^3}{3a^2}\frac{1}{x}-\frac{c^6}{3a^2}\frac{1}{x(c^2-x^2)^{\frac{3}{2}}}$$

$$u=c^2\left(\frac{cl}{2a^2}-\frac{c^2}{3a^2}-1\right)\frac{1}{\sqrt{c^2-x^2}}+\frac{c^3}{3a^2}\log\left(c+\sqrt{c^2-x^2}\right)$$

$$+\text{const} \qquad (3)$$

Since u must not be large when x differs slightly from c, the first term must vanish.

$$\therefore l=\frac{2a^2}{c}+\frac{2}{3}c \qquad (4)$$

Also for $x=0$, z is zero, so that $l-c+u_0=0$

$$\therefore u=\frac{c^3}{3a^2}\log\frac{c+\sqrt{c^2-x^2}}{2c}+c-l$$

The equation of the surface of meniscus is

$$z = c - \sqrt{c^2 - x^2} + \frac{c^3}{3a^2} \log \frac{c + \sqrt{c^2 - x^2}}{2c}$$

If the angle of capillarity ϕ is acute

$$\cot \phi = \frac{dz}{dx} \text{, for } x = r$$

$$\text{or } \cot \phi = \frac{r}{\sqrt{c^2 - r^2}} \left(1 - \frac{c^3}{3a^2} \frac{1}{c + \sqrt{c^2 - x^2}}\right)$$

$$\text{or } c = \frac{r}{\cos \phi} - \frac{r^3}{3a^2} \frac{1}{\cos^3 \phi} \frac{\sin^2 \phi}{1 + \sin \phi} \text{(appox)}$$

6. 9. Surface Tension— We have already seen in § 6. 2 that Thomas Young compared the free surface of a liquid to that of a membrane eqally stretched in all directions and obtained the differential equation of the free surface of a liquid on this hypothesis. Laplace's objection to this mode of treatment of the theory of capillarity has already been noted. We shall here indicate how the hypothesis of a uniform surface tension leads to the same results as already obtained.

Let *assume* that the free surface of the liquid is in a state of uniform surface tension T, so that the tension on the surface across any short length δs in the surface is T δs at right angles to the line δs.

Consider now a portion of the free surface ABCD of a liquid at rest under the action of gravity.

Let PQ, PS be elements of arcs of two principal sections of the surface at P. Draw the two principal sections OR and SR at the points Q and S. We thus obtain a small area PQRS of the free surface. Consider an element of the surface bounded by PQRS and of infinitely small thickness ε. It is in equilibrium under the action of

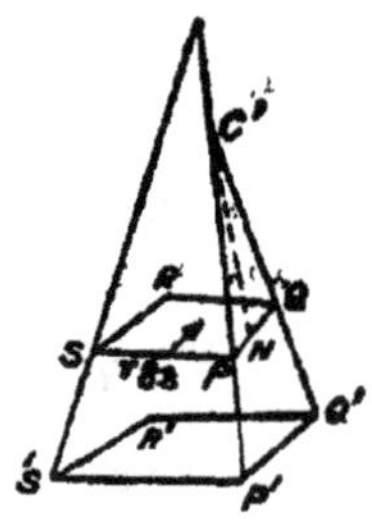

surface tensions acting across the contour, the weight, and the liquid pressure acting normally on the element. (We neglect atmospheric pressure at the top). We resolve all the forces along the normal PC′. If the pressure at P′, a point immediately below P is p, the total hydrostatical thrust acting on the element is p (PQ) (PS)$=pds\ ds'$, along C′P. The weight of the element is $g\rho\ ds\ ds'\varepsilon$, acting vertically downwards. If the angle between the normal and the vertical is α, the component of weight along PC′ is

$$g\rho\ ds\ ds'\varepsilon\ \cos\ \alpha.$$

If T is the tension per unit of length across PS, the whole tension across PS, (which acts at its middle point perpendicularly to PS) is T (PS)$=$Tds'. Its component along the normal PC′ is therefore

$$\text{T}ds'\ \cos\ \text{QPC}' \Big|\ \ \text{T}ds'\ \cos\ (\frac{\pi}{2}-\frac{\text{PC}'\text{Q})}{2}$$

$$=\text{T}ds'\ \text{Sin}\ \frac{\text{PC}'\text{Q}}{2}$$

$$=\text{T}ds'\ \frac{ds}{2\text{R}_1}$$

The tension across QR also gives a component of the same magnitude; hence the sum of these two components is $\dfrac{\text{T}ds\,ds'}{\text{R}_1}$

Similarly the sum of the normal components of the tensions acting on the sides PQ and SR is $\dfrac{\text{T}ds\,ds'.}{\text{R}_2}$

Hence the normal component of the tensions acting across the whole contour PQRS is

$$\text{T}\ (\frac{1}{\text{R}_1}+\frac{1}{\text{R}_2})\ ds\,ds'.$$

For equilibrium, therefore

$$p\,ds\,ds' = [T(\frac{1}{R_1}+\frac{1}{R_2}) + \varepsilon g^P \cos \alpha]\, ds\,ds'$$

Since ε is infinitely small compared with the other terms of the equation, this leads to

$$p = T\,(\frac{1}{R_1}+\frac{1}{R_2}).$$

Now for a liquid at rest under gravity we have $dp = g^P dz$. This equation will hold through-out the liquid until a distance ε from the free surface. Hence we can use it to determine pressure p at the point P', which is taken to be at a distance ε from the free surface.

Hence $p = g^P (z - h)$, h being a constant.

We, therefore, have

$$T \frac{1}{R_1}+\frac{1}{R_2}) = g^P(z-h).$$

Comparing this equation with that obtained in § 6· 7, we see that the "constant of capillary forces" $\frac{B}{2}$ is identical with the surface tension T of the liquid. That is why the constant $\frac{B}{2}$ was called the surface tension of the liquid.

Ex. 1. Show that the equation of a liquid film enclosing a mass of air at pressure $\overline{p}$ is given by

$$T(\frac{1}{R_1}+\frac{1}{R_2}) = \overline{p} - \pi$$

where T is the tension of the liquid film and π is the external pressure of the atmosphere.

Ex. 2. A plane plate is partly immersed in a liquid of density P and surface tension t. The angle of capillarity for the liquid and the substance is β and the plate is inclined at an angle

α to the horizontal. Prove that the difference of the liquid on the two sides of the plate above the undisturbed surface level is

$$4 \left\{ \frac{t}{g\rho} \right\}^{\frac{1}{2}} \cos \frac{\pi - 2\beta}{4} \cos \frac{\pi - 2\alpha}{4} \, .$$

We know that $h_1 = 2a \sin \dfrac{\alpha - \beta}{2}$

$$h_2 = 2a \sin \frac{\pi - \alpha - \beta}{2}$$

$$\therefore h_1 - h_2 = 2a \, 2\left[\cos \frac{\pi - 2\beta}{4} \cos \frac{\pi - 2\alpha}{4} \right]$$

$$= 4 \, a \cos \frac{\pi - 2\beta}{4} \cos \frac{\pi - 2\alpha}{4} \, ,$$

where $t = g\rho \, a^2$, or $a = \left(\dfrac{t}{g\rho} \right)^{\frac{1}{2}}$

Ex. 2. A volume $\frac{4}{3} \pi c^3$ of gravitating liquid and of density ρ is surrounded by an atmosphere of pressure π and contains a concentric cavity filled with air, whose volume at this atmospheric pressure is $\frac{4}{3} \pi a^3$. The surface tension of the liquid is t; prove that the radius x of the cavity in the configuration of equilibrium is given by

$$\pi \frac{a^3}{(x^3} - 1) = 2t \left\{ \frac{1}{x} + \frac{1}{\sqrt[3]{c^3 + x^3}} \right\} + \frac{2}{3} \pi \rho^2 \left\{ \frac{c^3 + 3x^3}{\sqrt[3]{c^3 + x^3}} - 3x^2 \right\}$$

Ex. 3. If two soap bubbles of radii r and r' are blown, from the same liquid and if they coalesce into a single bubble of radius R, prove that if π be the atmospheric pressure, tension is

$$\frac{\pi}{2} \frac{R^3 - r^3 - r'^3}{r^2 + r'^2 - R^2}$$

Ex. 4. A spherical balloon of radius r is made of a material which can sustain a maximum tensile stress of amount $T \div$ (thickness). It contains a quantity of gas of density σ at the pressure Π of the atmosphere on the surface of earth. The balloon rises vertically against gravity supposed constant, prove that it will burst when its velocity is given by

$$\tfrac{1}{2}\,v^2 = \frac{2T}{g\sigma r} + \frac{k}{g}\,\log\left(1 - \frac{T^2}{\Pi r}\right),$$

where $p = k\,\rho.$

(Higher I. C. S. 1934)

We have $dp = -g\rho\,dz$, for any point of the atmosphere at height z.

But $p = k\,\rho$

$$\therefore \frac{dp}{p} = -\frac{g}{k}\,dz$$

or, $p = \Pi e^{-\frac{g}{k}z}$ and $\rho = \frac{\Pi}{k}e^{-\frac{g}{k}z}.$

Now at any height z, the buoyancy of the fluid on the balloon is $g\rho V$, the weight of the ballon being appraximately $g\,\sigma\,V$, so that equation of motion of the balloon is

$$(g\,\sigma\,V)\,v\frac{dv}{dz} = g\,\rho\,V - g\,\sigma\,V$$

$$v\frac{dv}{dz} = \left(\frac{\rho}{\sigma}-1\right) = \frac{\Pi}{k\sigma}e^{-\frac{g z}{k}} - 1$$

$$\therefore \tfrac{1}{2}v^2 = \frac{\Pi}{k\sigma}e^{-gz/k}\left(-\frac{k}{g}\right) - z + C.$$

Since $v = 0$, when $z = 0$,

$$0 = -\frac{\Pi}{g\sigma} + C$$

or, $\tfrac{1}{2}v^2 = \frac{\Pi}{g\sigma}\left(1 - e^{-\frac{gz}{k}}\right) - z$

Now the balloon bursts when

$$\frac{2T}{r} = \Pi - p = \Pi - \Pi e^{-\frac{gh}{k}}$$

$$= \Pi \left(1 - e^{gh/k}\right).$$

$$\therefore \tfrac{1}{2} v^2 = \frac{2T}{g\sigma r} + \frac{k}{g} \, log \left(1 - \frac{2T}{\Pi r}\right).$$

Ex. 5. A circular cylinder is made to rest on a liquid with its axis fixed horizontally at a height h above the level surface of the liquid. If α be the angle of capillarity and 2θ the angle subtended at the axis by the arc of the cross section in contact with theliquid, prove that the surface of the liquid near the cylinder is a cylinder whose right section is the curve whose parametric equation is

$$x = \sqrt{\frac{T}{g\rho}} \left[log \cot \frac{\phi}{4} + 2 \cos \frac{\phi}{2} \right] + A$$

$$z = 2 \sqrt{\frac{T}{g\rho}} \sin \frac{\phi}{2}.$$

Also shew that

$$g\rho (c \cos \theta - h)^2 = 4T \sin^2\left(\frac{\theta - \alpha}{2}\right).$$

6. 11. *Liquid Films:* If we dip a frame work formed by rigid wires in a liquid e.g. a solution of soap and water and then draw it out slowly we obtain a system of infinitely thin films of the liquid which are bounded by the wires. We proceed to find the surface of equilibrium of these films. We have already proved in § 6. 6 that the force function, U, of a system consisting of a liquid resting in contact with solids is

$$- g\int\int\int \rho z \, dv + A - \frac{B}{2} \sigma + \left(E - \frac{B}{2}\right) \lambda,$$

where σ is the area of the free surface of the liquid and λ the area of the liquid in contact with the solid.

In the particular case of infinitesimally thin liquid films, we may neglect that last term as the area λ of the surface of contact of the liquid and solids is proportional to the thickness of the film, which is assumed to be exceedingly thin. The first term is also negligible in comparison with the third because it is also proportional to the thickness of the film, provided, of course, $\frac{B}{2}$, which is the surface tension of the liquid film, is not itself very small. The second term, which is a constant may also be ignored as the addition of a constant to the force function of a system makes no difference in the equations of equilibrium of the system derived from it.

We thus take the force function U in this particular instance to be $-\frac{B}{2}\sigma$.

The condition of stable equilibrium is that U or $-\frac{B}{2}\sigma$ be a maximum. That is, the area σ of the free surface must be a minimum. In the case of a single film, the free surface σ is composed of two faces of the film, whose surfaces are sensibly identical as the thickness of the film is very small. Hence in order that the equilibrium of a film be stable, it is necessary and sufficient that area $\frac{\sigma}{2}$ of one of the two faces be a minimum.

This conclusion is easily verified by means of a simple experiment due to Van der Mensbrugghe. Take a circular wire of copper and suspend it by means of three strings. Dip the wire in soap solution and withdraw it gently from the liquid by means of strings. A thin film is thus obtained. Form a loop of a piece of thread and moisten it with soap solution. Place it gently on the film. The thread can assume any form whatever. Now perforate the thin film inside the loop by means of a pin. It will be found that the loop of the thread is instantly drawn out into a circle c by the contracting film. Of the closed curves having a given perimeter circle has the maximum area. The area comprised between the circumference of the circle c and the metallic wire is thus least when the liquid is in equilibrium.

6. 12. *Liquid Films (Minimal Surfaces).*

Let A M B be one of the faces of a liquid film and $A_1M_1B_1$ a parallel surface infinitely close to it. If A MB is a surface of minimum area, the areas AMB and $A_1M_1B_1$ must differ by infinitesimals of the second order. Let us draw normals to this surface at every point of the contour of AB. These normals intersect the surface $A_1M_1B_1$ in a curve L', which encloses an area σ'. Let σ'' be the annular area between the contours A_1B_1 and $A'B'$. (See § 6. 6) we then have

$$\sigma_1 = \sigma' + \sigma''$$

Also $\delta\sigma = \sigma_1 - \sigma = \sigma' + \sigma'' - \sigma$

$$= \sigma'' + (\sigma' - \sigma)$$

$$= \int_L \frac{\delta n \cos\theta}{\sin\theta} ds - \iint_L (\frac{1}{R_1} + \frac{1}{R_2})\ \delta n\, dS,$$

by equation (6) of § 6.6.

The condition of equilibrium is therefore,

$$\iint (\frac{1}{R_1} + \frac{1}{R_2})\ \delta n\ dS - \int_L \delta n\ \cot\theta\ ds = o.$$

Since this condition must be satisfied for any value of δn arbitrarily taken, we must have

$$\frac{1}{R_1} + \frac{1}{R_2} = o,$$

and $\cot\theta = o.$

The two principal radii of curvatures of the surface must therefore be equal and of opposite signs. Such surfaces are called minimal surfaces The second equation expresses the fact that the angle of capillarity is $\frac{\pi}{2}$. Since the direction of the taugen plane to the wire with which the film is in contact is arbitrary, this is the same thing as saying that the surface of the film passes through the contour of the wire.

The problem of determining the surface of a liquid film is the same as that of finding a surface of minimum area passing through a given contour.

Ex. 1. Prove that the differential equation of a minimal surface is

$$\left\{1+\left(\frac{\partial z}{\partial y}\right)^2\right\}\frac{\partial^2 z}{\partial x^2}-2\frac{\partial z}{\partial x}\frac{\partial z}{\partial y}\frac{\partial^2 z}{\partial x\partial y}+\left\{1+\left(\frac{\partial z}{\partial x}\right)^2\right\}\frac{\partial^2 z}{\partial y^2}=0.$$

Ex. 2. Prove that a helicoide is a possible surface of equilibrium for a liquid film.

3. Prove that the surface of equilibrium of a liquid film supported by the circumferences of two circles whose planes are perpendicular to their line of centres is a catenoid formed by the revolution of a catenary about the line of centres

Ex. 4 Show that a surface whose mean curvature is zero every where is a surface of equilibrium for liquid films. Prove also that the equilibrium is stable   (Schwarz)

6 13   *Euqilibrium of a drop of oil.*

Let us consider the equilibrium of a drop of olive oil trapped between two wires of any shape or two circular discs) and inserted in a mixture of water and alcohol of the same density as itself.

In order to find the condition of equilibrium it is sufficient to determine the condition that the force function of the system formed by the oil and liquid is either a maximum or a minimum. Now the forces that act on the system are the weight and the capillary forces of the molecules   The centre of gravity of the liquid and oil does not chanze whatever may be the displacement of the oil drop since the surrounding liquid is of the same density. Hence the work done by weight in any virtual displacement is zero   It is therefore not necessary to take into account the external force of gravity.

The capillary actions are of several kinds. They are attractions.

   (1) of wires on the oil,

   (2) of oil on itself

   (3) of the mixture on itself,

   (4) of the mixture on oil,

   (5) of the mixture on the wires

We neglect the attractions of the material of the containing vase on the liquids which it contains because they do not figure in the variation of the force function when oil drop is slightly displaceed, provided that the oil drop is always at a great compared with ε), distance from the walls of the vase.

Let us denote by

$\sigma =$ the surface of contact of the oil and the mixture,

$\lambda' =$ the surface of contact of the oil and its solid supports,

$\lambda =$ the total surface of the solid supports,

$B' =$ the function relative to the mutual attractions of the molecules of the oil

$E_1 =$ the function relative to the attractions of the molecules of the oil and the solid supports

B_1', E_1' corresponding functions for the mixture and E_s, the function relative to the attractions of the oil and the mixture.

We have for the force function resulting from the capillary actions enumerated above,

$$(1) E_1 \lambda_1$$

$$(2) -\frac{B_1}{2}(\sigma + \lambda_1)$$

$$(3) -\frac{B_1'}{2}(\sigma - \lambda_1 + \lambda)$$

$$(4)\ E_2\ \sigma$$

$$(5)\ E_1'(\lambda - \lambda_1),$$

neglecting constant quantities.

Hence the total force function for the system is, (except for a constant),

$$\left(E_1' - \frac{B_1'}{2}\right)\lambda + \left(E_2 - \frac{B_1'}{2} - \frac{B_1}{2}\right)\sigma + \left(E_1 - \frac{B_1}{2} + \frac{B_1'}{2} - E_1'\right)\lambda_1$$

Now since the framework of wires is solid, the surface λ remains constant. We may therefore take

$$\left(E_2 - \frac{B_1'}{2} - \frac{B_1}{2}\right)\sigma + \left(E_1 - \frac{B_1}{2} + \frac{B_1'}{2} - E_1'\right)\lambda_1,$$

as our force function.

For equilibrium, therefore,

$$\left(E_2 - \frac{B_1'}{2} - \frac{B_1}{2}\right)\delta\sigma + \left(E_1 - \frac{B_1}{2} + \frac{B_1'}{2} - E_1'\right)\delta\lambda_1 = 0.$$

Comparing this with equation (1) of § 6. 6 giving the condition of equilibrium of a liquid in contact with solid walls we see that they are of the same form. They only differ by the values of the coefficients of $\delta\sigma$ and $\delta\lambda_1$ and by the disappearance of the term relating to weight. Following the same reasonings as there, it is easily seen that this condition of equilibrium leads to two conditions viz.

$$\frac{1}{R_1} + \frac{1}{R_2} = \text{const, and}$$

$$\phi = \text{const.}$$

Hence the mean curvature of the surface of separation of the oil drop and the mixture must be a constant and the surface must cut the solid supports at a constant angle.

6. 14. If the surface of equilibrium of the drop is a surface of revolution the meridian curve is the path of the focus of a conic rolling on a straight line. If the two wires holding the drop of oil be circles whose planes are perpendicular to the line joining their centres, the surface of the oil drop is evidently a surface of revolution, the line of centres being the axis of revolution.

Let F be any point on the meridian curve and let xy be the axis of revolution. Draw Fc the normal at F intersecting xy in I. Then it is well known that the principal radii of cur-

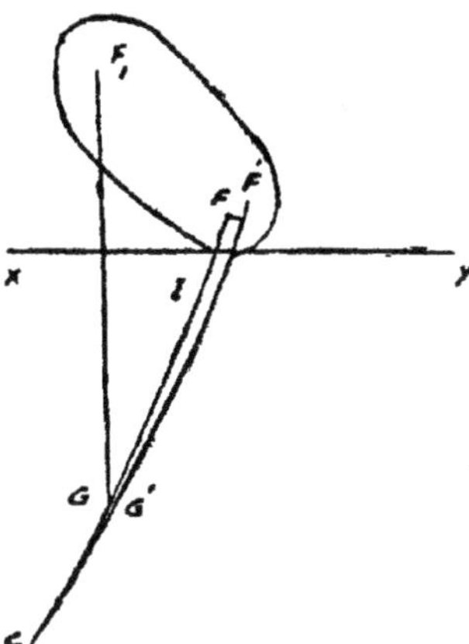

vature at F are FC, the radius of curvature of the meridian curve, and FI. Since the mean curvature of the surface must be constant in order that the drop be in equilibrium

$$\frac{1}{FI} + \frac{1}{FC} = \text{const.}$$

We proceed to show now that this condition is satisfied in the case of a curve generated by the focus a of conic rolling along a straight line.   Consider an ellipse whose focii are F,F.' The point of contact I is the instantaneous centre of rotation, therefore, we have

$$\frac{\text{Velocity of } F}{\text{Velocity of } F_1} = \frac{I\,F}{I\,F_1}.$$

Let G be the image of F_1 in the given straight line xy, on which the ellipse rolls. This point will have the same velocity as F_1.

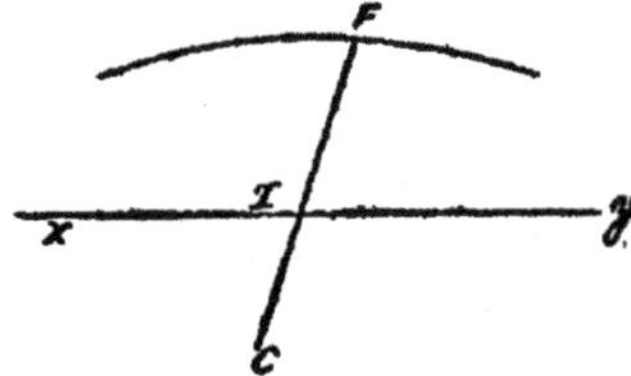

Also by a known property of the ellipse G will lie on F I, so that $I\,F_1 = I\,G$.

$$\text{Hence,} \quad \frac{\text{velocity of } F}{\text{velocity of } G} = \frac{IF}{IG} \qquad \ldots \qquad \ldots \qquad (1)$$

Through a point F' infinitely close to F on the locus of this point, draw a normal to this curve. Let this normal meet FI in C then this is the centre of curvature of the curve, for FIG is also normal to the curve

$$\text{Now } FG = FI + IG = FI + IF_1$$

$$= \text{major axis of the ellipse} = \text{const.}$$

Hence the locus of G is a curve parallel to that of F. Consequently the two infinitely small triangles FCF' and GCG' are similar,

(222)

$$\therefore \ \frac{FF'}{GG'} = \frac{CF}{CG}$$

$$\text{or, } \frac{\text{Velocity of } F}{\text{Velocity of } G} = \frac{CF}{CG}$$

$$= \frac{IF}{IG} \qquad \text{by (1)}$$

Hence the four points F, I, G and C form a harmonic range, so that

$$\frac{1}{IF} + \frac{1}{FC} = \frac{2}{FG} = const.$$

Hence the condition that must hold in the case of the meridian curve of the surface of equilibrium is satisfied by the locus of F. This curve is known as *Onduloide* Similarly it can be shown that the locus of the focus of a hyperbola rolling on a straight line has the same property. This curve is known as *nadoide*. In the case of a parabola, the locus of the focus is such that

$$\frac{1}{IF} + \frac{1}{FC} = o.$$

Such a curve is a catenary, with the straight line on which the parabola rolls as its directrix.

Ex. 1. A drop of oil rests in a liquid of the same density as itself without being in contact with any solid supports. Prove that the surface of equilibrium is a sphere.

[Hint : $\lambda = \lambda_1 = o$, so that the condition of equilibrim reduces to $\delta\sigma = o.$]

Ex. 2. If the drop in the above example is made to rotate about an axis passing through its centre with velocity ω, prove that the surface of the drop is a surface of revolution whose meridian curve is

$$x = \int \frac{c\,dy}{\sqrt{y^2 - c^2}},$$

where $c = \frac{\alpha}{4} y^3 + \frac{\beta}{2} y + \frac{\gamma}{y}$, $\alpha = \frac{\omega^2}{2T}$, T being the surface tension and β, γ arbitrary constants.

Let σ be the free surface and σ' a neighbouring surface obtained by an infinitesimal deformation of σ. The work done by capillary forces in a virtual displacement is, as we have seen,

$$-\left(\frac{B_1}{2} + \frac{B_1'}{2} - E_2\right)\delta\sigma = -T\,\delta\sigma,$$

where T is the surface tension.

Again, the rotation of the drop sets up centrifugal forces whose work in any virtual displacement is

$$\delta \Sigma \omega^2 r(m_i\,\delta r) = \tfrac{1}{2}\omega^2\,\delta I$$

where I is the moment of inertia of the drop about the axis of rotation.

Hence for equilibrium

$$\frac{\omega^2}{2}\,\delta I - T\,\delta\sigma = 0$$

$$\text{or, } \delta\sigma = \frac{\omega^2}{2T}\,\delta I = \alpha\,\delta I.$$

On account of the deformation of σ to an element $ab = dS$ of this surface, there corresponds an element $a'b' = dS'$ of the surface obtained by drawing normals along the contour ab to σ. The variation of σ is

$$\delta\sigma = \int\int dS' - \int\int dS$$

$$= \int\int \delta n\left(\frac{1}{R_1} + \frac{1}{R_2}\right)dS.$$

The variation of I is the sum of the moments of inertia of the elements of volume such as $ab\ a'b'$. If r be the distance of the centre of gravity of this element from the axis of rotation we have

$$\delta I = \int\int r^2\ \delta n\ dS.$$

$\therefore$ The condition of equilibrium is

$$\int\int \delta n\ dS \left(\frac{1}{R_1} + \frac{1}{R_2} - \alpha r^2\right) = 0,$$

for every δn such that

$$\int\int \delta n\ dS = 0,$$

which expresses the fact that volume of the drop does not change.

This is satisfied if

$$\frac{1}{R_1} + \frac{1}{R_2} - \alpha\ r^2 = const = \beta$$

If this surface is a surface of revolution, the principal radii of curvature are MC, the radius of curvature of the meridian curve, and MN. Hence

$$R_1 = MC = \frac{d\phi}{ds}\ , \ R_2 = MN = \frac{r}{cos\phi}$$

$$\therefore \frac{d\phi}{ds} + \frac{cos\ \phi}{r} = \alpha\ r^2 + \beta$$

This gives for the equation of meridian curve

$$\frac{d\phi}{ds} + \frac{cos\ \phi}{y} = \alpha\ y^2 + \beta$$

taking the axis of revolution as x—axis

$$dy = -\ sin\phi\ ds$$

$$\therefore - y\ sin\ \phi\ d\phi + cos\phi\ dy = (\alpha\ y^2 + \beta y)\ dy$$

$$\text{or, } y\ cos\ \phi = \frac{\alpha}{4}\ y^4 + \frac{\beta}{2}\ y^2 + \gamma = c,$$

γ being an arbitrary constant.

$$or,\ cos\ \phi = \frac{c}{y}$$

$$\therefore\ tan\ \phi = \frac{\sqrt{y^2 - c^2}}{c}$$

$$or,\ x = \int \frac{c\ dy}{\sqrt{y^2 - c^2}}.$$

Ex. 3.   A drop of liquid under no forces except uniform external pressure and surface tension rotates as a rigid body about an axis.   Shew that on the surface $(\frac{3}{R_1} - \frac{1}{R_2})$ is constant, R_1, R_2 being the principal radii of curvature of the surface.

6. 15.   *Closed liquid films.   Soap Bubble.*

If we dip a network of wires in a liquid we obtain in certain cases a system of liquid films, which form a closed surface enclosing a mass of air.   We shall now show that the surfaces of the equilibrium of these films are the same as the surfaces of equilibrium of a drop of oil placed in a mixture of water and alcohol of the same density.

Consider the system formed by these films and the mass of air enclosed within.   Imagine a virtual displacement of the system from its equilibrium position

The virtual work due to the weight of the system may be neglected, because the mass of the enclosed air and the mass of the liquid forming the films are very small.

Let σ be the total area of the faces of the films in contact with external air.   The area of the faces in contact with internal air is also sensibly σ, as the two faces of any film being very near each other can be regarded as parallel.   The virtual work of the capillary forces on account of a variation $\delta\sigma$ of this area is

$$2\left(-\frac{B_1}{2}\,\delta\sigma\right)$$

B_1, being the function relative to the action of the molecules of the liquid on themselves. If at the same time the area of contact of the liquid and the framework varies, we shall have to consider the virtual work of the capillary forces resulting from this variation. But this surface being proportional to the thickness of the films is very small and may therefore be neglected We, therefore, have only $- B_1\,\delta\sigma$ as the virtual work of capillary forces due to the displacement considered

To this we must add the virtual work of the pressures If p be the pressure of the air within and π that of the air without, the virtual works of the pressures due to a displacement of an elementary area dS are $p\delta n\,dS$ and $-\pi\delta n\,dS$ respectively.

The condition of equilibrium of the system is

$$- B_1\,\delta\sigma + \int\int_L(p-\pi)\,\delta n\,dS=o.$$

But we have already seen that

$$\delta\sigma=-\int\int_L \delta n\left(\frac{1}{R_1}+\frac{1}{R_2}\right)dS+ \int_L \delta n\,\cot\phi\,ds.$$

$$\therefore \int\int_L\left[p-\pi+\left(\frac{1}{R_1}+\frac{1}{R_2}\right)B_1\right]\delta n\,dS- B_1\int_L \delta n\,\cot\phi\,sds=o.$$

Since this is satisfied whatever the deformation we must have

$$-p+\pi=\left(\frac{1}{R_1}+\frac{1}{R_2}\right)\,B_1,$$

$$\cot\phi=o,\text{ or }\phi=\frac{\pi}{2}.$$

The pressures p and π being uniform, (since the weight of the air has been neglected), the first condition shows that the mean curvature of the surface is constant. This is one of the conditions of equilibrium of a drop of oil of the same density as the mixture in which it is inserted. The condition $\phi = \dfrac{\pi}{2}$ appears more restrictive than the analogous condition of $\phi =$ constant found for the drop. But in reality both the conditions are identical in as much as both express the fact that the surface of the films or of the drop must pass through the wires of the frame work.

In particular if we form a soap bubble passing through the contours of two parallel wires of the same radius we must obtain for figures of equilibrium, onduloide, or a right circular cylinder, or a nodoide, or a catenoide, This has been actually observed by Plateau.

Ex. 1. Two soap bubbles of radii R and R′ intersect one another in a circle through which passes a thin soap film. If the film forms part of a sphere whose radius is R″, prove that

$$\frac{1}{R'} - \frac{1}{R} = \frac{1}{R''}$$

Ex. 2. Two circular rings with a common axis at right angles to their planes support a closed liquid film containing air at a greater pressure than the external air; shew that the ends of the film are spheres of radius $a = 2\dfrac{T}{p}$, and that the surface between the rings is a surface of revolution of which the meridian curve has an intrinsic equation

$$\text{Sin } \phi = \frac{x}{a} + \frac{b}{x},$$

where ϕ is the inclination of the normal to the axis and x is the distance from the line of centres of the rings.

Ex. 3. A liquid film of total surface tension T is supported by two equal parallel circular discs of radius r, with their centres at a distance h apart on a line perpendicular to their planes. The film is in the form of a cylinder. If a pin hole is made in one of the discs so that the air slowly escapes, shew that a total quantity

$$P_o \, \pi \, r \left[\left(1 + \frac{T}{\Pi r} \right) hr - c^2 \left(\frac{h}{2r} + \text{Sinh}\,\frac{h}{2c} \right) \right]$$

will escape, where P_o and Π are atmospheric density and pressure and c is given by $\cosh \dfrac{h}{2c} = \dfrac{r}{c}$

Let the initial pressure inside the cylinder be p, so that

$$p - \Pi = \frac{T}{r} \qquad (1)$$

The mass of the air in the cylinder is $\pi r^2 \cdot (h) \; P$, P being the density of air inside the cylinder. Since $\dfrac{\Pi}{P_o} = \dfrac{p}{P}$, therefore mass of air

is $\pi r^2 \, h \dfrac{p P_o}{\Pi}$.

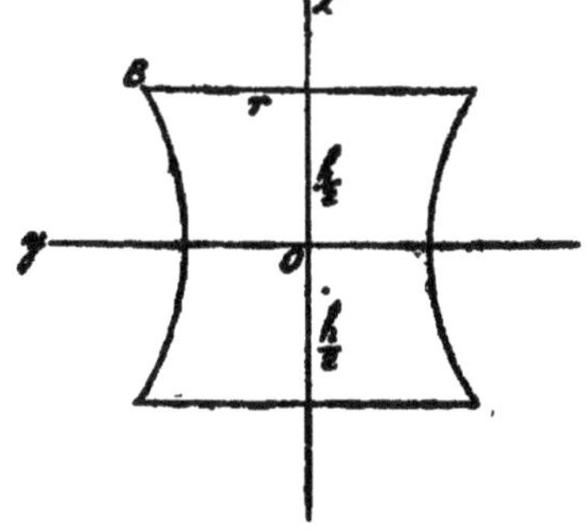

Now if a hole be made in one of the discs, air will escape till the pressures inside and outside are equal and the liquid film then assumes the form of a catenoid, that is the surface of revolution formed by revolving a catenary about its directrix, which in this case will coincide with the line of centres of the discs.

If v_o be the volume enclosed in the liquid film, the mass of the air remaining is $P_o v_o$, density of air being now the same as that of atmosphere.

The mass of air escaping is

$$\pi r^2 h \, \frac{P_o p}{\Pi} - P_o v_o$$

(229)

or by (1)

$$\pi r^2 P_o h \left(1 + \frac{T}{\Pi r}\right) - P_o v_o \qquad (2)$$

We have now to calculate the volume v_o of the surface of volution of the catenary

$$y = c \cosh \frac{x}{c}$$

about its directrix, which is the line of centres of the disc.

Since the point B $\left(\frac{h}{2}, r\right)$ lies on the catenary,

$$r = c \cosh \frac{h}{2c}$$

or, $\cosh \dfrac{h}{2c} = \dfrac{r}{c}$, whch gives c.

Now
$$v_o = 2 \int_o^{\frac{h}{2}} \pi y^2 \, dx$$

$$= 2\pi \int_o^{\frac{h}{2}} c^2 \cosh^2 \frac{x}{c} \, dx$$

$$= c^2 \pi \left[\frac{c}{2} \operatorname{Sinh} \frac{h}{c} + \frac{h}{2} \right]$$

$$= \pi c^2 \left[c\left(\frac{r}{c}\right) \operatorname{Sinh} \frac{h}{2c} + \frac{h}{2} \right]$$

$$= \pi r c^2 \left[\operatorname{Sinh} \frac{h}{2c} + \frac{h}{2r} \right]$$

Hence by (2) we have the required result.

Ex. 4 A wire in the form of a circle of radius a is placed in the surface of soapy water and raised gently, so as to draw after it a film. Prove that neglecting its weight, the meridian section of the film is a catenary. Also prove that the parameter of the meridian caternary, when the area of the film is equal to $\pi\, a^2$ is $\dfrac{a}{z}$ where z is given by

$$\cosh^{-1}\frac{1}{z} + z\,(\,z^2 - \,)^{\frac{1}{2}} = z^2$$

6. 16. *Equilibrium of a drop resting on liquid of greater density.—*

Let ABCD be the drop. Let σ be its free surface ABC and σ' the surface ADC in contact with the denser liquid on which it rests. Let σ'' be the free surface of the liquid itself. Let $\dfrac{B}{2}, \dfrac{B'}{2}, \dfrac{B''}{2}$ be the surface tensions of these surfaces. The work done by capillary forces in a virtual displacement of the drop is

$$-\frac{B}{2}\,\delta\sigma - \frac{B'}{2}\,\delta\sigma' - \frac{B''}{2}\,\delta\sigma''.$$

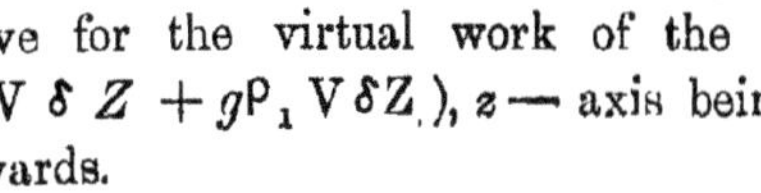

Let P be the density of the liquid and P_1 that of the drop. Let V, V_1 be the respective volumes of these liquids and Z, Z_1 the distances of their centres of gravity from the xoy plane; we have for the virtual work of the weights of the liquids $- (gP\, V\, \delta Z + gP_1\, V\delta Z_1)$, z — axis being supposed to be directed upwards.

The condition of equilibrium is, therefore

$$-g\,(PV\delta Z + P_1 V_1\,\delta Z_1) - \frac{B}{2}\delta\sigma - \frac{B'}{2}\,\delta\sigma' - \frac{B''}{2}\,\delta\sigma'' = 0.$$

The equations of constraint are $\delta V = o$ and $\delta V' = 0$,

since the volumes of the liquids do not change.

In order to transform these equations, let Σ, Σ', Σ'' be the new positions of σ, σ', σ''. If at each point of the original surfaces we draw normals to these surfaces the lengths δn of these normals comprised between these

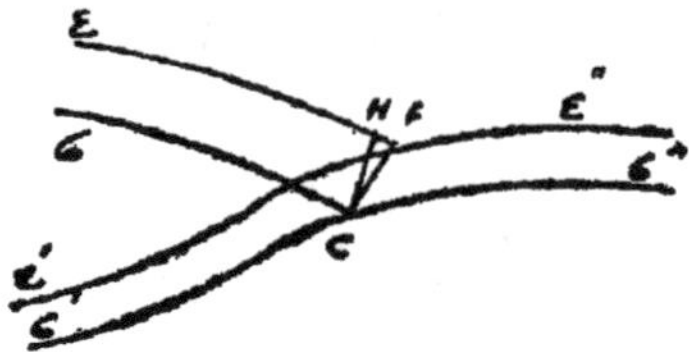

surfaces and those which result from their deformations will determine the latter surfaces. Let dS be the area of an element of σ, we have then

$$\delta \sigma = \iint \delta n \left(\frac{1}{R_1} + \frac{1}{R_2} \right) dS + \int \delta n \, ds \cot \phi$$

ds being an element of the curve of contact and ϕ the angle between the line CF, joining the two positions of a point of this curve with the tangent at F to the deformed surface. Now in the triangle CHF, where CH is normal to σ, the angle at H is sensibly a right angle. We, therefore, have

$$CH = CF \, sin \, HFC$$
$$\delta n = \delta n' \, sin \, \phi.$$

$\delta n'$ being the normal distance between σ'' and Σ''.

$$\therefore \; \delta \sigma = \iint \delta n \left(\frac{1}{R_1} + \frac{1}{R_2} \right) dS + \int \delta n' \, ds \cos \phi$$

Similarly we shall find

$$\delta \sigma' = \iint \delta n \left(\frac{1}{R_1'} + \frac{1}{R_2'} \right) dS + \int \delta n' \, ds \cos \phi'$$

$$\delta \sigma'' = \iint \delta n \left(\frac{1}{R_1''} + \frac{1}{R_2''} \right) dS'' + \int \delta n' \, ds \cos \phi''$$

For calculating δV_1 we remark that if the surface σ alone is deformed, we have for the variation of volume

$$\iint \delta n \, dS.$$

But since the surface σ' is also deformed we have

$$\delta V_1 = \int\int \delta n \, dS - \int\int \delta n \, dS'$$

Similarly

$$\delta V = \int\int \delta n \, dS' + \int\int \delta n \, dS''.$$

The volumes being constant

$$V_1 \, \delta Z_1 = \delta(V_1 Z_1) = \int\int \delta n \, z dS - \int\int \delta n z \, dS'$$
$$V \, \delta Z = \delta (VZ) = \int\int \delta n \, z dS' - \int\int \delta n \, z dS''.$$

The last members of these equations express the fact that the variation of the moment of the liquid with respect to $xo\,y$ plane is equal to the sum of the moments of the weight of their elements with respect to the same plane.

The equation of equilibrium becomes

$$-\int\int \delta n \, dS[\, g^{P_1} z + \frac{B}{2}\,(\frac{1}{R_1} + \frac{1}{R_2}\,)]$$

$$-\int\int \delta n \;\; dS'[\, g^{P}z - g^{P_1}z + \frac{B'}{2}\,(\frac{1}{R'_1} + \frac{1}{R'_2}\,)]$$

$$-\int\int \delta n \, dS'' [\, g^{P}z + \frac{B''}{2}\,(\frac{1}{R_1''} + \frac{1}{R_2''}\,)]$$

$$-\int \delta n' dS' (\frac{B}{2}\cos\phi + \frac{B'}{2}\cos\phi' + \frac{B''}{2}\cos\phi'\,) = o \;\;(1)$$

The equations of constraint are

$$\int\int \delta n \, dS' - \int\int \delta n \, dS' = o$$
$$\int\int \delta n \, dS' + \int\int \delta n \, dS'' = o \qquad \cdots \qquad (2)$$

Equation (1) must be satisfied for any δn satisfying equations (2). These are satisfied by taking

$$\int\int \delta n \, dS = \int\int \delta n \, dS' = \int\int \delta n \, dS'' = o \qquad (3)$$

Hence (1) leads to

$$g^{P_1}z + \frac{B}{2}\,(\frac{1}{R_1} + \frac{1}{R_2}\,) = \alpha$$

$$g\,(\,\mathsf{P}-\mathsf{P}_1\,)\,z + \frac{\mathrm{B}'}{2}\left(\frac{1}{\mathrm{R}_1'} + \frac{1}{\mathrm{R}_2'}\right) = \alpha' \qquad \ldots \quad (4)$$

$$g\,\mathsf{P}z + \frac{\mathrm{B}''}{2}\left(\frac{1}{\mathrm{R}_1''} + \frac{1}{\mathrm{R}_2''}\right) = \alpha'',$$

and $\mathrm{B}\cos\phi + \mathrm{B}'\cos\phi' + \mathrm{B}''\cos\phi'' = o,$

α^1, α'' being constants.

In order that equilibrium may be posible, equation (1) must be satisfied whatever be the displacement provided that it is compatible with the constraints. It must, therefore, be satisfied even when the conditions (3) are not satisfied provided equations (2) are.

But taking into account equations (4) we find that equation (1) reduces to

$$a\int\!\int \delta n\, d\mathrm{S} + a' \int\!\int \delta n\, d\mathrm{S}' + a'' \int\!\int \delta n\, d\mathrm{S}'' = o$$

$$\text{or, } (a+a'-a'') \int\!\int \delta n\, d\mathrm{S} = o,$$

by means of the equation (2) of constraint.

In order that this equation may be satisfied even when the integral $\int\!\int \delta n\, d\mathrm{S}$ is not zero,

$$a + a' - a'' = o.$$

This is the new condition that must be combined with equations (4 .

The first three equations of (4) give the equations of the surfaces σ, σ', σ'' respectively. The fourth equation expresses the fact that the sum of the projectious of the tensions at the point C on the straight line CF is zero, since ϕ, ϕ', ϕ'' are the angles this straight line makes with the tangents through F in the normal plane at this point to the curve of intersection As the direction of CF is arbitrary, this implies that the three tensions at C are in equilibrium.

6. 17. *Pressure on a solid of revolution immersed in a liquid.*

Let AαB be a solid of revolution whose axis is AB, which we take as vertical. We propose to calculate the pressure on the solid when it is in equilibrium in a liquid of density P. To do so let us give to the solid a slight displacement ε such that the form of the free surface Mα remains unaltered, so that this surface is simply prolonged so as to meet the solid in its new position A′α′B′. Let us now write the sum of the virtual works of all forces

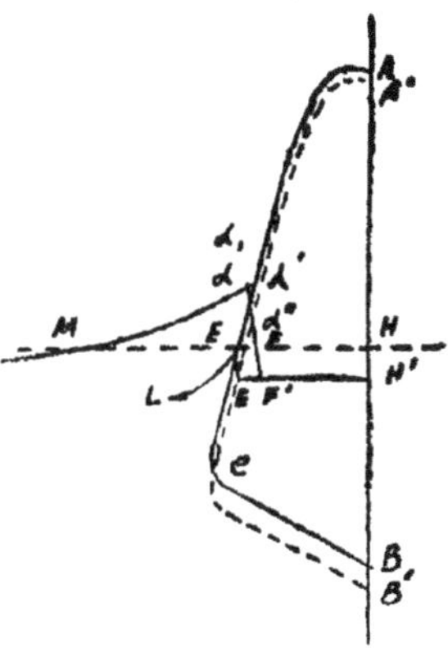

The virtual work of the capillary forces is, as we know already by §6.5

$$T_c = -\frac{B}{2}\,\delta\sigma + (E - \frac{B}{2})\delta\lambda$$

where $\delta\sigma$ is the variation of the free surface of the liquid and $\delta\lambda$ the variation of the surface of contact of the solid and the liquid. Let r be the radius of the parallel section passing through the curve of contact $\alpha\beta$. We have then

$$\delta\sigma = 2\pi r\alpha\alpha'$$
$$\delta\lambda = 2\pi r\alpha\alpha_1.$$

where α_1 is the original position of the point corresponding to α′ in the displaced position of the solid.

Also since $-\frac{B}{2}$ and $(E - \frac{B}{2})$ are related together by

$$-\frac{B}{2}\cos\theta = (E - \frac{B}{2}),$$

where θ is the angle of capillarity, (See Equation (10) of § 6.7)

$$\therefore Tc = \frac{B}{2} (2\pi r) (\alpha\alpha_1 \cos \theta - \alpha\alpha')$$

Now the term $(\alpha\alpha_1 \cos\theta - \alpha\alpha')$ is the projection of the contour $\alpha'\alpha\alpha_1$ on $\alpha\alpha'$. This is accordingly equal to the projection of the vertical $\alpha_1\alpha'$ on $\alpha\alpha'$. But $\alpha_1\alpha' = AA' = \varepsilon$. Hence this expression is equal to $\varepsilon \cos \phi$ where ϕ is the angle between $\alpha_1\alpha'$ and $\alpha\alpha'$ which is equal to the angle between the tangent plane at the point α to the free surface and the vertical.

Hence $T_c = \pi Br \, \varepsilon \cos \phi$.

Let us now evaluate the virtual work due to the weight. Since the solid is in equilibrium, its weight is equal and opposite to the pressure exercised by the liquid on it. Denoting it by X, the virtual work of the weight due to the displacement considered must be

$$X\varepsilon.$$

We have now to compute the virtual work due to the weight of the surrounding liquid. This is evidently equal to the variation of moment of the weight of the liquid with respect to any horizontal plane e.g. the free surface of the liquid at a great distance from the solid. Assuming that the virtual displacement is such that the free surface of the liquid remains unaltered so that it just extends to the solid in its new position, the variation of this moment is

$$T_w = - \text{Moment of } e\text{BB} + \text{moment of } \text{EL}e + \text{moment of } \alpha\alpha'\text{EL}$$

$$= - \text{Moment of } \text{LH}e\text{B}' + \text{moment of } \text{EH}e\text{B} + \text{moment of } \alpha\alpha'\text{EL}$$

But moment of $\text{LH}e\text{B}' = \text{moment of } \text{E}'\text{H}'e\text{B}' + \text{moment of } \text{LE HH}'$,

where EE' is the vertical drawn through E, the point of intersection of the meridian curve of the solid and the horizontal plane Now the volume $LE' HH'$ differs little from that of a right circular cylinder of height $H H' = \varepsilon$; it is therefore an infinitesimal of the first order and its moment with respect to the horizontal plane ELH is therefore of second order. We can accordingly neglect its contribution.

$$T_w = -(\text{moment of } E'H'eB' - \text{moment of } EHeB) + \text{moment of } aa'EL.$$

But $E'H'eB'$ is merely volume $EHeB$ displaced vertically through ε, the difference of their moments is equal to the product of the displacement ε by the weight of any one of these volumes,

$$\therefore T_w = -\varepsilon g P \text{ Vol } EHeB + \text{moment of } aa'EL.$$

It remains now to evaluate the moment of volume $aa'EL$. The surface of the triangle $aa'a''$, being an infinitesimal of second order, the volume generated by its revolution can be neglected in comparison with that generated by the revolution of area $aa'EL$, so that we have

$$\text{moment of } aa'EL = \text{moment of } aa''EL$$

or, moment of $aa'EL = \text{moment of } aEF - \text{moment of } a''LF$, where F is the point of intersection of the vertical aa'' with the horizontal EH. If we prolong this vertical length to FF' so that $FF' = \varepsilon$ we obtain a triangle $a''E'F'$ generating a volume whose moment differs from that of the volume $a''LF$ by infinitesimals of second order,

$$\therefore \text{moment of } aa'EL = \text{moment to } aEF - \text{moment of } a''E'F'$$

The volumes generated by aEF and $a''E'F'$ being equal, the difference between their moments with respect of the same horizontal plane is equal to the product of the weight of this volume and a quantity ε by which the centre of gravity has moved.

$$\therefore \text{moment of } aa'EL = \varepsilon g P. \text{ Vol } a \, EF.$$

$$\therefore T_w = -\varepsilon g P \text{ Vol } EHeB + \varepsilon g \, P\text{Vol. (annular } aEF)$$

Since the sum of the various virtual works is zero, we have

$$T_c + T_w + X\varepsilon = \pi B r\varepsilon \; \cos \phi - g\rho\varepsilon \; (\text{Vol } EH eB - \text{Vol } \alpha EF)$$
$$+ X\varepsilon = 0.$$

or, $X = -\pi B r \cos \phi + g\rho \; (\text{Vol } EHeB - \text{Vol } \alpha EF),$

giving the vertical thrust of the liquid on the solid.

If the surface of the liquid were plane, the vertical thrust has the value

$$g\rho \quad \text{Vol} \quad EHeB.$$

We see then that if ϕ is acute, the capillary forces diminish the vertical thrust X acting on the solid. If the angle of capillarity is obtuse, then so is angle ϕ in general. Moreover it is easy to see that the term $g\rho$ Vol αEF must take the positive sign when the point α is below the horizontal plane.

Hence the capillary forces sometime enhance the vertical pressure exerted on a solid and thus enable it to float even if its density is greater than that of the liquid.

Ex. 1. Prove that in the case of a cylinder floating with its axis horizontal, the vertical pressure is given by

$$- B \, l \cos \phi + g\rho \; (\text{Vol } EHeB - 2 \text{ Vol } \alpha EF).$$

where l is the height of the cylinder.

Ex. 2. Prove that conditions of equilibrium of a floating needle are.

$$-B \operatorname{Sin} (\phi - i) + g\rho \; (c^2\phi + c^2 \operatorname{Sin} \phi \cos \phi - 2 \, hc \operatorname{Sin}\phi) = w$$
$$\text{and } B \operatorname{Sin}^2 \tfrac{1}{2} (\phi - i) = g\rho (c \cos \phi - h)^2$$

where i is the angle of capillarity, w is the weight per unit length of the needle, c its radius, h the height of its centre above the natural level of water and 2ϕ is the angle subtended at the surface by the curve of contact.

Here the angle made between the tangent α T at α to the free surface of the liquid and the vertical through α is clearly $(\frac{\pi}{2}-\phi+i)$ where $<\alpha OP=\phi$

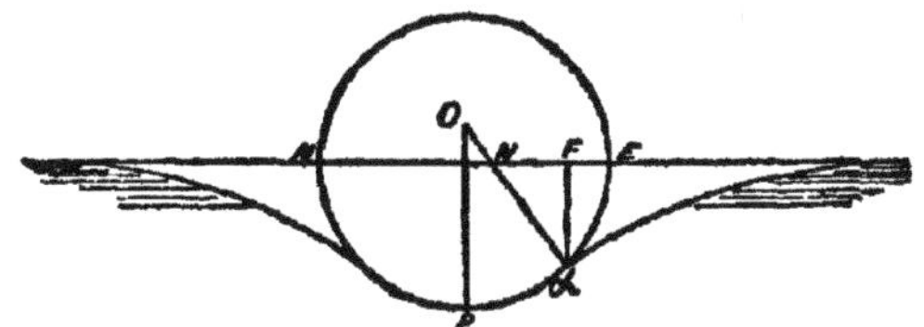

Hence by Ex. 1 the vertical pressure on the needle is

$$-Bl \cos \left(\frac{\pi}{2}-\phi+i\right)+g^P \text{ (Vol EPH}-2 \text{ Vol}\alpha\text{EF)}$$

$$=-Bl \sin (\phi-i)+g^P \text{ (Vol EPH}-2\text{Vol } \alpha\text{EF).}$$

Now Vol. EPH $=l \{ \frac{1}{2}c^2 (2\theta)-\frac{1}{2} h (2c \sin \theta) \}$

$$=l (c^2\theta-ch \sin \theta), \text{ where}\theta = <\text{EOP.}$$

Volume αEF$=l \{ \text{ area } \alpha\text{EF} \}$

$$=l \{ \text{ area of sector } \alpha\text{OE}-\text{area of triangle OEN}$$

$$-\text{area of triangle } \alpha\text{FN} \}$$

$$=l \{ \frac{1}{2}c^2 (\theta-\phi)-\frac{1}{2}h (c \sin \theta -h \tan \alpha)$$

$$-\frac{1}{2} (c \cos\phi-h) (c \sin \phi-h \tan \phi) \}$$

where N is the intersection of Oα with EH.

$\therefore$ Vol EPH -2VolαEF $=l \{ c^2 \alpha+c^2 \sin \phi \cos \phi-2hc \sin \phi \}$

The vertical pressure is, therefore,

$$-Bl \sin (\phi-i)+g^Pcl \{ c\phi+c \sin \phi \cos \phi-2h \sin\phi \},$$

and this must be equal to the weight of needle viz wl. We have, then,

$$-B \sin (\phi-i)+g^Pc \{ c\phi+c \sin\phi \cos \phi-2h \sin \phi \} =w,$$

which is the first condition to be proved.

To obtain the second condition we refer to § 6. 9 from which we obtain the equation of the free surface in the form

$$\frac{1}{[1+(\frac{dz}{dx})^2]^{\frac{1}{2}}} = 1 - \frac{z^2}{2a^2},$$

where z is measured from the level surface and $a^2 = \dfrac{B}{2g\rho}$.

If ψ be the angle made by a tangent to the free surface with the horizontal, we have

$$\frac{dz}{dx} = \tan \psi,$$

so that the differential equation of the surface leads to the relation

$$z^2 = 2a^2 (1 - \cos \psi) = 4a^2 \sin^2 \frac{\psi}{2}$$

Now at the point a, $z = (c \cos\phi - h)$ and $\psi = i - \phi$,

$$\therefore (c \cos\phi - h)^2 = 4 a^2 \sin^2 \frac{i - \phi}{2}$$

$$= \frac{2B}{g\rho} \sin^2 \frac{i - \phi}{2}.$$

Ex. 3.   A needle floats on water with its axis in the natural level of the surface; if ω be the specific gravity of steel with respect to water, i the angle of capillarity, and 2α the angle subtended at the axis by the arc of a cross section in contact with water, prove that

$$(\pi\omega - \alpha) \sin \tfrac{1}{2} (\alpha - i) = \cos \alpha \cos \frac{\alpha + i}{2}.$$

CHAPTER VII

The Figures of Equilibrium of a Mass of Rotating Liquid.

7. 1. We shall study in this chapter the shapes assumed by masses of rotating liquids which are acted upon by no other forces save their own gravitation, confining ourselves to the simplest case in which matter is supposed to be homogeneous and incompressible. Even this simple case is complicated enough to have taxed the ingenuity of some of the greatest mathematicians.

7. 2 *History of the Problem:*

Newton had seen that the law of gravitation must account for the figure of stars as well as their movements. He showed that the centrifugal force combined with its weight must make earth an ellipsoid of revolution flattened at the poles. He calculated the ellipticity of the earth assuming it to be of homogeneous density. Maupertuis studied the equilibrium of a plane figure turning round an axis normal to its plane, on taking account of a central attraction and a centrifugal force. But it was Maclaurin who in 1742 applied to a homogeneous mass of liquid in rotation the principle of Pascal regarding the equality of pressure even before the principles of hydrostatics were firmly established. He showed that the ellipsoid of revolution is a possible figure of equilibrium. Simpson in 1743 studied the conditions of existence of these ellipsoids of Maclaurin He also discovered an upper limit to $h = \dfrac{w^2}{2\pi \gamma \rho}$ on taking w, the angular velocity as a parameter. This expression, where ρ is the density and γ, the constant of gravitation, must be less than ·2247 for ellipsoidal equilibrium.

Clairaut, in his remarkable book Figure de la Terre (1743) gave to these results and demonstrations their definite form.

He further extended the calculations to the study of a heterogeneous mass, as the earth and planets actually are. He gave formulae connecting the ellipticity and the weight with the density and centrifugal force in the case of a sufficiently slow angular velocity. In 1776 Laplace remarked that a general solution of the problem was impossible and that only particular cases could be studied and purely empircal solutions given.

A little later Legendre made known his fundamental method which permitted one to search directly the figures of equilibrium in the neighbourhood of a sphere. It is this method that is of primary importance in Mathematical Physics and to this is due most of the recent progress in this Problem, Poincarè and Liapounoff have generalised this method of spherical harmonics and applied to ellipsoids by using Lame's functions instead of spherical harmonics.

For a long time it was believed that there were no other figures of equilibrium except the Maclaurin ellipsoids and the ring round a central body. It was in 1834 that Jacobi showed that an ellipsoid with three unequal axes turning round the least axis is also a possible form of equilibrium. Liouville gave an analytical proof of this. Otto Meyer gave a complete discussion of the equations obtained in this case by taking 'w' as the variable.

In a celebrated paper which appeared in Acta Mathematica, 7, 1885, Poincarè discussed the problem of figures of equilibrium in a more general manner. He pointed out that the possible figures of equilibrium form a linear series depending on a single parameter, such as the angular velocity, and such that to each value of the parameter corresponds either one and (only), one or else a finite number of figures and that these figures vary in a continuous manner as the parameter is varied. Among others who have specially worked at the problem be mentioned Liopounoff, Darwin, Lord Kelvin, Jeans, Appell, Globa—Mikhailenko.

For a more detailed account of the latest researches on the subject the reader is referred to Chapter I of Paul Appell's 'Traitè De Mecanique Rationnelle" tome quatrième, from which the above historical account is taken.

7. 3 *Mass without rotation.*

We shall first take up the problem of determining the form of equilibrium of a mass of liquid whose elements attract according to Newton's law and are at rest

Let P (a constant) be the density of the liquid. Let S be the free surface, supposing the equilibrium to exist. Apply the equations of equilibrium to the liquid mass.

We have then

$$dp = P\,(X dx + Y dy + Z dz)$$

$$= -P\,(\frac{dV}{dx} dx + \frac{dV}{dy} dy + \frac{dV}{dz} dz)$$

$$= -P d V$$

$$\therefore\ p = -PV + \text{cons.}$$

On the free surface, S, we have $p = o$, hence at every point on S we must have

$$PV = \text{cons.}$$

That is S, the free surface, must be an equipotential surface.

We arrive at the same result even if the pressure at the free surface (p_o) be not zero.

An evident form of equilibrium is, therefore, a sphere; since sphere is also an equipotential surface

The sphere is a solution of the problem. But is this the only solution? It is probable; but this cannot be rigorously demonstrated. To prove this it would be necessary to show that if the potential of a homogeneous mass bounded by surface S is such

that S itself is an equipotential surface then S must necessarily b
a sphere.

7 4. *General Equations.*

Suppose a homogeneous mass of a liquid of density ρ rotate
round Z—axis with angular velocity w. The conditions $\cdot$
relative equilibrium are given by the equations

$$\frac{\partial p}{\partial x} = -\rho \, \frac{\partial V}{\partial x} + w^2 \rho x$$

$$\frac{\partial p}{\partial y} = -\rho \, \frac{\partial V}{\partial y} + w^2 \rho y$$

$$\frac{\partial p}{\partial z} = -\rho \, \frac{\partial V}{\partial z}$$

Here p is the pressure at the point $(x,y,z,)$ and V is th
gravitational potential. Since ρ is a constant

$$dp = -\rho \, dV + w^2 \rho (x\,dx + y\,dy),$$

or, $p = -\rho V + \tfrac{1}{2}w^2 \rho (x^2 + y^2).$

The pressure must be zero (or constant) over the fre
surface. Thus the necessary and sufficient condition that an
configuration shall be a possible figure of equilibrium for
homogeneous liquid of density ρ rotating with angular velocit
w is that

$$V - \tfrac{1}{2}w^2(x^2 + y^2)$$

shall be constant over its surface, V being the gravitationa
potential of the mass.

7. 5. Let us now apply this result to the ellipsoidal confi
guration given by

$$\frac{x^2}{a^2} + \frac{y^2}{b^2} + \frac{z^2}{c^2} = 1 \tag{1}$$

The necessary and sufficient condition that ellipsoid (1) shall be a figure of equilibrium for a homogeneous mass rotating with angular velicity w is that

$$V_i - \tfrac{1}{2}w^2(x^2 + y^2)$$

shall be constant over the boundary.

Now, $V_i = \pi \gamma \rho\, abc \int_0^\infty (\frac{x^2}{A} + \frac{y^2}{B} + \frac{z^2}{C} - 1)\frac{d\lambda}{\triangle}$

where $A = (a^2 + \lambda)$, $B = (b^2 + \lambda)$, $C = (c^2 + \lambda)$, $\triangle = (ABC)^{\frac{1}{2}}$

Set $J = \pi \gamma \rho\, abc \int_0^\infty \frac{d\lambda}{\triangle}$, $J_A = \pi \gamma \rho\, abc \int_0^\infty \frac{d\lambda}{A\triangle}$

$J_B = \pi \gamma \rho\, abc \int_0^\infty \frac{d\lambda}{B\triangle}$, $J_c = \gamma \rho\, abc \int_0^\infty \frac{d\lambda}{C\triangle}$

Hence $(x^2 J_A + y^2 J_B + z^2 J_c - J) - \tfrac{1}{2}w^2 (x^2 + y^2)$

shall be constant over the surface (1).

It follows that

$$a^2 (-\tfrac{1}{2}w^2 + J_A) = b^2 (-\tfrac{1}{2}w^2 + J_B) = c^2 (J_C) \qquad (2)$$

$$\text{or } \tfrac{1}{2}(a^2 - b^2)w^2 = a^2 J_A - b^2 J_B \qquad (2')$$

$$\tfrac{1}{2}a^2 w^2 = a^2 J_A - c^2 J_C \qquad (3)$$

Equation (2) can also be rewritten

$$(a^2 - b^2) \left\{ \frac{w^2}{2\pi \gamma \rho\, abc} - \int_0^\infty \frac{\lambda d\lambda}{\triangle(a^2 + \lambda)(b^2 + \lambda)} \right\} = 0 \qquad (4)$$

This equation is satisfied in two ways viz (i) if $a = b$, or (ii) if

$$\frac{w^2}{2\pi \gamma \rho\, abc} = \int_0^\infty \frac{\lambda d\lambda}{\triangle(a^2 + \lambda)(b^2 + \lambda)} \qquad (5)$$

7. 6. **Maclaurin's Spheroids.** Taking the first case viz. when a $=$ b we see that an ellipsoid of revolution is a possible form of equilibrium provided w is given by (3).

$$\frac{a^2 w^2}{2\pi \gamma \rho a^2 c} = \int_0^\infty \frac{d\lambda}{\triangle} \left(\frac{a^2}{a^2+\lambda} - \frac{c^2}{c^2+\lambda} \right)$$

or, $$\frac{w^2}{2\pi\gamma\rho} = (a^2-c^2)c \int_0^\infty \frac{\lambda d\lambda}{\triangle(a^2+\lambda)(c^2+\lambda)} \qquad (6)$$

As the integral on the right hand side of this equality is necessarily positive, w is real only if a $>$ c.

Thus only an oblate spheroid is a possible form of equilibrium; a prolate spheroid is not a possible form of equilibrium.

In order to evaluate the integral on the right hand side of (6 we write

$$\frac{w^2}{2\pi\gamma\rho c} = \int_0^\infty \frac{a^2 d\lambda}{(a^2+\lambda)\triangle} - \int_0^\infty \frac{c^2 d\lambda}{(c^2+\lambda)\triangle} \qquad \dots (7)$$

But $$\int_0^\infty \frac{a^2 d\lambda}{(a^2+\lambda)\triangle} = \int_0^\infty \frac{a^2 d\lambda}{(a^2+\lambda)^2 \sqrt{c^2+\lambda}} \ , \text{ putting } u^2 = c^2+\lambda$$

$$= \int_c^\infty \frac{2a^2 du}{(c^2 l^2 + u^2)^2}.$$

where $a^2 - c^2 = c^2 l^2$

Now, $$\int_c^\infty \frac{du}{a^2+u} = \frac{1}{a} \left(\frac{\pi}{2} - tan^{-1} \frac{c}{a} \right)$$

$$= \frac{1}{a} cot^{-1} \frac{c}{a}$$

Differentiating with respect to 'a'

(246)

$$\int_0^\infty \frac{2a\,du}{(a^2+u^2)^2} = \frac{1}{a^2}\cot^{-1}\frac{c}{a} - \frac{1}{a}\left(\frac{c}{a^2+c^2}\right)$$

Hence replacing 'a' by cl we have

$$\int_0^\infty \frac{2\,du}{(c^2l^2+u^2)^2} = \frac{1}{c^3l^3}\cot^{-1}\left(\frac{1}{l}\right) - \frac{1}{c^2l^2}\frac{c}{(c^2+c^2l^2)}$$

$$= \frac{1}{c^3l^3}\left\{\tan^{-1}l - \frac{l}{1+l^2}\right\}$$

$$\therefore \int_0^\infty \frac{a^2 d\lambda}{(a^2+\lambda)\triangle} = \frac{a^2}{c^3l^3}\left\{\tan^{-1}l - \frac{l}{1+l^2}\right\}$$

Simlarly,

$$\int_0^\infty \frac{c^2\,d\lambda}{(c^2+\lambda)\triangle} = \frac{1}{l^3c}\left\{2l - 2\tan^{-1}l\right\}$$

Hence equation (7) becomes

$$\frac{w^2}{2\pi\gamma\rho} = \frac{1+l^2}{l^3}\left(\tan^{-1}l - \frac{l}{1+l^2}\right) - \frac{1}{l^3}(2l - 2\tan^{-1}l)$$

$$= \frac{(3+l^2)\tan^{-1}l - 3l}{l^3} \qquad \ldots \qquad \ldots \qquad (8)$$

where $a^2 = (1+l^2)c^2$.

Thus if w be given, equation (8) determines the ellipticity of the spheroid of equilibrium. Such spheroids are called Maclaurin's spheroids.

7.7. *Discussion of equation (8).*

Set

$$h = \frac{w^2}{2\pi\gamma\rho} = \frac{(3+l^2)\tan^{-1}l - 3l}{l^3}$$

(247)

Since $tan^{-1} l = l - \dfrac{l^3}{3} + \dfrac{l^5}{5}$, ...for small values of l, we have from (8), $h = \dfrac{4}{15} l^3$.

Hence for $l = o$, $h = o$, and for l increasing $h > o$. When l tends to infinity, h is of the order $\dfrac{1}{l}$ and, therefore, tends to zero. Thus h is zero between these two limits of l and increases in the beginning.

Differentiating h with respect to l we have

$$\frac{dh}{dl} = \frac{9 + l^2}{l^4} \, f(l)$$

where $f(l) = \dfrac{7 l^2 + 9}{(1 + l^2)(9 + l^2)} \, l - tan^{-1} l.$

The sign of $\dfrac{dh}{dl}$ is the same as that of $f(l)$. For small values of l, we have

$$f(l) = l\left(1 - \frac{l^2}{3} + \frac{7}{27} l^4 \ldots\right) - tan^{-1} l$$
$$= \frac{8}{135} l^5 \qquad \ldots$$

The derivative is at first zero, then becomes positive. At infinity $\Psi(l)$ reduces to $-\dfrac{\pi}{2}$ and the derivative becomes negative.

Let us now take the derivative of $f(l)$ with respect to l

$$f'(l) = \frac{8l^4(3 - l^2)}{(1 + l^2)^2 (9 + l^2)^2}$$

This expression is at first positive, zero for $l = \sqrt{3}$, and then becomes negative for ever afterwards. The expression $f(l)$ is, therefore, zero for $l = o$, increases till $l = \sqrt{3}$ when $f'(l)$

becomes zero, then begins to decrease for $l > \sqrt{3}$ and tends to $-\frac{\pi}{2}$. Hence $f(l) = o$ has one and only one root, $l_0 > \sqrt{3}$. It will, therefore, be the same for $\frac{dh}{dl}$. Let us designate by l_0 this value of l for which $\frac{dh}{dl}$ and $f(l)$ are zero. It is given by

$$\tan^{-1} l = \frac{9 + 7l^2}{(1 + l^2)(9 + l^2)} l.$$

We find $l_0 = 2'53\dots$ and the corresponding value h_0 of h is $h_0 = '224\dots$

For $l < l_0$ we have $\frac{dh}{dl} > o$; the function h, therefore, increases; for $l > l_0$, $\frac{dh}{dl} < o$; h, therefore, decreases and is maximum for $l = l_0$.

Taking two axes Oh and Ol we represent the curves

$$h = \frac{(3 + l^2)\tan^{-1} l - 3l}{l^3}$$

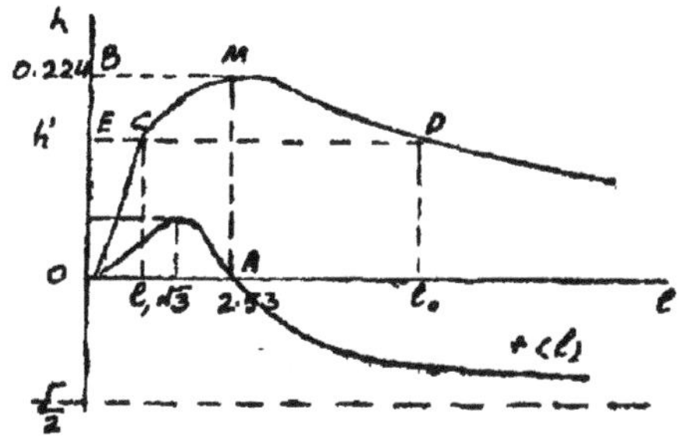

and $h' = f(l)$

The curve h touches Ol at O, its ordinate increases till $h = h_0 = .224$ for $l = l_0 = 2.53\dots$; then it decreases and approaches Ol asymptotically.

For a given value of $h <.224$ there correspond two values of l. Hence as $h = \dfrac{w^2}{2\pi\gamma\rho}$, for a given w there are two possible ellipsoids of revolution, provided $\dfrac{w^2}{2\pi\gamma\rho} < \cdot 224$.

If $\dfrac{w^2}{2\pi\gamma\rho} < \cdot 224$, there are two spheroids of Maclaurin;

if $\dfrac{w^2}{2\pi\gamma\rho} = \cdot 224$, there is only one spheroid of equilibrium;

if $\dfrac{w^2}{2\pi\gamma\rho} < \cdot 224$, there is no ellipsoid of revolution, which can be a figure of equilibrium.

Maclaurin's spheroids cannot be a form of equilibrium if the velocity of rotation becomes greater than $(.448\,\pi\gamma\rho)^{\frac{1}{2}}$.

Remark (i) If the celestial bodies like the earth or planets are Maclaurin's spheroids, these must correpond to the lower root of l, assuming the ellipticity to be small. For if $l > 2.53$ ellipticity

$$\varepsilon = \frac{a-c}{a} = 1 - \frac{1}{\sqrt{1+l^2}} > 1 - \frac{1}{\sqrt{1+4}} > \tfrac{1}{2};$$

and ε is known to be much smaller than $\tfrac{1}{2}$ in the case of the earth and planets.

Remark (ii). Ellipticity of the earth. We have

$$\frac{w^2}{2\pi\gamma\rho} = \left(\frac{2\pi}{24\times 60^2}\right)^2 \left(\frac{2a}{3g}\right), \text{ for } g = \frac{4\pi\gamma\rho a^3}{3a^2}$$

$$= \frac{4\pi\,2\pi a}{24^2.\,6_\circ{}^4.3g}$$

$$= \frac{4\times 3.14\times 40{,}000{,}000}{24^2\times 6_\circ{}^4\times 3\times 981}$$

$$= .00227.$$

For this value of h, we solve the equation

$$h = \frac{(3+l^2)\tan^{-1}l - 3l}{l^3},$$ and take the lower root.

The corresponding ellipticity ε is $\dfrac{1}{231}$. This value certainly disagrees with the geodetic measurements. The ellipticity given by Helmert in 1901 is $\dfrac{1}{298}$ and by Hayford in 1909 is $\dfrac{1}{297}$. It is necessary to conclude that if the earth is an ellipsoid of revolution and if it was fluid sometime it is not homogeneous.

Remark (iii) when w tends to zero, one of the values of l tends to zero, and the corresponding spheroid is accordingly a sphere.

The other increases indefinitely. If l is very large, we have, assuming the mass M of the liquid to be finite,

$$M = \frac{4\pi}{3}\, a^2 c\, \rho = \frac{4\pi}{3}\frac{a^3\rho}{(1+l^2)^{\frac{1}{2}}} = \frac{4\pi}{3}\, c^3\rho(1+l^2)$$

Hence $c^3 = \dfrac{3M}{4\pi\rho}\,\dfrac{1}{1+l^2}$ and $a^3 = \dfrac{3M}{4\pi\rho}\,\sqrt{1+l^2}$

It follows that $c \longrightarrow 0$ and $a \longrightarrow$ infinity. We have a figure resembling a disc of infinitely large radius and infinitely small central thickness.

7. 8. *Jacobi's Ellipsoids.*

Let us now take the second alternative of satisfying. equation (4) of §7.5 *viz.*

$$\frac{w^2}{2\pi\gamma\rho abc} = \int_0^\infty \frac{\lambda d\lambda}{(a^2+\lambda)(b^2+\lambda)\Delta} \tag{9}$$

From equations (2′) and (3) of § 7.5 we also have

$$a^2 b^2(J_A - J_B) + c^2(a^2 - b^2,\ J_c = 0 \tag{10}$$

(251)

$$\text{or, } (b^2 - a^2) \int_0^\infty \left[\frac{a^2 b^2}{(a^2+\lambda)(b^2+\lambda)} - \frac{c^2}{c^2+\lambda} \right] \frac{d\lambda}{\triangle} = 0 \quad (11)$$

Since $b \neq a$, we have to discuss now the equations

$$\frac{w^2}{2\pi\gamma\rho} = abc \int_0^\infty \frac{\lambda \, d\lambda}{(a^2+\lambda)(b^2+\lambda)\triangle} \quad (12)$$

$$\text{and, } \int_0^\infty \left[\frac{a^2 b^2}{(a^2+\lambda)(b^2+\lambda)} - \frac{c^2}{c^2+\lambda} \right] \frac{d\lambda}{\triangle} = 0 \quad (13)$$

To reduce these integrals let us set $\lambda = c^2 x$ we have then

$$\frac{w^2}{2\pi\gamma\rho} = abc \int_0^\infty \frac{c^4 x \, dx}{(a^2+c^2x)(b^2+c^2x)\sqrt{(a^2+c^2x)(b^2+c^2x)(c^2+c^2x)}}$$

$$= st \int_0^\infty \frac{x \, dx}{(1+sx)(1+tx)\,\phi(x}, \quad (14)$$

where $\phi(x) = \sqrt{(1+sx)(1+tx)(1+x)}$, and

$$\frac{c^2}{a^2} = s, \quad \frac{c^2}{b^2} = t. \quad (15)$$

And equation (13) becomes

$$\int_0^\infty \frac{(1-s-t)\, x - ts x^2}{\phi^3(x)} dx = 0$$

$$\text{or, } (1-s-t) \int_0^\infty \frac{x \, dx}{\phi^3(x)} = st \int_0^\infty \frac{x^2 \, dx}{\phi^3(x)} \quad (16)$$

These equations give s, t when we are given w. The problem is to reduce these equations.

Note : From equation (16) it is evident that $(1-s-t) > \,^\circ$ since both the integrals must be positive and s, t are also positive. Hence $s+t<1$. Since s, t are positive,

$$\text{therefore } s<1, t<1$$
$$\text{or, } c^2<a^2 \text{ and } c^2<b^2.$$
$$\therefore\ c \text{ is the least axis.}$$

For equilibrium it is necessary that the axis of rotation must be the least axis.

7. 9. Discussion of equations (14) and (16).

$$\text{Set } h = \frac{w^2}{2\pi\gamma\rho} = f(s, t)$$

$$= \int_0^\infty \frac{x\,dx}{(1+sx)(1+tx)\triangle}\cdot$$

$$\text{Also } o = \Psi(s,t) = (1-s-t)\int^\infty \frac{x\,dx}{\triangle^3} - st \int_0^\infty \frac{x^2\,dx}{\triangle^3}\ .$$

$$\text{where } \triangle = \sqrt{(1+sx)(1+tx)(1+x.)}$$

We proceed to show that $\Psi=o$ has always a root and only one root in s for every value of t, and that the expression h has always one value and only one for every value of t or s, with its maximum for $s=t=t_o$.

There is in every case one ellipsoid of Jacobi as a figure of equilibrium.

These two equations define a curve of space by means of the three variables h, s, t. A point P of the curve projects into a point R on the $s-t$ plane. The coordinates (s, t) of the point R will clearly satisfy $\Psi(s,t) = o$.

Hence to trace the above skew surve it is only necessary to trace $\Psi(s, t) = o$ on the $s-t$ plane and then to erect at

(253)

point R of this curve an ordinate RP equal to the corresponding value of h. The locus of points P is the required curve.

(i) $\psi (s, t) = o$ has only one root in s when t is given between zero and one

Set $s+t=p$ and $st = q$,

then $dp=ds+dt$ and $dq = t\, ds +s\, dt$

Denoting by **A** and B the integrals in ψ

$$\psi = (1-p)\, A - q\, B, \qquad \ldots \qquad \ldots \qquad (17)$$

$$\text{where } A = \int_{o}^{\infty} \frac{x\, dx}{\triangle^{3}} \ , \ B = \int^{\infty} \frac{x^{2}\, dx}{\triangle^{3}} .$$

Now, $\triangle^{2} = (1+x)\,(1+sx)\,(1+tx)$

$$= (1+x)\,(1+px + qx^{2}).$$

Differentiating ψ with respect to s

$$\frac{\partial \psi}{\partial s} = - A - tB + (1-p)\, \frac{\partial A}{\partial s} - q\, \frac{\partial B}{\partial s}$$

$$\text{and } \frac{\partial A}{\partial s} = - \tfrac{3}{2} \int_{o}^{\infty} \frac{x^{2}(1+x)\,(1+tx)}{\triangle^{5}}\, dx, \ldots\ldots\ (18)$$

$$\frac{\partial B}{\partial s} = - \tfrac{3}{2} \int_{o}^{\infty} \frac{x^{3}(1+x)\,(1+tx)}{\triangle^{5}}\, dx, \ldots\ldots\ 19)$$

$$\text{Hence } (1-p)\, \frac{\partial A}{\partial s} - q\, \frac{\partial B}{\partial s} = - \tfrac{3}{2} \int_{o}^{\infty} \frac{x^{2}(1+x)\,(1+tx)}{\triangle^{5}}\, (1-p-qx)$$

$$= - A_{1} - B_{1}t,$$

$$\text{where } A_{1} = \tfrac{3}{2} \int_{o}^{\infty} \frac{x^{2}(1+x)\,(1-p-qx)}{\triangle^{5}}\, dx,$$

(254)

$$B_1 = \tfrac{3}{2} \int_0^\infty \frac{x^3(1+x)(1-p-qx)}{\triangle^5} dx.$$

$$\therefore \frac{\partial \psi}{\partial s} = -(A+A_1) - (B+B_1)\, t = -A_0 - B_0 t, \dots \quad (20)$$

$$\text{where } A_0 = \int_0^\infty \frac{x(1+x)}{2\triangle^5} (2 + 3x - px - qx^2)\, dx$$

and similar expression for B_0.

Consider now the equation

$$\frac{d}{dx} \frac{x^2(1+x)}{\triangle^3} = \frac{x(1+x)}{2\triangle^5} (4 + 3x + px - 2qx^2 - 3qx^3)$$

$$= \int_0^\infty \frac{x(1+x)}{2\triangle^5} (4 + 3x + px - 2qx^2 - 3qx^3)\, dx = \left| \frac{x^2(1+x)}{\triangle} \right|_0^\infty$$

$$= 0.$$

Then $2A_0 = 2A - C = \tfrac{3}{2} \int_0^\infty \frac{x^2(1+x)}{\triangle^5} (1 - p + qx^2)\, dx.$

As $p < 1, A_0 > 0.$

From this value of A_0 we have

$$2A_0 + 3B_0 = \tfrac{3}{2}(3-p) \int_0^\infty \frac{x^2(1+x)^2}{\triangle^5}\, dx$$

$$= \tfrac{3}{2}(3-)p D$$

The integral denoted by D being always positive.

$\therefore 2A_0 + 3B_0$ is always positive.

Now we may write

$$-\frac{\partial \psi}{\partial s} = A_0 + B_0 t = A_0 \left(1 - \tfrac{2}{3} t\right) + \tfrac{t}{3} (2A_0 + 3B_0.)$$

As we have $t < 1$, the second member of the above equation

is always positive so that $\dfrac{\partial \Psi}{\partial s}$ is always negative.

Hence Ψ is a decreasing function of s. It varies in the same sense and, therefore, cannot be zero for more than once when s varies between its limits, t being a given constant. The same is true with respect to t when s is given.

Now let us put $s = o$ and $s = 1$ in Ψ we have

$$\Psi_o = (1-t) \int_o^\infty \frac{x\,dx}{(1+x)^{3/2}(1+tx)^{3/2}} > o,$$

$$\Psi_1 = - t \int_o^\infty \frac{x\,dx}{(1+x)^2 (1+tx)^{3/2}} < o$$

It follows therefore that for a given $t < 1, \Psi = o$ has one and only one root in s between zero and one. Thus if one of the two ellipticities is known, so is the other.

Considering s as a function of t, the functional relation being defined by $\Psi = o$, we will have

$$\frac{d\Psi}{dt} = \frac{\partial \Psi}{\partial s}\frac{ds}{dt} + \frac{\partial \Psi}{\partial t} = o,$$

$$\therefore \frac{ds}{dt} = - \frac{\dfrac{\partial \Psi}{\partial t}}{\dfrac{\partial \Psi}{\partial s}}$$

But $\dfrac{\partial \Psi}{\partial s} < o$ and $\dfrac{\partial \Psi}{\partial t} \angle o$, hence $\dfrac{ds}{dt}$ is negative. Hence s

and t always vary in opposite directions. For $s = o$, $t = 1$, and for $t = o$, $s = 1$ and so on for every value of s and t. To each pair of values of s_1 and t_1 of s and t corresponds another pair viz

t_1 and s_1 since the expression Ψ involves s, t symmetrically. The ellipsoids corresponding to these two pairs of values are identical where merely the a and b axes have been interchanged.

The two values of s and t become equal at an intermediate value, say t_o, we have then for $s = t = t_o$, where t_o is given

$$(1-2\,t_o)\int_o^\infty \frac{x\,dx}{\triangle^3} = t_o{}^2 \int_o^\infty \frac{x^2 dx}{\triangle^3}\ .$$

Here $\triangle = (1+t_o x)\,\sqrt{1+x}$.

The curve $\Psi\,(s,t)=o$ in the sOt plane can now be traced.

We notice that

(i) s,t are essentially positive and lie between o and 1;

(ii) $\Psi\,(s,t)$ is symmetrical with respect to s and t, the curve is therefore symmetrical with respect to the bisector of angle sOt;

(iii)   If $s=o$, $t=1$ and vice verca;

(iv)   If s increases t decreases and vice versa;

(v)   Since $s+t \angle 1$ the curve is always below the straight line $s+t = 1$;

(vi)   Given a value s_1 of s between zero and one, there is always one and only one value of t corresponding to it. That is, any line through P parallel to Ot axis meets the curve once and once only.

The coordinates of the point C situated on the bisector of the angle sOt are given by the relation $s=t=t_o=\cdot3396$, which we will calculate shortly. The curve $\Psi\,(s,t) = o$ is drawn below.

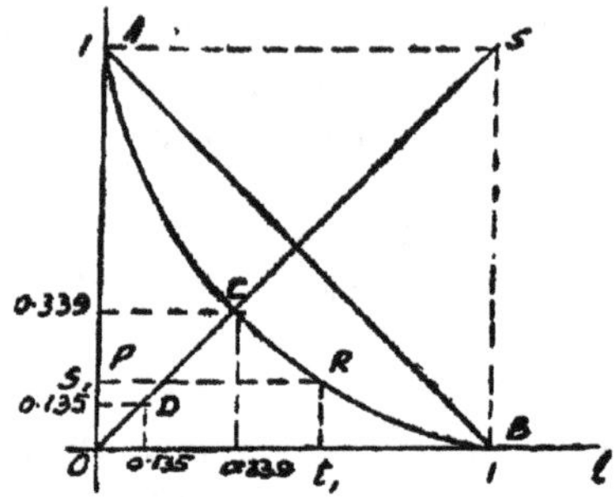

We have now to examine the equation $h = f(s,t)$.

Taking t as defined by the relation $\Psi(s,t) = 0$,

We have

$$- d\Psi = - \frac{\partial \Psi}{\partial s} ds - \frac{\partial \Psi}{\partial t} dt = 0$$

$$= - \Psi'_s \Psi \left(\frac{dq - s dp}{t - s} \right) + \Psi'_t \left(\frac{dq - t dp}{t - s} \right)$$

substituting for ds, dt from $dp = ds + dt$ and $dq = t ds + s dt$.

$$\therefore - d\Psi = - \frac{dq}{t - s} \left(\Psi'_s - \Psi'_t \right) + \frac{dp}{t - s} \left(s \Psi'_s - t \Psi'_t \right)$$

$$= - \frac{dq}{t - s} \left(- A_0 - B_0 t + A_s + B_0 s \right)$$

$$+ \frac{dp}{t - s} \left(- A_0 s - B_0 st + A_0 t + B_0 st \right),$$

Substituting for Ψ'_s and Ψ'_t by their values already found;

$$= A_0 \, dp + B_0 \, dq$$

Now set $r = (s - t)^2 = p^2 - 4q$, so that $2\, p \, dp = dr + 4\, dq$. r is always positive, being zero for $s = t = t_0$, and varies from o to 1. We can consider h as a function of r and q, and q as function of r defined by $\Psi = o$. On replacing the value of dp by its value in terms of r we have

$$- 2p \, d\,\Psi = A_o \, dr + (4A_o + 2p \, B_o) \, dq.$$

But $4A_o + 2p \, B_o = 4A_o + 2p \, B_o - 2C$

$$= (3 - p)B,$$

where B and C are integrals already defined.

Hence $-\, 2\, p \, d\Psi = A_o \, dr + (3-p) \, B \, dq = o$.

Since A_o and B are positive, $\dfrac{dq}{dr}$ is always $< o$.

Let us now consider the equation $h = f \, (s,t)$ giving h in terms of s and t, or q and r. We shall prove that h varies in the same sense as r and that it is maximum for $r = o$ or $s = t = t_o$.

$$h = st \int_o^\infty \frac{x(1+x)}{\triangle^3} \, dx = q(A+B)$$

$$= (1-p+q)A = (1-s) \, (1-t) \int_o^\infty \frac{x \, dx}{\triangle^3} \; ;$$

since from (17), $\Psi = (1-p) \, A - q \, B = o$.

Hence, $dh = (-\, dp + dq)A + (1-p + q)(A_s' \, ds + A_t' dt)$.

But $A_s' \, ds + A_t' \, dt = -\tfrac{3}{2} \int_o^\infty \frac{x^2(1+x)}{\triangle^5} \, (dp + x \, dq)$,

from values of A'_s, A'_t already found vide equation (18).

$$\therefore dh = (-dp+dq) \int_o^\infty \frac{x \, dx}{\triangle^3}$$

$$-\tfrac{3}{2} (1-p + q) \int_o^\infty \frac{x^2(1+x)}{\triangle^5} \, (dp + x \, dq)$$

$$= (- dp + dq) \int_0^\infty \frac{x\,dx}{\Delta^5} (1+x)(1 + px + qx^2)$$

$$-\tfrac{3}{2}(1-p+q)\int_\bullet^\infty \frac{x^2(1+x)}{\Delta^5}(dp + x\,dq).$$

$$\text{or, } 2p\,dh = \int_0^\infty \frac{x(1+x)}{\Delta^5}\,dx \left\{ (1+px+qx^2)(-2pdp+2pdq) \right.$$

$$\left. -\tfrac{3}{2}(1-p+q)\,x\,(2pdp+2pxdq) \right\}$$

$$= \int_0^\infty \frac{x(1+x)}{\Delta^5}\,dx \left\{ (1+px+qx^2)(2pdq-dr-4dq) \right.$$

$$\left. -\tfrac{3}{2}(1-p+q)x(2pxdq+dr+4dq) \right\} \qquad (21)$$

$$= -\tfrac{3}{2}\,\mathrm{D}(qdr-rdq)+\tfrac{1}{2}p\mathrm{B}dq \qquad (22)$$

On taking count of the expression $\mathrm{C}=o$

$$\therefore -4p\frac{dh}{dr}=3q\mathrm{D}-(3r\mathrm{D}+p\mathrm{B})\frac{dq}{dr}.$$

Hence we have always $\dfrac{dh}{dr} < o$, since $\dfrac{dq}{dr} < o.$

This proves that h varies in the opposite sense with r.

The expression for $d\Psi$ gives if we make $s=t$

$$-d\Psi=(\mathrm{A}_o+s\mathrm{B}_o)dp, \text{ for } dq=sdp.$$
$$=o.$$

Hence for $s=t$, $dp=dq=o$ and therefore from (21) $dh=o$ and from (22) $dr=o.$

That is, $dp=dq=dh=dr=o.$

Also h varies in the inverse sense as r and dh is zero for $r=o$. Hence h increases for s between 1 and $t=t_o$ and decreases for s between t_o and o; h is, therefore, maximum for for $s=t=t_o$.

Moreover on replacing dr by its value in terms of ds and dt we have $\dfrac{dh}{ds}=[\,2(t-s)\,(\dfrac{dt}{ds}-1)]\dfrac{dh}{dr}$ with $\dfrac{dt}{ds}<o$.

$\therefore \dfrac{dh}{ds}$ is $+$ive if $t>s$ and $-$ive if $t<s$. Hence when s increases from o to t_o, s remains less than t so that h increases when s increases.

We now proceed to determire t_o and h_o.

For $s=t=t_o$ the two fundamental equations become

$$h_o=t_o{}^2\int_{o}^{\infty}\frac{x\,dx}{(1+t_ox)^3\,\sqrt{1+x}},$$

$$\Psi=(1-2t_o)\int_{o}^{\infty}\frac{x\,dx}{(1+t_ox)^3(1+x)^{\frac{3}{2}}}-t_o{}^2\int_{o}^{\infty}\frac{x^2\,dx}{(1+t_ox)^3(1+x)^{\frac{3}{2}}}$$
$$=o.$$

In order to evaluate these integrals let us put $\dfrac{1}{t_o}=1+l^2$, and transform the integrals by substituting $1+x=\dfrac{1}{u^2}$, and then resplacing u by x

$$h_o=2(1+l^2)\int_{o}^{1}\frac{x^2(1+x^2)\,dx}{(1+l^2x^2)^3}$$

$$\Psi_1=\int_{o}^{1}\frac{x^2(1-x^2)(1-l^4x^2)}{(1+l^2x^2)^3}\,dx=o.$$

Hence, $\dfrac{1+3l^2}{2} h_0 - (1-l^2)\Psi_1$

$$= 2l^2 \int_0^1 \frac{x^2\,dx}{1+l^2x^2} + l^2(1+l^2)\int_0^1 \frac{3x^2-(5+l^2)x^4-l^2x^6}{(1+l^2x^2)^3}.$$

The last intergral on the right hand side is

$$\left| \frac{x^3(1-x^2)}{(1+l^2x^2)^2} \right|_0^1 = 0. \text{ Also } \Psi_1 = 0.$$

$$\therefore \frac{1+3l^2}{4l^2} h_0 = \int_0^1 \frac{x^2\,dx}{1+l^2x^2} = \frac{l - \tan^{-1} l}{l^3}$$

· Also for an ellipsoid of revolution, wo have already seen (Maclaurin's spheroid that

$$h_0 = \frac{3+l^2}{l^3}\tan^{-1} l - \frac{3}{l^2}$$

Eliminating h_0, we have

$$F = \tan^{-1} l - l\frac{3+13l^2}{3+14l^2+3l^4} = 0.$$

For $l=0$, the above expression is zero. Its derivative

$$\frac{16\, l^4(l^2-1)\,(3l^2+1)}{(1+l^2)\,(3+14l^2+3\,l^4)^2}.$$

For $l<1$, the derivative is negative, and positive for $l>1$. The function F, which vanishes for $l=0$ decreases at first and is negative, but when $l>1$, it begins to increase and tends to $\dfrac{\pi}{2}$ It therefore has only one root for $l>1 \cdot$ This root l is determined by the equation $F=0$. Substituting for $\tan^{-1} l$ its expansion in powers of l in the expression for h_0 we have

$$h_0 = \frac{4l^2}{3+11 l^2 + 3l^4}.$$

The calculations give $l_0 = 1\cdot395$, $t_0 = \cdot3396$, $h_0 = \cdot1871$
For an ellipsoid of 3 unequal axes to be a possible figure of
equilibrium $-\frac{w^2}{2\pi\gamma\rho} < .1871$. This value being less than the
ccorresponding maximum for Maclaurin's spheroids, we also
have two Maclaurin's ellipsoids of revolution as possible figures
of equilibrium for the same values of w.

We may now draw the skew curve defined by the surface

$h = f(s\,t$, and cylinder $\Psi(s,t) = o$.

Recalling the remark made in §7 9 we see that points on
this curve are obtained by erecting ordinates of the height
$h = f(s,t)$ at the various points of the plane curve $\Psi(s,t) = o, h = o$,
already drawn.

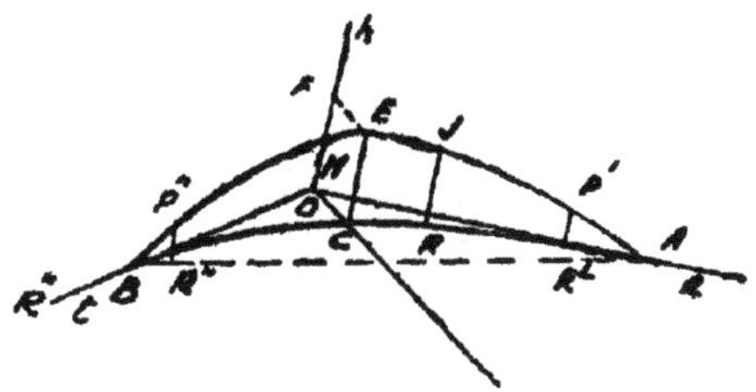

h being symmetrical with respect to s,t; the skew curve is
symmetrical with respect to the plane hOs. It is sufficient,
therefore, to trace the curve on the one side of this plane.
Starting from point A of the curve $\Psi(s,t) = o$, $h = o$ we find that
at this point $t = o$, $s = 1$ and therefore $h = o$. Hence A is a point
of the skew curve we are searching. When s decreases from 1
to t_c, h increases from o to $.1871$, its maximum value. This
point is represented by E in the figure. To have the ellipsoids
corresponding to a given value of w, we merely search for the
two points P', P'' on this curve in which the horizontal plane at
height h intersects the skew curve. These points, P',P'' are

clearly symmetrically situated with respect to the plane hOs. Boths these points give rise to the same ellipsoid as already remarked. Only the axes a and b are interchanged.

Remark: When w tends to zero, the limiting form of equilibrium assumed by the corresponding ellipsoid of Jacobi is very different from that assumed by Maclaurin's spheroid. Here for $w=o$ we have $h=o$ and $s=o$ or $t=o$, both the values giving the same ellipsoid. If $s=o$, $c=o$, and a is infinite, $b=o$ but $\frac{b}{c}$ tends to 1. Hence when w tends to zero, the larger axis extends indefinitely, the other two axes shrink indefinitely in such a way that their ratio tends to 1. The form of equilibrium is therefore a needle shaped figure, "sensibly round but infinitely large." Poincaré called it "Une aiguille allongèe" (See Poincaré's Figures d' Equilibre d' Une Masse Fluide, *page* 162).

7. 10. *Graphical Representation of the results.*

We have found that when

$w=o$, there are 3 figures of equilibrium: The sphere, the elliptic disc, and the elongated needle or "1^2 aiguille allongèe".

$$\frac{w^2}{2\pi\gamma\rho} \angle .1871\ldots\ldots \begin{cases} 2 \quad \text{Spheroids of Maclaurin,} \\ 1 \quad \text{Ellipsoid of Jacobi.} \end{cases}$$

$$\frac{w^2}{2\pi\gamma\rho} = .1871\ldots\ldots \begin{cases} 2 \quad \text{Spheroids of Maclaurin,} \\ 1 \quad \text{Ellipsoid of Jacobi, which} \\ \quad\;\; \text{in the limiting case is an} \\ \quad\;\; \text{ellipsoid of revolution.} \end{cases}$$

$$.1871 \angle \frac{w^2}{2\pi\gamma\rho} < .2247\ldots\ldots\ldots 2 \quad \text{Spheroids of Maclaurin.}$$

$$\frac{w^2}{2\pi\gamma\rho} = .2247\ldots\ldots\ldots 1 \qquad \text{''} \qquad \text{''} \qquad \text{''}$$

$$\frac{w^2}{2\pi\gamma\rho} > .2247\ldots\ldots \quad \begin{cases} \text{There are no ellipsoidal forms} \\ \text{of equilibrium.} \end{cases}$$

We have already traced the curve which represents Maclaurins' spheroids taking l as the variable. In order to facilitate comparison with corresponding results pertaining to Jacobi's ellipsoid let us take the same variable $s = \dfrac{c^2}{a^2}$, Hence $l = \sqrt{\dfrac{1-s}{s}}$

We have then $h = \dfrac{w^2}{2\pi\gamma\rho} = \sqrt{s}\ \dfrac{(1+2s)\tan^{-1}\sqrt{\dfrac{1-s}{s}} - 3\sqrt{s}(1-s)}{(1-s)\sqrt{1-s}}$

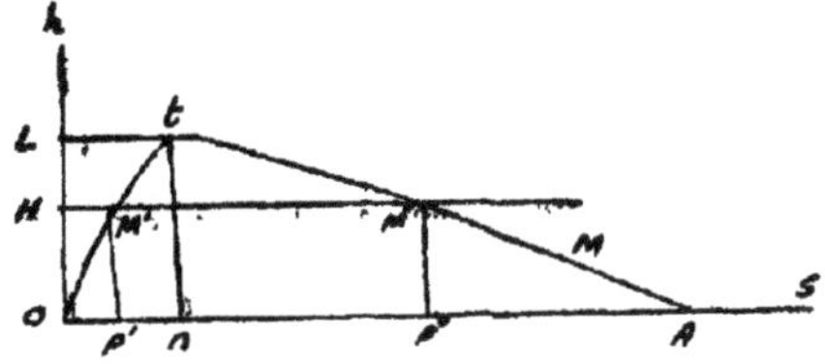

s varies from o to 1. For $s = o$, $h = o$, and for $s = 1$, $h = o$; h is maximum for $s = \cdot 135$; for any other value of h less than this maximum we have two values of s, viz op', op''.

The totality of above results is very simply represented graphically. The skew curve in Fig. 2 of § 7·9 is the line of Jacobi's ellipsoids and the above curve which lies in the plane hOs of Fig. 2 of § 7·9 represents the line of Maclaurin's spheroids. Both the curves are shown in the Fig. below. It is evident

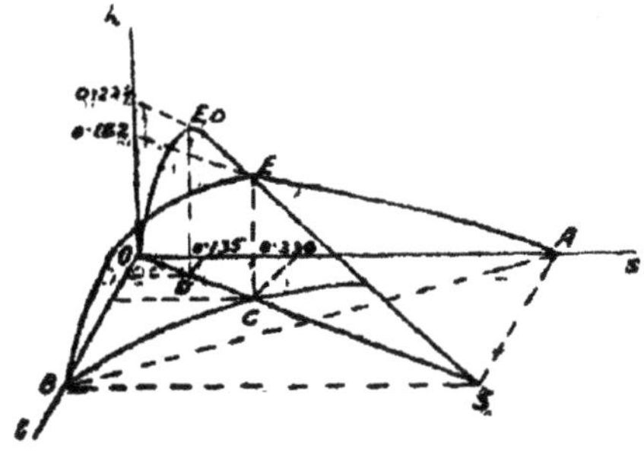

that the maximum ordinate CE of the curve of Jacobi's ellipsoids is also an ordinate of the line of Maclaurin's spheroids so that E is the common point of the two curves. Moving along the line of Maclaurin's spheroids from the point S (which corresponds to a sphere) we reach point E. The ellipsoid represented by the point E is common to both series viz. the series of spheroids and the series of ellipsoids. At E the series of Maclaurin's spheroids "bifurcates" into that of Jacobi's ellipsoids. The e lipsoid represented by E is called the "ellipsoid of bifurcation" Thus the various forms of equilibrium constitute a continuous series or a "linear" series when w is regarded as a variable parameter, th e series of Maclaurin's spheroids bifurcating into the series of Jacobi's ellipsoids.

For further details reference may be made to Appell's Mècanique Rationnell tome IV, Poincaré's Figures' d Equilibre d'une Masse Fluide, and "Astronomy and Cosmogony" by Jeans.

(1). Show that an elliptic cylinder is a possible form of equilibrium for an infinite mass of homogeneous gravitating liquid, rotating as if rigid, about the axis of the cylinder

If a, b be the semi-axes of the cylinder an w the angular velicity, prove that

$$\frac{a-b}{a+b} = \sqrt{1 - \frac{w^2}{\pi \gamma \rho}},$$

ρ being the density of of the liquid   Deduce that elliptic cylinder cannot be a possible form of equilibrium unless $\dfrac{w^2}{\pi \gamma \rho} < 1$

[Hint: The potential V! at an internal point (x, y) is given by $V_i = -\dfrac{2\pi \gamma \rho}{a+b} (bx^2 + ay^2)$.

Ex (2) A solid gravitating sphere of radius a and density ρ is surrounded by a gravitating liquid of volume $\frac{4}{3} \pi (b^3 - a^3)$

and density σ. Show that the form of the free surface of the liquid is the spheroid of small ellipticity ε given by

$$r = b \left(1 - \frac{2}{3} \varepsilon\, P_2\right)$$

where, $\varepsilon = \dfrac{15\, w^2\, b^3}{8\pi \left\{5 \,(P - \sigma)\, a^3 + 2\sigma b^3\right\}}$

P_2, being Legendre's coefficient of the 2nd order.

(I. C S., 1935)

To solve this problem we recall the fact that the potential of a liquid of density σ bounded by a surface $r = b\ (1 + \lambda\ P_2)$ at an internal point is given by

$$-\left[\frac{4\pi}{3}\left(b^2 - \frac{r^2}{3}\right)\sigma + \frac{4\pi}{5}\sigma b^2 \left(\frac{r}{b}\right)^2 \lambda\, P_2\right]$$

Hence the potential of a solid sphere of density P and of a homogeneous liquid of density σ surrounding the sphere and bounded by the surface $r = b\ (1 + \lambda\ P_2)$

$$-V_1 = \frac{2\pi}{3}\left(b^2 - \frac{r^2}{3}\right)\sigma + \frac{4\pi\,\psi\,\sigma}{5} r^2\ P_2 + \frac{4\pi}{3}(P - \sigma)\frac{a^3}{r}$$

For equilibrium to be possible

$$V_1 - \tfrac{1}{2}\,\omega^2\,(r^2 - z^2) = V_1 - \tfrac{1}{2}\omega^2\,r^2(1 - \cos^2\theta)$$

$$= V_1 - \tfrac{1}{2}\,\omega^2 r^2\left(\frac{2 - 2P_2}{3}\right)\ \text{since}\ P_2 = \frac{3\cos^2\theta - 1}{2},$$

$$= V_1 - \frac{\omega^2 r^2}{3}\,(1 - P_2)$$

must be constant over the surface $r = b\ (1 + \lambda P_2.)$

Replacing r by $b\ (1 + \lambda P_2)$ and neglecting powers of λ higher than unity and products of ω^2 and λ, this expression reduces to

$$-\frac{4\pi}{3}\sigma\, b^2 - 4\pi\, (\rho-\sigma)\frac{a^3}{b} - \tfrac{1}{3}\omega^2 b$$

$$+ P_2\left\{ \frac{4\pi}{3}\sigma\lambda\delta^2 - \frac{4\pi\lambda}{5}\, b^2\sigma + \frac{4\pi}{3}(\rho-\sigma)\frac{a^3\lambda}{b} + \frac{\omega^2 b^2}{3}\right\}$$

As this must be a constant, the coefficient of P_2 must be zero.

$$\therefore\; 4\pi\lambda\left\{ \frac{b^2\sigma}{3} - \frac{b^2\sigma}{5} + \frac{(\rho-\sigma)a^3}{3b}\right\} = -\frac{\omega^2 b^2}{3}$$

or, $\lambda = -\dfrac{5\omega^2 b^3}{4\pi\left\{5(\rho-\sigma)\,a^3 + 2\sigma b^3\right\}}$

Hence $\quad \varepsilon = -\tfrac{3}{2}\lambda = \dfrac{15\omega^2 b^3}{8\pi\left\{5(\rho-\sigma)\,a^3 + 2\sigma b^3\right\}}$

Ex. (3): A homogeneous gravitating fluid just does not fill a rigid envelope in the form of an oblate spheroid. The fluid is rotating in relative equilibrium round the polar axis with kinetic energy E. If it rotates with kinetic energy E_1 the envelope is a free surface of zero pressure. Prove that for all values of E whether greater or less than E_1, the tension per unit length across the equatorial section of the envelope is

$$\frac{15}{32}\frac{E-E}{A}$$

where A is the area of a polar section of the ellipsoid.

(I. C, S. 1933. Higher Applied Mathematics)

Ex. (4): Prove that the ellipticity ε of a nearly spherical mass of liquid rotating round its axis of symmetry is $\dfrac{15\omega^2}{16\pi\rho}$, ω being the angular velocity

Ex. (5): Two gravitating liquids which do not mix and whose densities are ρ, σ ($\rho>\sigma$) are enclosed in a rigid spherical envelope. The whole rotates in relative equilibrium with a small uniform angular velocity ω about a diameter of the sphere. Show that the possible form of common surface of the two liquids is an oblate spheroid of ellipticity $\dfrac{15\omega^2}{16\pi(\rho+\frac{2}{3}\sigma)}$.

Ex. (6): A mass of homogeneous liquid of density ρ subject to its own gravitation and the gravitational attraction of any number of other external masses If the liquid rotates round an axis with angular velocity w, prove that relative equilibrium is impossible, whatever may be the form assumed by the liquid mass, if $\dfrac{w^2}{2\pi\gamma\rho} > 1$

(Poincaré's Theorem)

For equilibrium to exist it is necessary that the resultant of the forces of attraction and centrifugal force, be directed towards the interior of the liquid, for otherwise a part will be detached.

Let us take the axis of rotation as z—axis and ox, oy two other lines perpendicular to it as axes of x and y respectively, Let V be the potential of the external masses at any point inside the liquid mass or on its surface. Let V' be the potential of the liquid mass itself at the same point.

If, therefore, we set

$$U = V + V' - \tfrac{1}{2}w^2\,(x^2 + y^2),$$

the force per unit mass acting at a point of the liquid is derivable from the potential U. At a point on the free surface force along the outward normal is, therefore, $-\dfrac{\partial U}{\partial n}$.

Now by Green's theorem

$$\iint_s \left(\frac{\partial U}{\partial n}\right)dS = \iiint_v \nabla^2 U\,dr,$$

the surface integral being taken on the free surface and volume integral through the liquid mass

But $\triangle^2 V = 0$ and $\nabla^2 V' = 4\pi\gamma P$, by Poisson's Theorem.

$$\therefore \iiint \triangle^2 U\, dv = \iiint (4\pi\gamma P - 2w^2)\, dv$$

$$= 2\,(2\pi\gamma P - w^2)\, v,$$

where v is the volume of the liquid mass.

If $\dfrac{w^2}{2\pi\gamma P} > 1,\ \iiint \triangle^2 U\, dv$ is clearly negative.

Hence $\iint \left(\dfrac{\partial U}{\partial n}\right) dS$ is negative,

or, $\iint \left(-\dfrac{\partial U}{\partial n}\right) dS$ is positive.

But $\left(-\dfrac{\partial U}{\partial n}\right)$ at any point on the face surface is the resultant force acting along the outward normal. It follows from the above, that $\left(\dfrac{\partial u}{\partial n}\right)$ is positive at some points of the surface, that is the resultant of the forces of attraction and centrifugal force at some points of the free surface acts outward. Equilibrium is therefore impossible.